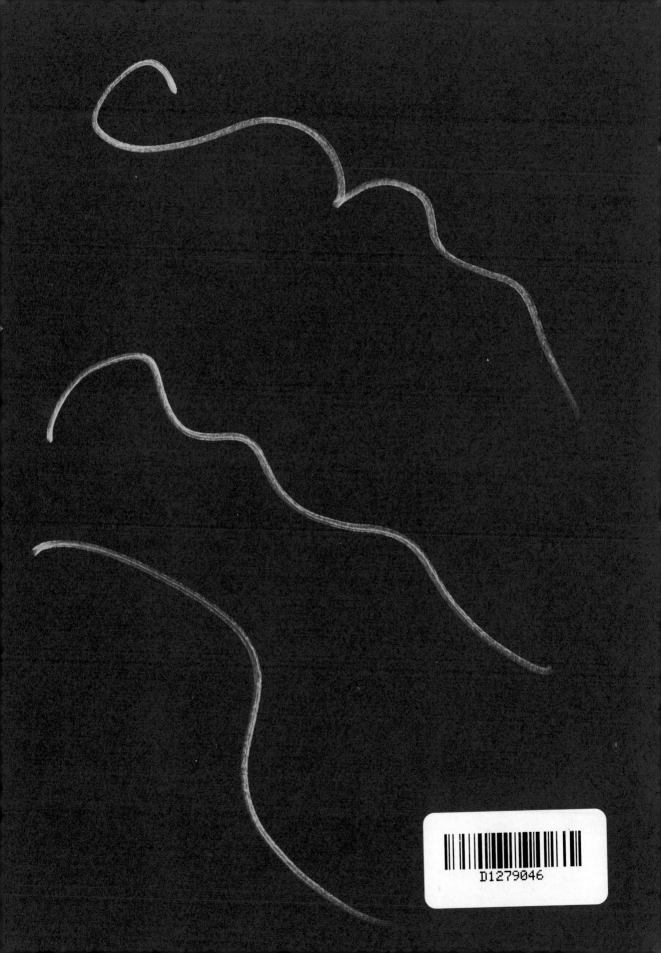

The Indianapolis "500"

The Indianapolis "500"
THE WORLD'S MOST EXCITING AUTO RACE

Produced by Lyle Kenyon Engel
and the editors of
Auto Racing magazine

REVISED EDITION

FOUR WINDS PRESS / NEW YORK

EDITORIAL STAFF
Ross R. Olney
George S. Engel
Marla Ray

STATISTICAL SECTION PREPARED BY
Donald C. Davidson

PHOTOGRAPHERS
Will Barbeau
Major Baynes
Don Blake
Arnie de Brier
Charles Duffy
George S. Engel
Lyle K. Engel
Joe Farkas
Firestone Tire & Rubber Company
Ford Motor Company
Goodyear Tire & Rubber Company
Indianapolis Motor Speedway
Bud Jones
Robert Kluesner
John R. Mahoney
John P. May
Dennis Torres

Published by Four Winds Press
A Division of Scholastic Magazines, Inc., New York, N.Y.
Copyright © 1970, 1972 by Lyle Kenyon Engel.
All Rights Reserved
Printed in the United States of America

Library of Congress Catalogue Card Number: 76-105336

CONTENTS

[illegible]

Jim Malloy

Sam Sessions

George Follmer

[illegible]

[illegible]

Sonny Ates

Jim McElreath

Jim Hurtubise

Larry Dickson

Art Pollard

Leader Card Racers
Bob Wilke owner
3 Indie champs
3 Nat'l champs
1 Monza champ
6 Car owner champ

Bruce Walkup

Lee Roy Yarbrough

Gary Bettenhausen

Arnie Knepper

Rick Muther

Mel Kenyon

Ronnie Bucknum

Rick Mears

Bobby Unser

Peter Revson

Gordon Johncock

Wally Dallenbach

Johnny Rutherford

Andy Granatelli

Joe Leonard

JC Agajanian
#98 & 97

George Bignotti

Roger McCluskey

Carl Williams

The Indianapolis "500"

▲ Millions of people, both in the packed
grandstands and in front of closed-circuit
television, await the start of the world's
most exciting auto race. As the cars sit in
their starting positions on the main
straightaway and the crews await the signal
to start their engines, the band plays "Back
Home Again in Indiana."

INTRODUCTION: 1911-1962

It has been said that the Indy "500" is the most exciting event in all of sports, and it is true that more fans attend the 500-mile race than any other single event in any sport. Over a quarter of a million pack into the sprawling racing plant on Memorial Day, and many millions more view the drama on closed-circuit television. Each year more fans return to find newer, larger grandstands to hold them and smoother methods of handling the great crush.

Yet who would have guessed, when Carl Fisher first looked at those acres of planted beans back in 1909 and envisioned a race track that so many millions of people would be touched, that the result would be so very far-reaching? Fisher himself, a man of wonderful foresight, could not have imagined that his decision would mean riches for some, death for others, and blood-pounding excitement for many millions more. But it has.

So the track was carved out, paved with bricks and finally in 1911—with 3000 hitching posts provided by a thoughtful management for the fans who came on horseback—Ray Harroun drove his 6-cylinder Marmon "Yellow Jacket" (shortened by reporters to "Wasp") to victory in the very first 500-mile race. The fans were thrilled at the thundering excitement—Harroun's average speed was 74.6 miles per hour.

That was in 1911. In 1969 Mario Andretti drove 156.867 mph to win, and in the interim the competition has been fierce, the excitement often unbearable. In 1912 the fans were wondering if one of the hot young rookies could win. Today they still wonder. Then they wondered if the Stutz could actually outrace the marvelous Peugeot, and later if the Miller could outrace them both. Still later they wondered if the silent turbine could lay to rest the little rear-engined race car which had buried the traditional roadster.

The drivers have changed from leather-helmeted, mustachioed daredevils handling huge, ungainly machines to modern young jousters in low-slung bombs. The race is faster, sleeker, more colorful and certainly cleaner, and the drama of Jimmy Murphy, Tommy Milton, Leon Duray, and Frank Lockhart has passed on through Mauri Rose, Bill Holland, Rodger Ward, and Bill Vukovich to become the drama of Mario Andretti, A. J. Foyt, Bobby Unser, and Dan Gurney.

The sons of great men now carry on the hazardous play though their fathers died at the game. Bettenhausen's sons now gamble for the gold, with everything on the line, as their father once did. Vukovich and Parsons had sons who now race, and so did Carter.

Then they screamed encouragement to the favorite Ralph DePalma who, with the race in the bag in the few last miles, snapped a connecting rod and ground to a halt. Attempting to shove his heavy car the rest of the way, he looked up to see a grinning, exultant Joe Dawson thunder by to take the prize.

And later they cheered for the likes of Parnelli Jones as his odd turbine-powered race car coasted to a halt within sight of what could have been the greatest victory of his winning career.

The races have blasted away annually, uninterrupted by anything but the World Wars. The price of admission has gone up from a dollar and a half for the best seat in the house to thirty-nine dollars. And there's a long waiting list of willing buyers. The track has been smoothed and paved and repaved until the bricks, save for a yard-wide strip at the starting line, are buried memories. But the place is still called ''the brickyard'' in deference to tradition and the fine old-timers who remember.

The grandstands have been transformed from rickety old wooden structures which would today be banned at the local ballpark into monsters of sleek steel and concrete with every comfort and convenience for fans.

But still every year a new man with a new machine reaches for the gold, and produces more drama. In the old days it was men like Jimmy Murphy trying with Miller's new car, and winning. Wilbur Shaw came back in a foreign Maserati after flying his Duesenberg over the wall. He won the great race three times. Lou Meyer won three times. Shaw became the president of the track, and Meyer went on to further develop the marvelous Meyer-Drake engine (formerly the Offenhauser). Mauri Rose won once, then came back in a sleek new Blue Crown Spark Plug Special and won two more times. Other men, though, have tried again and again, and with all their great skill and experience have won only once, or not at all: Cliff Bergere, a driver of great skill, raced sixteen times at the brickyard, and yet in spite of the fact that he frequently led, he never once won.

In the early sixties an odd new car appeared, but this had happened often before. Usually these new machines were talked about and then forgotten. The Novi was one such machine, a brute of power and speed and yet a non-winner, and there were many others over the years. They came to the track, they established certain records, they captured the fancy of the crowd, and then they failed to qualify, dropped out of the race with mechanical problems, or destroyed themselves—often taking a man with them.

◀ Shortly after taking the checkered flag for an unexpected win in the 1912 Indy "500," Joe Dawson slipped away from the well-wishers who crowded Victory Lane and drove to his home nearby. When his mother, who had refused to go to the race, learned of his victory, she could only ask: "Joe, did you get any bumps or bruises?"

▲ Ralph DePalma led for 196 of the 200 laps during the 1912 race. Many people, convinced of his victory, were already beginning to leave the grandstands when his Mercedes started slowing down. The car ground to a halt on the 199th lap. DePalma and his mechanic Rupert Jeffkins tried to push the car, but to no avail.

◄ The third Indy "500" saw an influx of European entries. Frenchman Jules Goux, driving a French Peugeot, spoke no English and conversed with American coach Johnny Aitken through a translator. Imagine Aitken's amazement when the translator informed him that Goux must have some chilled wine waiting for him the next time he stopped at his pit! Aitken was opposed to the idea but Goux was insistent. Translator Faroux disappeared for a while, and when Goux next pitted a bucket of ice and six pints of champagne were waiting for him. Much refreshed, he went on to win the 1913 race.

◄ The 1914 race was the scene of the most complete foreign domination in the history of the "500." French drivers captured the first four finishing positions while American Barney Oldfield brought his white #3 Stutz home in fifth position. Oldfield was back in good standing with the AAA after his fourth "lifetime suspension"—for racing on outlaw tracks and for competing against animals and airplanes—and he was considered America's best chance for winning this year's race. Although he never won the "500," Oldfield's long list of major accomplishments included the 1903 National Driving Championship and the 1910 Land Speed Record of 131.724 mph for the measured mile.

◄ Ray Harroun came out of retirement to drive in the first Indy "500." Refusing the services of a riding mechanic, Harroun mounted an eight-by-three-inch mirror on a framework over the cowling of his Marmon. The car's long tail and black-and-yellow paint job earned it the nickname "The Wasp." Harroun predicted that an average speed of 75 mph would be fast enough to win the race. While other cars led during the leading stages of the race, his prediction proved correct: he won at 74.59 mph!

▲ Ralph DePalma, who competed in ten 500-mile races at Indy and led for a total of 613 laps, (a record which still stands) is shown here taking the checkered flag for his only "500" victory, in 1915. But he almost didn't finish. A connecting rod broke on the 197th lap, the same mechanical trouble that had plagued him during the race in 1912. This time, however, the car kept running and he finished three and a half minutes ahead of Dario Resta, who had challenged him for most of the race.

In 1920 Gaston Chevrolet became the first American driver in an American car to win the "500" since 1912. He also became the first winner to go the entire 500 miles without changing tires. As the race drew to a close, Chevrolet's team cars began dropping out with faulty steering arms. When Gaston's brother Louis congratulated him on his good fortune, he nudged the steering arm on his car—and it promptly broke.

When Pete DePaolo won the 1925 "500," he became the first man to finish the race at an average speed of over 100 mph. His record of 101.13 mph was not beaten for seven years.

▲ Young Californian Frank Lockhart had never driven on the Indy bricks and could not get a ride for the 1926 race. He made a deal to help prepare Bennett Hill's car in exchange for round-trip transportation and the chance that he might relieve Hill. However, on the first day of time trials Peter Kreis took ill, Lockhart qualified the car and went on to win the rain-shortened race.

◄ In 1936, Lou Meyer became the first three-time winner in Indy history as he drove his red-and-white Miller-engined car to victory over Ted Horn. The track had been extensively revamped for this year's race, with asphalt paving on the turns, wide safety aprons replacing the infield wall and a new concrete retaining wall built on the outside edge of the turns at right angles to the track.

◄ Wilbur Shaw was so sure that he would win the 1939 "500" in this sleek, black Maserati that he made a deal with his car owner that he would either win or he would not receive one cent of pay. He not only won this race but the 1940 race as well in the same car, becoming the first man ever to win the race twice in succession and only the second man to have won it three times.

▲ Norman Batten, relief driver for the victorious Pete DePaolo in the 1925 Indy "500," guides his flaming Miller Special through the pit area. His bringing the car to a safe stop in spite of painful burns on his face and arms won him the acclaim of the racing fraternity for one of the most heroic performances in the history of the sport. The following year he finished fifth.

▼ In 1948 Mauri Rose beat teammate Bill Holland to the checkered flag for the second year in a row, and this time his victory was much less controversial. The previous year, with the race apparently clinched, owner Lou Moore gave both drivers the EZ sign. Holland slowed down considerably but Rose kept his pace and passed Holland on the 193rd lap. Holland, thinking himself a lap ahead, had waved Rose by for the win.

▲ In 1954 Bill Vukovich won the "500" for the second year in a row, becoming the third man ever to do so. Vukie was actually of Yugoslav parentage, although he was nicknamed the "Mad Russian." Having seen victory in the 1952 race snatched from his grasp, Vukie came to the Speedway in 1955 determined to become the only man ever to win the race for three consecutive years. He was well in the lead on the 57th lap when he was involved in a multiple car crash and he died of injuries received when his car flipped.

▲ Undoubtedly the world's most famous "oval"
racetrack, The Indianapolis Motor Speedway is not
really an oval. The track is actually rectangular in
shape with two long straightaways, each five-eighths
of a mile; two short straightaways, each one-eighth of
a mile; and four ninety-degree turns, each one-quarter
of a mile long and banked nine degrees and twelve
minutes. Since the original track surface broke up
badly during the races prior to the first "500," it was
decided to pave the track with brick, the finest material
available at that time. More than three million bricks,
each weighing ten pounds, were used and the
monumental task was completed in sixty-three days.
Over the years portions of the track have been paved
with asphalt, and today, except for a symbolic yard of
brick at the start/finish line, the entire surface is asphalt.

▲ Indy veterans were certain that the flimsy-looking rear-engined Lotuses would disintegrate in the event of a mishap. However, when Dan Gurney crashed during a last-minute practice session, the car held up extremely well despite the loss of the right front tire. The car was repaired over night by the Lotus crew, and Gurney qualified at 149.019 mph, for twelfth starting position. He finished the 500 miles in seventh position.

◄ Indy oldtimers viewed Jimmy Clark and his "funny-looking little racer" with skepticism. The car, however, proved both fast and reliable, and Clark qualified fifth and finished second.

and this time the machine was very light, flimsy-looking and small, with the engine at the wrong end. It had come from England, and everybody *knew* that race drivers on the continent were no match for the Indy men. Then too, this race car was powered by a Detroit engine, a Ford of all things! This Ford-powered, English-built, rear-engined lightweight was preparing to challenge the brute strength of the standard Indy roadster.

It did! And once again the pure excitement of the "500" caused hearts to pound. First appearing in 1963, the Lotus Ford which looked pretty meek next to the hefty Indy roadster brought chuckles from devoted fans. Still

it had certain things going for it, everybody admitted, not the least of which was the fact that the great Scottish driver Jim Clark would be at the wheel.

The race ended after a wild last few laps, during which leader Parnelli Jones either was or was not dropping oil onto an already slick track—an offense for which he almost received the black flag. Parnelli took the big prize, but buzzing quickly after him was Jim Clark in his Lotus powered by Ford. So another revolution had begun at Indy, much to the delight of the fans and the chagrin of the car owners.

▶ The spectators loved Eddie Sachs, "The Clown Prince of Racing." While running in third, Sachs spun in the first turn and scraped the wall. He continued in the race without making the required stop for inspection. Before he could be black flagged, a wheel came off and he crashed into the outer wall at the opposite end of the course. He coolly climbed out of the wrecked machine, picked up the loose wheel and rolled it back to the pits, smiling and waving to the cheering fans.

◄ The lightweight, rear-engined Lotus was a tight fit even for a driver of Clark's slight build. The car was based on the design that had proved so successful in Formula 1 racing. The chassis was of monocoque construction, and the car was both light and agile. In addition, it was built on the centerline originally instead of being offset to the left, as in common Indy practice.

▼ Dan Gurney (93) passes Dempsey Wilson's Offy-powered roadster on the main straightaway. The difference in size between the two car designs is clearly illustrated in this picture. The Lotus' rear engine eliminates the need for a drive shaft running from the engine in front to the drive wheel in back, resulting in a lower, more aerodynamic car.

▼ USAC National Driving Champion Rodger Ward started this front-engined Offy roadster in fourth place and could get no higher in the race—his poorest finish in five consecutive Indianapolis "500" appearances. It was the last time Ward would drive a roadster at Indy. After seeing how fast the rear-engined cars were, he switched.

▲ Parnelli Jones' faithful "Calhoun" takes the checkered flag from starter Pat Vidan for Jones' only victory in seven years at the Speedway. The next year, while leading the race, Jones pitted for fuel and Calhoun burst into flames as he left his pit. The car was carefully restored and today is on display in the Speedway Museum.

► Car owner J. C. Agajanian (white Stetson) beams with joy in Victory Lane. He convinced the officials to take a second look at Parnelli's car in the closing stages of the race to see if he really was dropping oil on the track. It was decided that no oil was being dropped. The black flag was put away and Jones raced to the checkered flag.

◀ 1963 was a year of great change at the Indianapolis Motor Speedway. These cars, posed in back of the timing tower, show the extreme differences in designs that were tried that year. *Left,* the flat, pancake-shaped creation of California hot-rodder Mickey Thompson; *center,* the tried-and-true Offy roadster of A. J. Watson; *right,* the new rear-engined Lotus designed by Colin Chapman.

▲ Jim Hurtubise brought tears of joy to the eyes of his chief mechanic Jean Marcenac and other members of his crew by qualifying one of the powerful Novi cars at 150.257 mph for second fastest qualifying position. He retired on the 102nd lap with an oil leak and was awarded twenty-second position.

▲ Walt Hansgen, in the MG Liquid Suspension Special (a rear-engined Offy-powered Huffaker) looks as though he's about to be gobbled up by the much larger front-engined Offy-powered Watson driven by Johnny White. Hansgen started tenth but was flagged at 176 laps and awarded thirteenth finishing position. White started twenty-first and finished fourth.

and the lightweight, rear-powered entry was obviously the race car of the future at the brickyard, and as if to prove this fact twelve of the thirty-three starters this year were rear powered (six Offy, six Ford). Some veterans went along with the new trend, including past winner Rodger Ward, and some other champions chose to stay with the so-called dying dinosaur (front-engined roadster), including past winners A. J. Foyt, Parnelli Jones, and Troy Ruttman.

Heralded as a race for supremacy, a hot contest to decide once and for all the form and power of future race cars, the event was shaping up as a fan's delight. It promised everything.

Yet most fans would sooner forget that black year at the brickyard. With all the customary pomp and magnificent pageantry the thirty-three gleaming race cars blasted away at new record speeds at precisely eleven o'clock. The fans, as always, stood to cheer them away.

But before the second lap was completed, at the fourth turn coming back onto the main stretch, a driver lost control. Skidding, he bounced from the wall, exploded and stopped directly in the center of the track, burning. Speeding cars tried to get around him and through the sheet of flames. Spectators screamed in horror. Eddie Sachs, a crowd favorite and the fine ''clown prince of racing,'' could not avoid the burning race car of young Dave MacDonald and plowed directly into the flames at high speed.

Another terrible explosion, and both men were dead.

Many fans went home, most wept, and very few were able to recapture the spirit of the day as A. J. Foyt went on, after a restart, to win his second 500-mile race, again in a standard roadster.

Of the rear-engined cars Ward placed second, Don Branson twelfth, Walt Hansgen thirteenth, Len Sutton fifteenth, and Dan Gurney seventeenth.

The lightweights were at the brickyard to stay.

▶ The rear-engined lightweights were here to stay, and some of the Indy veterans switched to them. Two-time ''500'' winner Rodger Ward qualified this Offy-powered, rear-engined Watson at 156.406 mph, which was third fastest. This filled the front row with rear-engined cars—the Lotuses of Jim Clark and Bobby Marshman grabbed the first two spots. Clark's speed was 158; Marshman's, 157 mph.

▲ Another Indy veteran who switched to the rear-engined cars but did not fare as well was Eddie Sachs. He qualified his Ford-powered Halibrand at 151.439 mph for seventeenth starting position. However, on the second lap, his car tangled with Dave MacDonald's and exploded in flames. The ever-smiling, always exuberant Eddie, loved and respected by fans and competitors alike, was gone from racing forever.

▶ Thick, black clouds of smoke from the violent gasoline fire boil skyward at the start of the main stretch as MacDonald crashes, involving Sachs, Rutherford, Duman, Unser, Stevenson and Hall. MacDonald and Sachs died, but Ronnie Duman leaped from his wrecked car and rolled about on the grass inside the safety barrier in an effort to smother his flaming driving suit. The cars of Johnny Rutherford, Bobby Unser, Chuck Stevenson and Norm Hall were too seriously damaged to continue the race, but the men themselves were not injured. As a result of this tragic accident, the USAC Rules Committee made several important changes in regulations for the following year: all fuel tanks must be constructed of metal with approved rubber bladder inserts; fuel tanks on either side of the cockpit must not extend beyond a line formed by the inside edge of the wheels; and no fuel tank could be located directly in front of the driver.

▶ Promising young rookie Dave MacDonald qualified his rear-engined Ford-powered Mickey Thompson racer at 151.464 mph for fourteenth starting position. MacDonald lost control coming out of the fourth turn to complete the second lap of the race. The car spun into the inside wall and exploded in flames in front of Eddie Sachs. MacDonald died later that day in the hospital.

▲ A. J. Watson built an Offy-powered, rear-engined car for Indy veteran Don Branson, who qualified well at 152.672 mph for ninth starting position. Branson dropped out with clutch troubles after 187 laps for an assigned finishing position of twelfth. Following Branson in this picture is an Indy veteran who chose to stay with the old roadster design. Jim Hurtubise built his own Offy-powered car which was only slightly slower than Branson's. Hurtubise qualified at 152.542 mph but he only managed to complete 141 laps.

▼ Fastest qualifier Jimmy Clark (nearest camera) passes two-time World Driving Champion Jack Brabham. Driving a rear-engined, Offy-powered car of his own design, Brabham is considered to be the man who started the modern rear-engined trend at Indianapolis. He had come to the Speedway in 1961 with a vastly underpowered Formula 1 Cooper Climax whose added maneuverability in the turns compensated for the power deficiency enough to get Brabham a ninth place finish. This year, however, he dropped out after 77 laps with a split fuel tank.

▼ A. J. Foyt goes down low to pass Art Malone in the Studebaker STP Novi. Although often among the fastest cars at the Speedway, the Novis never managed to find their way to victory. Previous winners A. J. Foyt and Parnelli Jones, with both front- and rear-engined cars to choose from, elected to go once more with the proven roadsters. They qualified fourth and fifth behind the rear-engined creations that they dubbed "funny cars," although there was nothing funny about the speeds these cars attained while qualifying. Clark's rear-engined Ford-powered Lotus was more than four miles per hour faster than Foyt's front-engined Offy.

▲ Veteran Lloyd Ruby also remained faithful to the Offy roadster and was rewarded by finishing third, his highest placing in five years of competition at the Speedway. Ruby's car was built by A. J. Watson, as were all the cars that finished in the top four this year. After six straight "500" victories (1959–1964) Watson-built cars would never again finish in the top three.

◄ A. J. Foyt, Sr. (A. J.'s father and crew chief) rushes to his son's side to be the first to congratulate him on his second "500" victory.

◄ After proving his Lotus the fastest car at the track by capturing the pole position and leading in the early stages of the race, Jimmy Clark was forced out when a huge portion of the tread of one of his tires flew off. This unbalanced his wheel to such an extent that the resulting vibration broke the suspension. A fine driver, Clark safely drove the car off the course without further mishap. Teammate Dan Gurney's Lotus was fitted with identical tires and he was withdrawn from the race.

▼ During practice before the race, Jimmy Clark tried various means of protecting his face from the buffeting wind and small flying objects thrown up from the track by the tires of other cars. Shown here in a heavy mask of the kind worn by USAC drivers on dirt tracks, Clark finally decided on just a few pieces of adhesive tape. The black masking tape on his goggles is for protection from the glaring sun.

◄ In his tenth and final appearance at the Speedway, Dick Rathmann drove this Offy-powered Watson to a seventh place finish. Note that Rathmann is wearing one of the old-style leather helmets.

◄ If the rear-engined revolution at Indy can be attributed to the actions of a single person—other than Jack Brabham—that person should be Dan Gurney. He personally brought Lotus builder Colin Chapman to the United States to see the Indy "500" and the Ford Motor Company.

▲ The Mustang pace car pulls off the track into the pits and the field roars down the main straight to take the green flag for the start of the race.

▼ Jimmy Clark goes wide into the first turn on the second lap, allowing A. J. Foyt to take the lead—but Jimmy took it back on the following lap. Afterwards Clark said, "I didn't make any real effort to stay ahead of Foyt when he started to pass me . . . When I passed him on the next lap without running flat out, I knew I could take him anytime I wanted to."

▲ *Middle,* Parnelli Jones also made the transition to a rear-engined car this year and qualified fifth fastest. Shown here during the race signaling his pit crew that he will stop on the next lap, Jones had fuel consumption problems and made three stops while the first and third place winners made only two. Even so, Jones' car barely made it across the finish line before running out of fuel.

▲ *Bottom,* Rookie Mario Andretti qualified fourth and ran with the leaders all during the race and competed fiercely with Parnelli Jones for second place in the closing stages of the race. Running third on the final lap, Andretti closed to within six seconds of Jones as Jones' car sputtered across the finish line.

IT WAS 1965

and the stage was set for the running of the great classic. From May 1st, when the track had opened for practice, the drama built, and the full import of the events of the previous year became increasingly obvious in the garages as more and more spidery little race cars were hauled in. Suddenly the grand old roadster was in the minority. Even Jones and Foyt, who had won in the roadsters and had remained with them to the bitter end were assigned—or chose to drive—the new cars. And somebody else was present that year who would rock the racing world and become its number one driver. He was a classy young rookie up from the Eastern dirt tracks—Mario Andretti. The veterans were there, except for Eddie Sachs, and he was missed. Branson, who would later die in a dirt track race in California, was there, along with other veterans Al Miller, Lloyd Ruby, Bud Tinglestad, and sentimental favorite Jim "Hercules" Hurtubise. Rodger Ward wasn't there. For the first time in many years, the popular veteran and past winner had been unable to qualify his car.

The "funny cars," the little lightweights, were recognized as the only real formula for victory. Only six front-engined cars qualified in the thirty-three-car lineup.

Nearly three hundred thousand fans poured into the racing plant for the big event in auto racing—and they were not disappointed. In contrast to last year's race, this one was perhaps the smoothest, cleanest, most injury-free race in the history of the track.

A foreign driver had not won the big race since World War I, but Jimmy Clark, the precise Scotsman, was totally familiar with the "new" Indy race cars, and he won easily. Fighting a dry fuel tank, Parnelli Jones coasted across in second place—he didn't have enough fuel left to complete his slow-down lap—and young Mario Andretti flashed across in third place to easily take "Rookie of the Year" honors. Of the first nine cars, only one (driven by Gordon Johncock into fifth place) was a front-engined roadster.

The revolution was nearly complete, and it was difficult to imagine a more perfect machine for the great old track. The safety factor was good. Even in apparently severe crashes, no injuries were recorded. The smaller cars seemed to disintegrate upon impact, with wheels flying in all directions, but with the body remaining intact and a roll cage protecting the driver (who lies almost on his back to drive). The weight was right and properly displaced, the power was far more than a driver needed, and the reliability was finally there.

► Co-owners J. C. Agajanian (seated on the car) and George Hurst (*right,* hat in hand) join their crew as they push Parnelli Jones' car down the pits. Jones had pushed the car to the pit entrance after completely running out of fuel at the north end of the track on his slowdown lap.

▼ Another stock car member of the Lotus team was driver Bobby Johns, who managed to qualify in twenty-second place. He drove a steady race to finish seventh, passing Don Branson on the final lap to win the position by .032 seconds. This was his only USAC appearance of the year; he finished the season driving in NASCAR Grand National events.

▲ After two years of indifferent pit work, the Wood Brothers of NASCAR stock car racing fame were hired to handle the refueling chores in the Lotus pits. Rival crews couldn't believe their watches when Clark spent only 19.8 seconds in the pits on his first stop. Two former "500" winners serving as commentators for television coverage assumed that his tanks had not been completely filled and predicted that he would have to make extra stops. Clark's tanks had been filled, however, and his second and final stop took only 24.7 seconds.

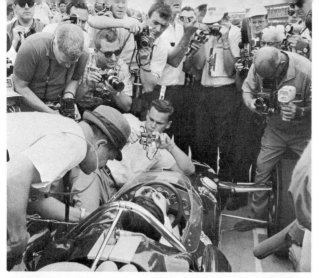

◄ Clark had developed a large following of fans, and after he broke the qualifying record for the second year in a row, he was surrounded by photographers. Clark's speed would soon be bettered by A. J. Foyt, but for the time being he had the pole position.

◄ With the demise of Foyt's transmission midway through the race, Clark's only real competition was gone, and his lead over Jones increased as the race went on. Here a member of the pit crew prepares to show Clark a signal board to inform him that he is 126 seconds ahead. As the race drew to a close, "The Flying Scot" began driving slower to save his car. In spite of this he still finished a minute and fifty-nine seconds ahead of Jones.

▼ Jim Clark became the first foreign driver to win the "500" since Dario Resta in 1916. His victory also marked the first time the race had been won by a rear-engined car and by a car powered by a V8 engine. In addition, it was the first "500" victory for a Ford-powered car.

▲ Members of the Lotus team including owner/builder/designer Colin Chapman (nearest camera in dark glasses) run toward Victory Lane as Clark takes his slowdown lap. In marked contrast to the previous year's finish, rear-engined cars held all but two of the top seventeen places.

▲ Mario Andretti gets a drink and a pair of clean goggles during his second pit stop. The once spotless white car is now streaked with oil as the track becomes slicker with every lap. The pattern of air flow over the windscreen is plainly etched in oil. This was his first full season on the Championship Trail and his first time at Indy, and Andretti had never run so fast or so long. His third place finish was remarkable for one so inexperienced and easily won him Rookie of the Year honors. His driving remained of the same high caliber throughout the year, and he became USAC National Driving Champion.

▼ Another European race car builder joined the ranks of Indy competitors as more car owners realized that the Lotus was the car to beat. Bud Tinglestad, competing in a rear-engined car for the first time, completed 115 laps in this Lola before hitting the wall in the northeast turn. Tinglestad qualified the car in twenty-fourth position and was awarded sixteenth place.

▲ *Middle,* In his final racing appearance at the Speedway, Len Sutton drove this rear-engined, Ford-powered Vollstedt to twelfth place after having qualified twelfth. He completed 177 laps before being flagged. His best showing at Indy was in 1962 when he placed second to teammate Rodger Ward.

▲ *Bottom,* Jimmy Clark raises his hand in the air as he flashes across the finish line at a record average speed of 151.388 mph, fully four miles per hour faster than the winning speed of the year before. This marked the first time the race had been run at an average speed of over 150 mph.

◀ For the first time in fifteen straight years at the Speedway, two-time Indy winner and twice USAC National Driving Champion Rodger Ward, *left*, failed to qualify for the "500." A veteran of ten years of racing, Johnny Boyd, *center*, successfully made the transition to the rear-engined cars, but went out after 140 laps with gearbox trouble. Rookie Jerry Grant, *right*, qualified well in the middle of the field, but only managed to finish thirty laps before the magneto packed in.

◀ Glen Wood and other members of Clark's crew frantically point out to a safety marshal that Clark is coming in for a pit stop. Since he would have to cut directly in front of Al Unser's car (45) which would be leaving its pit at any moment, there was a chance that a serious accident might result. All turned out well, and rookie Unser finished ninth behind the winning Clark.

▼ Al Miller brought his rear-engined Ford-powered Lotus in fourth behind Clark, Jones and Andretti to make it a clean sweep for the first four places for Ford. Miller had qualified at 157.805 mph for seventh starting position. Even though he made five pit stops for fuel, Miller recorded his highest finish at the Speedway.

▲ The Lotus invasion of Indy was complete this year: the top three qualifiers were Ford-powered Lotuses. Even A. J. Foyt, *right,* who broke Clark's record to capture the pole position did it at the wheel of one of those "funny cars that would never make it at the Speedway." Filling in for teammate Jimmy Clark is Bobby Johns, *center.* Clark was in Monaco for the Grand Prix at the time this picture was taken. Dan Gurney, *left,* was third fastest qualifier.

and one lonely Offy roadster qualified well back in the field. Bobby Grim was driving this Watson-designed roadster.

It had long been a fear of fans that the thundering start of the 500-mile race was a courtship with disaster. Speeds had increased dramatically, yet the start remained the same—efficient but potentially deadly. Lined up in their qualifying positions along the main stretch, the cars pull away behind a pace car. First they circle the track in a "parade lap" to perfectly align themselves and to give the fans a last view before the eye-blurring speeds to come; then there is a pace lap to pick up speed, and finally they hurtle out of the fourth turn and down the straightaway, three across, eleven deep, inches apart—and accelerating.

At the last moment the pace car sweeps down into pit lane and the green flag drops. The packed cars then streak down into the sweeping first turn, a ninety-degree bend, still accelerating rapidly.

It is a heart-stopping moment in sports. The sound often brings tears to the eyes and the drama and excitement of this moment are impossible to describe.

So in 1966 they blasted away as the pace car released them, and they flashed under the fluttering green flag—and in another instant pandemonium reigned. A race car lagged briefly, and another swerved slightly to miss the first. A third moved to fill the hole and instantly every driver tensed to avoid what he knew was coming. One second

they were thirty-three sleek cars, shining and roaring, multi-colored and snarling; the next they were a skidding, twisting group of candidates for an auto wrecking yard. Car parts skidded about the track and wheels flew in all directions—one sailed into the grandstand. A car burned. When the chain-reaction crash finally ended, eleven racing cars were junk and several others were damaged. Fans, stunned into silence at the violence of the crash, awaited word of injuries and deaths.

But, amazingly, there were no deaths, and the only injury was a mild one to the finger of champion A. J. Foyt caused by a sharp wire as he vaulted over the fence to escape the holocaust.

After the restart, delayed an hour while the track was cleaned and wrecked cars were towed away, rookie Graham Hill breezed along smoothly and when the checkered flag snapped down he had won. He became the first rookie driver to win the race since George Souders accomplished it in 1927, but Hill was a rookie only at Indy. He was already a recognized Grand Prix driver on the European circuits.

Grim's roadster, the only one in the race, had been in the middle of the first lap crash, and was destroyed before it ever reached the first turn.

The revolution was complete.

Or was it?

◄ At the start of the race, the first two rows—with the exception of Gordon Johncock (arrow 1)—pulled away from the rest of the field. In maneuvering around Johncock, Billy Foster was forced into the wall. He lost two wheels and the nose piece of the car upon contact. Foster kept his car against the wall (arrow 2) to keep the track clear. However, the nose piece (arrow 3) flew across the track. Mel Kenyon and Don Branson spun out, avoiding the nose piece, and Gary Congdon, unable to stop or swerve, drove right over Branson (arrow 4), leaving tire tracks on his helmet, but not in any way injuring him. Coming off Branson's car, Congdon hit the inside wall and bounced out toward the middle of the track, closing it to the rest of the cars. In all, sixteen cars were involved in this, the worst crash in Speedway history. Damage to five of the cars was slight, and they were repaired and continued in the race. The cars of A. J. Foyt (seeking his record-tying third "500" victory), Dan Gurney, Billy Foster, Don Branson, Gary Congdon, Al Miller, Cale Yarborough (making his Indy debut), Ronnie Duman, Larry Dickson, Bobby Grim and Arnie Knepper were damaged too badly to be repaired for this race.

▼ Gary Congdon's car continued sliding down the track all the way to the pit exit before coming to a stop. Gary is seen climbing out of the car as Jim Hurtubise, who had managed to pick his way through the wreckage, drives by. In the center photo fire control crews smother Al Miller's car with foam. The car had burst into flames after he had climbed out. Miller, *far left,* assures an ambulance attendant that he has not been injured in any way. Bottom photo shows track completely blocked with rescue equipment and crews whose job it was to clear the track after the race had been stopped. It took one hour and forty minutes to complete this monumental task and get the race restarted. Incredible as it may seem, save for a few minor cuts and bruises, not one driver was injured. Several of the cars slid long distances against the inner and outer walls, and some, with one or more wheels torn off, slid along the track, but with the exception of Miller's car there were no fires. The fuel cells developed after the deaths of Sachs and MacDonald in 1964 had done their job.

◄ Graham Hill may have been a former World Driving Champion, but since he had never competed at Indy before, he was, according to the rules, a rookie. In the background, partially hidden by the Victory Lane crowd and Hill's upraised hand, are Andy Granatelli and members of the STP crew standing around Jimmy Clark in his Lotus (not visible). Through an error in scoring, Clark and the crew thought they had won the race and went to Victory Lane.

▼ After threading his way through the wreckage of the first lap accident—Hill had qualified in the middle of the field—he drove a steady and consistent race. He moved up in position as one car after another dropped out, took over the lead on the 191st lap, and became the first rookie to win the "500" since 1927.

▲ Gordon Johncock, farthest from camera, passes Jim McElreath, who finished third. Johncock's car was one of the five that was involved in the crash but got back into the race. However, the rules at that time stipulated that no work could be done on a car while the race was stopped. After the race had been restarted his crew quickly repaired the nose of his car and Johncock roared out onto the track. Not counting his handicap start from the pits, Johncock actually completed his 200 laps in less time than the winner Graham Hill. This fine driving resulted in a fourth place finish.

▼ The first fifteen laps of the race were run under the caution flag. The drivers had the opportunity to run into the surface the oil-absorbent materials that had been spread on the track after the crash, and to familiarize themselves with the "feel" of the track where these materials had been spread. Mario Andretti's car burned a valve during these slow laps and dropped out soon after the green flag was shown.

▼ For the second year in a row Jimmy Clark qualified second and recovered from two spinouts into the infield to finish second for the second time in four years at the Speedway. A scoring error in the pits led Clark to believe he was in the lead late in the race. He slowed down and cruised to the checkered flag at a reduced pace.

▶ Clark, who ran under the STP banner this year, had the Granatelli brothers Vince and Joe and Vince, Jr., Andy's son, as members of his pit crew. The Wood Brothers had left their mark on the pits at Indy and for the second straight year Clark's stops were consistently shorter than anyone else's.

▼ Never having led in any of his previous six years at the Speedway, Lloyd Ruby, driving one of the new Eagles built by Dan Gurney, led for a total of 68 laps and earned over ten thousand dollars in lap prize money alone—more than any other driver that year. Ruby was in the lead at the three-quarter mark when a broken cam stud forced him to retire.

▲ Young Scotsman Jackie Stewart, who inherited the lead after Ruby dropped out, seemed a sure winner as he led the race for the next forty laps. However, with just ten laps to go, his engine lost its oil pressure and Stewart shut it off and coasted to a stop at the south end of the course. He was awarded fifth finishing position and was voted Rookie of the Year.

▲ On the day of the race, people are up and about in Gasoline Alley, as early as six o'clock in the morning, making last minute preparations for the big Memorial Day Classic. Soon the garage area will be jammed with drivers, mechanics, owners, representatives of accessory manufacturers, and everyone else connected with the 500-mile race run for the USAC Championship.

▶ After parking his disabled car in the infield, Jackie Stewart made the long walk back to the pits. En route he received a standing ovation from the spectators who had quickly become his admirers. In an unusual pre-race episode, Stewart assisted the Indiana State Police in apprehending thieves who were escaping in a stolen car. As a result he was made an honorary member of the Police Department and came to the driver's meeting brandishing an unusual souvenir—his own personal policeman's nightstick.

◄ *Top left,* Parnelli Jones, driving a new Shrike in its first appearance at the Speedway, qualified well at 162.484 mph for fourth starting position, but dropped out after only 87 laps when a wheel bearing went bad. He was awarded fourteenth place.

◄ *Middle left,* Dan Gurney's teammate Joe Leonard managed 170 laps before dropping out with engine trouble. He was awarded ninth place. In their very first year Eagles captured five of the starting positions with Leonard's being the highest finisher.

◄ *Bottom left,* After being unable to qualify the year before, Rodger Ward came back to capture a starting position near the middle of the field. He survived the first lap crash, but dropped out with handling problems after 74 laps. When asked how it felt to have driven through that wild melee at the start of the race, Ward replied that it was no fun and that when racing stops being fun, it's time to quit. After a Speedway career that spanned sixteen years and included fourteen consecutive starts, two wins, two seconds, a third and a fourth place finish, and after having gone the entire 200-lap distance in seven races, Ward retired.

▲ Knocked out in the first lap crash was Bobby Grim's old-style roadster, the only one in the race this year. The car managed to qualify after its Offenhauser engine was fitted with a turbocharger, but it was the slowest car in the field. No one could deny that the grand era of the Offy roadster was gone forever.

▲ The STP Turbocar was truly the first space-age racing vehicle. It was powered by a small 260-pound Pratt & Whitney turbine engine which was designed for use in small aircraft, boats and helicopters. It was rated at 550 horsepower and propelled the bright red racer down the back straight at Indy at 200 mph. The engine could run on any combustible liquid, including alcohol, kerosene, gasoline or perfume. The car was considered by many to be one of the safest machines in history. A major contribution to safety was the placement of the 48-gallon fuel supply deep inside the rigid spinal chassis, within a riveted aluminum structure of enormous (30 G) crash resistance. The unique side-by-side placement of the driver and engine on either side of the central chassis gave the car a squat, bulging, somewhat ungainly look. With its great handling, however, it easily left all others behind.

and car builders had their customary
eleven months of the year to experiment with
new techniques, new chassis forms, and
new methods of power. Though the funny car
was plainly the car of the day, a few builders,
particularly the Granatelli brothers, were
contemplating further advances. With a name for
trying new things at Indy (they had
campaigned the crowd-pleasing, though losing,
Novi), they appeared at the track on
May 1, 1967, with a race car so odd that many
veteran fans laughed out loud. Not that the
design had not been tried before—it had, but
always with a notable lack of success.
Still, the Granatellis seemed very confident.

The new car was turbine-powered, and was
immediately dubbed the "swooshmobile" by
reporters because it was so quiet. It was
different. With the cockpit and the engine, side
by side, and painted a bright red, the car
appeared squat and stubby.

It couldn't be competitive, decided the fans,
and the general consensus was that Andy
Granatelli was only fooling himself. He had put
three years of design and construction into
the race car, and over a million dollars—and
people laughed. He expected to compete
with the likes of Mario Andretti and A. J. Foyt
and all the other great drivers and their
proven rear-engined piston-driven race cars.

The laughter quieted down a bit when
Granatelli announced that his driver was to be
Parnelli Jones, a fine driver and a shrewd
businessman. Parnelli, the fans knew, had had
his choice of machines, and he had *chosen*
to drive the Turbocar.

Andy, calm and confident on his stool in the
pits with his brothers on each side,
smiled serenely.

Qualification days came, and suddenly the
racing world knew what Granatelli had
known all along. It was a superb machine. It
stuck to the curves as though it were
nailed to the track; it had fantastic acceleration
with its four-wheel drive and it had far
fewer moving parts to break down under the
500-mile grind. It had power to spare
and it handled beautifully. It was obvious that
Parnelli was not driving the car for the
money alone. He was driving the car to win.

New plans went on the drawing boards in
garages across the country, and 1968
plans were made even before the 1967 race.
The trend toward a new generation of
racing machines was obvious.

Art Lathrop, at one time the owner of a fleet of
Offy-powered roadsters during the
Lotus-powered-by-Ford revolution, pointed to
his machines one afternoon and said
calmly to reporters, "Gentlemen, you are
looking at a million dollars worth of junk!"

Now owners were suddenly saying the same
about their rear-engined lightweights.

So it was Jones and his Turbocar against
thirty-two now-standard Indy machines, and as
they blasted away on that day in 1967,
the future became the present. In the first
turn, Jones, who had qualified in sixth position,
moved outside and by the end of the
second turn he was in the lead and moving

away easily. At the end of the very first lap he was alone and far ahead of the thundering pack. He was in absolute command of the race, and a rain delay with a restart the following day made no difference.

Throughout nearly 500 miles the race was for second place, because most of the time Jones and his swooshmobile were out of sight. Fans screamed their delight, or disgust, at the ease with which Jones was winning in a race which normally called for every single ounce of a driver's skill and concentration and energy. Jones was breezing along effortlessly.

Behind him came Gurney and Foyt and Andretti and all the other great drivers who had qualified, but they began to drop out one by one as their machines failed under the strain of trying to catch the turbine. Foyt stayed in, but he was far behind in second place. The race pounded on, with Jones in the lead on every single lap except those during which he was in his pit for fuel —after which he promptly regained the lead and moved far ahead. In the Turbocar pit, Granatelli smilingly readied himself for a long-awaited trip to Victory Lane to accept his well-deserved rewards.

But suddenly, incredibly, Jones slowed down!

With less than ten miles remaining of the original five hundred, Jones pulled sadly into the pits. A six-dollar bearing in the transmission of the turbine had failed. Threading through a crashing, spinning, last-lap accident, A. J. Foyt swept to the victory which had been snatched from Jones' grasp. It was A. J.'s third win at Indy.

But even though it had not won, the turbine was the obvious next step at Indy, and car owners redoubled their efforts at the drawing boards.

▲ At the start of the race pole-sitter Mario Andretti jumped into the lead as the cars headed for the first turn. But Parnelli Jones, starting in sixth position in the STP Turbocar, passed Joe Leonard, A. J. Foyt, Gordon Johncock, Dan Gurney and Andretti in the first two turns and was leading the race in less than half a lap. The "funny car" of 1967 was not only leading, it was rapidly pulling away.

▲ Jones in the STP Turbocar #40, shown here lapping Jochen Rindt, led every lap of the race when not in the pits for fuel (after which he quickly regained this position)—until the 197th lap.

▶ Andy Granatelli (stopwatches in hand) goes over practice times with Parnelli. Assuming the car's potential to be even greater than it actually was, many critics claimed that Jones was sandbagging (not running it as fast as it would go) when his practice speeds were not the fastest at the Speedway that year. Jones replied that he ran the car as fast as it would go and still hold together.

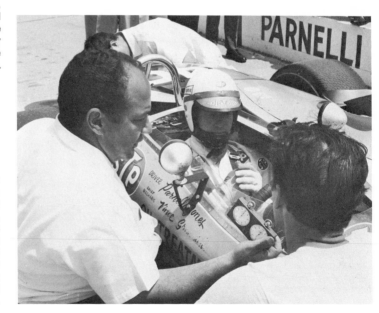

▶ STP also sponsored the Lotuses of Jim Clark and Graham Hill. Last year's winner Hill, however, had great difficulty in qualifying his car, and it began to look as if he might not make the race. A trackside discussion with Granatelli that included some tips on driving at Indy did the trick. Hill started on the last row, his worst position ever at Indy.

▶ Lotus chief, Colin Chapman, sits in Hill's car totally frustrated in all his efforts to make this and Clark's car competitive. In his previous three years at the Speedway Clark had qualified his Lotus either first or second fastest. This year he barely made the race and dropped out after only thirty-five laps with a burned piston.

▶ Hill's troubles carried over onto race day and the car wouldn't start. As the rest of the field pulled away for the parade lap, Hill was pushed into the pits where the Lotus crew managed to start the car. Here Hill is accelerating down the pit lane to join the rest of the field as they begin the pace lap. Hill's troubles were far from over, however, as he burned a piston after only twenty-three laps.

▲ Mario Andretti burned his clutch attempting to keep up with Jones in the "Silent Screamer." Andretti pulled into the pits thinking the race was over for him, when a rainstorm halted the "500." Revised rules now allowed crews to work on their cars while the race was stopped. The car was repaired, but when the race was restarted the following day, Andretti was several laps behind. Driving at a furious pace, Andretti was finished when he lost a wheel.

▶ Parnelli Jones (nearest camera) was involved in one of LeeRoy Yarbrough's three spins. Both cars spun down off the track onto the infield grass but were able to continue. In fact, Jones was able to maintain his position at the head of the field.

▲ A. J. Foyt (14) passes Bobby Unser, who finished ninth. Confident that the Turbocar would not go the distance, Foyt drove in a steady and conservative manner, very unlike his usual hard-charging style, and held second place for a total of 117 laps. When the Turbocar broke, Foyt glided into first place.

▶ Lou Meyer, *left,* and Foyt each hold up three fingers at the Victory Banquet, signifying their three "500" victories. Of the triple "500" winners—Meyer, Foyt, Wilbur Shaw and Mauri Rose—only Foyt is still racing and looking for a record-breaking fourth victory at Indy.

▲ Obviously pleased with his third visit to Indy's
Victory Lane, Foyt gladly suffers the barrage of
questions from the many reporters who broadcast live
interviews with the winner. In one of the wildest
finishes in "500" history, Foyt threaded his way through
a multiple-car last lap crash in the fourth turn to take
the checkered flag from starter Pat Vidan, who
immediately waved the red flag to halt the race. For
the first time in Speedway history only one car
completed the entire 200 laps.

▲ On the seventy-fourth lap rookie Wally Dallenbach, who had qualified well in the middle of the field, spun coming down the main straightaway and hit the pit wall twice, smashing the rear end of his car. He was uninjured, however, and quickly leaped from his car and sprang to safety over the pit wall.

▶ New Zealander Denis Hulme came to the Speedway for the first time and qualified Smokey Yunick's City of Daytona Beach Special (an Eagle built by Dan Gurney's All American Racers) at 163.376 mph. Starting from twenty-fourth place, Hulme moved up twenty positions to finish fourth and capture Rookie of the Year honors.

▲ Jackie Stewart qualified car #43 at 162.221 mph, which proved too slow as he was bumped from the field. Since Indy regulations prohibit qualifying a car more than once, Stewart climbed into car #24 which he qualified at 164.099 mph for a starting position. He had worked his way from twenty-ninth place to third when his engine blew on the 169th lap. Stewart was out of the race in exactly the same place as he had been the year before when he dropped out with engine troubles while leading.

▲ Roger McCluskey (12) overtakes Carl Williams, who had tangled with Bob Veith in the third turn. McCluskey's Eagle dropped out after 165 laps with a blown engine. Williams and Veith both lost the noses of their cars but continued in the race to finish tenth and eleventh respectively.

▲ *Top,* Al Unser (Bobby's younger brother) in only his third start at the Speedway qualified ninth and finished second. A team car to the one driven by Jackie Stewart, this Lola was the highest placed British-made car in the race. Al also finished second in four other Championship races and finished fifth again in the point standings to retain the #5 on his car.

▲ *Middle,* Joe Leonard, three-time National Motorcycle Champion and four-time runner-up, qualified this Foyt-built Coyote next to teammate A. J. Foyt on the second row. Two pit stops in three laps a third of the way through the race dropped him from ninth to nineteenth position. Although his final pit stop cost him two positions, he moved up steadily to finish third.

▲ *Bottom,* Rookie Art Pollard started thirteenth and was running third when he made his first pit stop. A spin on the northwest turn and a penalty lap for a push to restart dropped him to an eighth place finish.

▲ Bobby Unser, who qualified eighth and finished
ninth, seen here during a normal pit stop for fuel. He
had managed to work his way up to fourth place
midway through the race when an extended pit stop
(over six minutes) dropped him to sixteenth place,
his lowest at any time during the race. Unser managed
to work his way back to ninth place when the
race was flagged.

▲ Andy Granatelli amassed a formidable team for this year's "500." Seen here with Andy are Parnelli Jones in the rebuilt #40, Colin Chapman, and Jim Clark in the new Lotus Turbocar that featured a sharp, wedge shape with the engine in the rear. Andy's team also included Graham Hill, Jackie Stewart and several more Lotus Turbocars. But the team dwindled with the death of Clark in Europe, the retirement of Jones and a broken wrist sustained by Stewart during practice for a Formula 2 race.

▶ Ex-Lotus Formula 1 team driver Mike Spence was hired for the Indy effort and he quickly adapted to the unusual four-wheel-drive Turbocars and their different handling. Though he had never raced at the Speedway before, Spence began turning laps of over 169 mph, just short of Andretti's qualifying record. As everyone was well satisfied with his car, Spence began testing the car to be driven by Greg Weld, another new team member. Inexplicably, Spence crashed Weld's car and died that same night of his injuries.

IT WAS 1968

and surely this was the year of the turbine. Other machines were entered in the 500-mile race, but as all eyes had once been on the little Lotus-powered-by-Ford racers, now all attention was focused on the beautiful turbine-powered racers in the garage area.

Carroll Shelby had brought a stable of turbines, designed by ex-Granatelli designer Ken Wallis (engine and driver side-by-side), and Andy Granatelli had brought last year's model plus four brand new, wedge-shaped Turbocars designed by Lotus chief Colin Chapman. These had the jet engine in the rear of the car.

Another noise, however, was in the air. The turbocharging of piston engines was under test, and several top drivers were entered in this type of racer. Still, the turbine machines were favored.

In spite of his protestations that due to changes in the rules the turbines were sadly underpowered, Granatelli's machines rushed out on the first qualification day and captured the first two positions in the field, establishing astounding new track records along the way. Meanwhile, Shelby's turbines were withdrawn as not yet ready for competition. Third in the field was Bobby Unser in a turbocharged Offy, a lightning-fast, piston-driven racer.

So race day dawned damp and gray-looking, and fans split their attention between a threatening sky and the upcoming battle for supremacy. The racers were pushed to their assigned spots on the grid and the final ceremonies were conducted. The bombs exploded overhead, the balloons drifted up into a partially overcast sky and the announcement came:

"Gentlemen, start your engines!"

Moments later, after the traditional parade and pace laps, the field thundered—or "swooshed" in the case of the three Turbocars —into the first turn. True to every prediction, Joe Leonard in the pole-winning Granatelli Turbocar rocketed into the lead. Close on his square tail was the racer of Bobby Unser, and within striking distance was the Turbocar of former World Driving Champion Graham Hill.

The race, for all practical purposes, seemed over as soon as it started, for everybody knew that the turbines were practically failure-proof—especially after 1967 and Jones' near victory. It would simply be a matter of pushing the race to tremendous speeds and forcing the conventional cars to fail one by one. The rumor spread through the stands that Granatelli was going to have his turbines sweep across the finish line in formation—one, two, three—a worthy dream after years of frustration with the dramatic Novi racer, and the near win of 1967, but it was not to be.

Although Leonard either led or dogged the heels of the leader throughout the entire race, and was leading at 190 laps, his Turbocar failed near the very end—almost at the same moment that the Turbocar of Art Pollard was failing (Hill's had crashed)—and the dream was over. Bobby Unser swept by the stalled Leonard car and on to victory in his turbocharged Offy racer. Once again the Turbocars had almost tasted victory, and then had been beaten.

Turbines may never be seen again at Indy, for owners of conventional cars are attempting to have them banned once and for all as having no place on an "automobile" track. Nevertheless, for a time the turbines injected a new life and drama into the brickyard—and they may yet return to win.

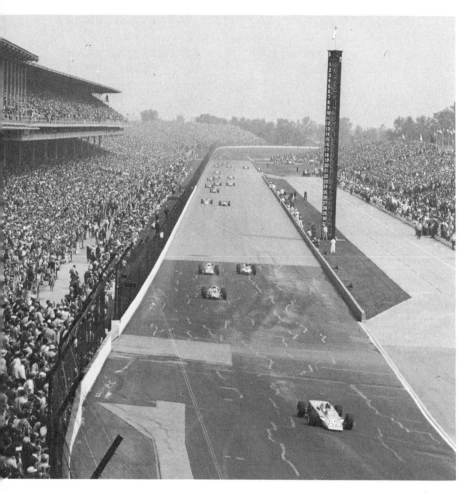

▲ At the start of the race it began to look like another
STP Turbocar pullaway as Leonard, from his pole
position, shot into the lead and pulled a short
distance away from Bobby Unser in second place.
Unser held on, however, and eight laps later
passed Leonard for the lead.

▶ Parnelli Jones, in the pits with Andy Granatelli
during the race, points out early trouble for the team,
as Art Pollard, driving the third Turbocar, makes
an unscheduled pit stop.

▶ When Jones decided the #40 Turbocar would not be competitive, despite its having been redesigned for this race, Joe Leonard was assigned to drive the car. He crashed during practice, and although Leonard escaped without injuries, the car was never raced again.

▶ History repeats itself as the STP Turbocar breaks down and coasts to a stop while leading late in the race. Here the STP crew have turned the car around and are pushing it back to the pits from the first turn where Leonard had abandoned it. The cars had been running under the caution flag for ten laps when the green flag was shown again on lap 191. As Leonard hit the throttle a fuel pump shaft snapped and the engine stopped.

▲ This shot shows Bobby Unser trailing Joe Leonard—which proved to be the exception, not the rule, during the race. Leonard led for only thirty-one laps while Unser's turbocharged Offy led for 127 laps.

◀ An Eagle crew member fans Denis Hulme with a pit signal board to keep the eye-watering, nose-searing nitromethane fumes away while the engine is being warmed up for his qualifying run. Hulme's decision to wait until the last minute before leaving for Monaco in the hopes that he might get another attempt to qualify paid off. Hulme qualified at over 164 mph, stopped for just a moment to have his picture taken by the Speedway photographer and then jumped from the car. He ran through Gasoline Alley to a waiting helicopter which took him straight to the airport. After finishing fifth at Monaco, he returned to Indy and for the second consecutive year, now driving for Dan Gurney's All American Racers, finished fourth. Had he not had to make an unexpected pit stop to change a tire that had been punctured by debris left on the track (from a crash late in the race) Hulme would have finished third behind Unser and teammate Dan Gurney.

▶ Ex-racing driver Carroll Shelby also thought turbines were the way to go at Indy. He entered two turbines designed by Ken Wallis, who had designed the #40 STP car. The cars were to be driven by Bruce McLaren, *left,* and Denis Hulme (in cockpit). The cars did not handle at all well and were withdrawn.
McLaren later said: "I have never spent so much time in or around a race track and so little time actually *in* a racing car *on* it! I wasn't able really to appreciate what Indy is all about because the car was so bad."

◄ Denis Hulme provided more than his share of pre-race excitement while trying to qualify his Eagle. Hard-pressed for time on the final Saturday of qualifying (he was also scheduled to race in the Grand Prix of Monaco the following day) his problems began when in a last minute practice session before attempting to qualify, his engine blew. Getting a ride back to the pit area, Hulme was informed by the crew that the engine could be replaced in a few hours. He decided to wait until the last possible minute before leaving for Monaco.

▲ Here we see Graham Hill in the #70 STP Turbocar lose a wheel in the number two turn after 110 laps, spin around and crash into the outer retaining wall near the start of the back stretch, Hill's car slides backward along the wall as his right rear tire and wheel (with portions of the suspension still attached) go bouncing down the track towards the path of the other cars. Note the driver with his hand raised in the air (in the lower left hand portion of the photo) warning those behind him to slow down. The photo on the left shows how badly damaged this Lotus racer was, though Hill was not injured.

► When the car Ronnie Bucknum (in cockpit) had qualified was mistakenly disqualified for weighing less than the legal minimum, preparations were made for Bucknum to qualify Mario Andretti's backup car. Seen here with Andretti's co-chief mechanics Clint Brawner (in hat) and Jim McGee, Bucknum was just about to make his qualifying attempt when it was discovered that the scales used to weigh the cars were not working properly and that Bucknum's car and qualifying attempt were legal.

▲ Andretti's backup car was qualified by Larry Dickson, who was relieved by Andretti during the race after Mario's car had burned a piston. Here he attempts to pass Dan Gurney in an effort to make up time lost in the pits. His efforts were to no avail, however, as this car also burned a piston after only twenty-four laps. Gurney went on to capture second place, his best finish at the Speedway.

▲ Dan Gurney's pit stop, shown here, is typical of
the planned hysteria of such stops in all major races.
Each member of the pit crew has a job to do and
will rarely do any other. Things went smoothly for
Gurney this year, and after qualifying his stock block
Ford-powered Eagle tenth fastest, he drove a fast,
steady race to finish second with an average speed of a
mile an hour slower than winner Bobby Unser.

◀ Lloyd Ruby's pit crew helps him out of his car at the end of the race. Now in a state of near-exhaustion, forty-year-old Ruby had driven an extremely fast race and was the last car to complete the full 200 laps. After his dead-last finish of the year before when his car bent a valve after only three laps, Ruby was again running with the leaders. His fifth place finish was his second best at the Speedway.

▲ Rookie Mike Mosley loses control and spins his car in front of Mel Kenyon. Ably controlling the spin, Mosley got back into the race and went on to complete 197 laps and finished eighth, nineteen positions better than his twenty-seventh place start. Mel Kenyon qualified in the middle of the field and drove a fine race to finish third in his Gerhardt, splitting up the Eagles of Unser, Gurney and Hulme.

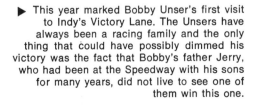

▲ Ruby (25) and Leonard (60) dice for position in the turns. Ruby posted the fastest lap of the race when he turned in a lap at 168.666 mph. Although most of the race had been a battle between Leonard and Bobby Unser, it was Ruby who was leading with twenty-five laps to go. However, a late-race pit stop to fix a coil cost him his victory.

▶ Bobby Unser, seen here with car owner Bob Wilke, (wearing cap), holds up pit signal board with his fastest practice lap speed on it. Unser's was the only non-turbine-powered car to go over 170 mph.

▶ This year marked Bobby Unser's first visit to Indy's Victory Lane. The Unsers have always been a racing family and the only thing that could have possibly dimmed his victory was the fact that Bobby's father Jerry, who had been at the Speedway with his sons for many years, did not live to see one of them win this one.

▼ Billy Vukovich, son of the late two-time Indy winner Bill Vukovich, qualified his turbocharged Shrike at 163.510 mph for twenty-third place starting position. Despite a spin in the fourth turn, Vukovich finished in seventh place and captured Rookie of the Year honors.

▲ The son of another famous driver was a rookie at the Speedway this year. Gary Bettenhausen, son of the late two-time National Driving Champion Tony Bettenhausen, nervously smokes a cigarette as he awaits his turn to qualify for the "500." The pressure and tensions are so great as the number of places open in the field shrinks that many drivers, particularly rookies, crack. Bettenhausen remained cool, however, and qualified in twenty-second position, only to drop out of the race after forty-three laps with oil cooler problems.

▲ Dan Gurney ponders the weighty problem of how to modify the quick-raising jack so that it will work with the newly revised suspension design on his Eagle.

◄ Mel Kenyon, three-time USAC Midget Champion, had a good year at Indy despite the setback of insufficient sponsorship money for the car. His hometown, Lebanon, Indiana, raised thousands of dollars in contributions toward his Indy effort. With the addition of this money he entered the car as the City of Lebanon Special. Kenyon is used to overcoming setbacks. In 1965 his left hand was so severely burned in an accident that even surgery could not save the fingers on that hand. He now drives with a special glove that has a socket which fits over a pin clamped to the steering wheel.

▼ The attempt of three-time "500" winner A. J. Foyt to become the only four-time winner was thwarted after 86 laps when the engine blew. In each year after Foyt had won the "500," his finish was usually way down. He finished twenty-third the year after his first victory, fifteenth following his second win and this year he finished twentieth.

▼ Gasoline Alley appears strangely vacant as rain sends everyone running for the shelter of the garages. Many days of practice and qualifying were lost as the month of May proved unusually wet in Indianapolis this year. Unlike sports car or Formula racers, Championship cars, and particularly tires, are not designed for racing on wet tracks. Consequently, all racing activity at Indy stops whenever it rains.

◀ Some cars are pushed back to their garages in Gasoline Alley while others are hastily covered with blankets and tarpaulins as practice is stopped and the track closed on account of rain.

▶ Burning the midnight oil is not unusual for a race mechanic. After qualifications and before the race, each car is completely stripped and cleaned and every part is carefully inspected before the car is rebuilt. Garages brightly lighted in the middle of the night—and sometimes all through the night—are a common sight in Gasoline Alley.

▲ Mario Andretti's new turbocharged Ford-powered
four-wheel-drive Lotus was easily the fastest car at the
Speedway—Andretti became the first man this year
to go over 170 mph. However, the car was demolished
during a practice crash brought about when a wheel
snapped. Andretti's only injuries were painful
burns around his nose and upper lip.

and the turbines were dead. One was entered, the Jack Adams Special (with an annulus inlet area of only 12.5 square inches), but it barely qualified and was finally bumped by faster cars. Then, to officially bury these controversial racers, USAC announced that the Jack Adams turbine would have been banned in any case for an air guidance vane mounted in the inlet area.

Another type of air compression had a firm hold, though. This was the turbocharger being used on a vast majority of the thirty-three qualified cars. Driven by exhaust gases, the turbocharger rams air into the engine, adding more power to already powerful piston-driven engines. The first nine cars in the field had turbos; then came Dan Gurney's stock block engine. Then the next eighteen had turbos. In the last five, three more were turbocharged, and two were Repco Brabham engines.

Mario Andretti crashed his four-wheel-drive Lotus turbo Ford just before the second two days of qualification (the first weekend had been rained out). Although Andretti suffered only minor facial burns, the stupendous crash completely demolished the prime car. Andretti was forced to turn to his two-wheel-drive turbo Ford Hawk backup car for the race.

A. J. Foyt took the pole position with a speed of 170.568, a record for piston engine cars, with Mario taking second fastest time for the middle of the front row of starters. The 1968 winner, Bobby Unser, captured the outside front row.

Many eyes were on the flashy rookie Mark Donohue, who did as expected and beat a number of veterans as he qualified for the second row pole with an average speed of 168.903 miles per hour. The field was filled on the second weekend with Peter Revson, another rookie, bumping Rick Muther for thirty-third spot.

Of eleven cars entered under the STP label, Andy Granatelli, the former turbine king, managed to get three into the field—Andretti, Art Pollard, and Carl Williams. All eleven were conventional piston-powered racers. The Granatelli/Andretti combination was the favorite of most fans. Each man had suffered many frustrating defeats at the brickyard and had still returned to the battle. Mario was perhaps the most popular driver in the field, and Andy had become a popular car owner with thousands of fans who felt that USAC had been too strict with him and his Turbocars. Now the two men had combined their talents, and the fans were watching hopefully.

Race morning was bright, clear, and hot as Tony Hulman ordered, "Gentlemen, start your engines!" Everybody obeyed the command but eighth-place starter LeeRoy Yarbrough who was having trouble with his portable starter. By the time Yarbrough finally got moving, the field had completed the parade lap and was well into the much faster pace lap. But Yarbrough caught up and threaded his way into his position as the field headed into the main stretch, and the sparkling, aligned racers were waved away in perfect order.

And the great thunder which announces the Indy field in the first turn blasted up, to be heard for miles around, and around the world on closed-circuit television. But was it 1967 . . . or 1968? . . . Pulling away from the pack was a bright red STP Special, just as in previous years. Only it wasn't "swooshing,"—it was roaring. Mario Andretti, in the Granatelli-owned Hawk, had jumped into the lead.

But the race is 500 miles long. Much could happen, and Granatelli knew that better than any man. Still, Andretti streaked smoothly along, leading the field lap after lap.

But A. J. Foyt, anxious for an historic fourth victory in the "500," grabbed the lead from Mario and widened the gap. Following Foyt around Andretti was Foyt's teammate Roger McCluskey, in an identical turbo Ford Coyote.

Then, in rapid order, McCluskey ran out of gas, Andretti and Foyt pitted for fuel, and popular veteran Lloyd Ruby swept into the lead, followed closely by Wally Dallenbach with still another turbocharged engine, an Offy. With a Ruby pit stop, Dallenbach inherited the lead, then it was Foyt again as Wally pitted.

By lap forty, eight cars were out. The day was hot and the speeds were new records—tough on machinery. Billy Vukovich was out, Art Pollard was out, and so were Bruce Walkup, Ronnie Bucknum, Gary Bettenhausen, Johnny Rutherford, George Follmer, and Jim McElreath, who had steered his burning car up and out of the groove in the first turn to protect the other racers.

A. J. Foyt, running a fine race in the lead, had suffered turbocharger waste-gate problems during practice, and they started again. Ruby grabbed the lead followed by Andretti as Foyt faltered and finally pitted. But Lloyd Ruby was due for some heartbreak too.

With the fans screaming at Ruby to hurry, he pitted for fuel for the second time. A mistake in the pits tore out the entire fuel mechanism from the left side of his car and he was out for the day. He had been running the finest race of his career, and every fan felt deep sympathy for the ace driver as he wearily hauled himself from his disabled car.

Meanwhile, veteran Arnie Knepper had lost a wheel and crashed directly in the middle of the main stretch. Rather than running for

▲ After leading the early laps, Andretti (2) eased the pace slightly as his car began to overheat and is seen here running third behind A. J. Foyt (6) and Lloyd Ruby (4) at about the 60-lap mark. Andretti later said he had been certain he could outrun Foyt if necessary in the closing laps, but he hadn't been too sure of Ruby. Foyt had slipped back to fourth place midway through the race but then dropped out of contention when turbocharger problems kept him in the pits for nearly half an hour. Ruby was then leading with Andretti close behind.

safety, Knepper stood atop his wrecked car and waved the oncoming field safely around through the dust and smoke of the wreck. It was a fine act of bravery, and no doubt prevented a simple accident from becoming a tragic one.

On lap 152 Mario Andretti came in for his last scheduled fuel stop. He was leading Denny Hulme and Dan Gurney by over a lap, and McCluskey by even more. Although the fans once again screamed at him to hurry, the STP crew worked slowly and carefully, and Andretti finally pulled away after a long stop, still in the lead. Hulme dropped out, Joe Leonard hit a piece of the Knepper wreckage and dropped out for a long repair job, and Mark Donohue moved up. On lap 170 it was Andretti, Gurney, Donohue, Unser, and Mel Kenyon, with rookie Peter Revson moving up. Then a charging Mark Donohue slowed with problems.

The fans counted away the last few laps with Mario, who had slowed the pace considerably in an effort to nurse his car to the finish. Andy Granatelli watched intently from the pits, never making a move to Victory Lane, never even glancing that way. He'd been so close before, as Mario had. Could this be his year?

Five . . . four . . . three . . . two . . . the white flag came out for Mario Andretti. Nearly 300,000 fans at the track held their breath as Mario cruised around the last 2½ miles. He was certainly in "Granatelli country" where last-second failures change triumph to heartbreak. This time, though, Andretti took the checkered flag to win the 1969 500-mile race at Indy . . . at last!

▲ Despite his painful facial burns, Andretti quickly adjusted his driving technique to extract the maximum performance out of his backup car, a two-wheel-drive design that handled quite differently from the four-wheel-drive Lotus.

When his car caught fire as he came out of the fourth turn, Jim McElreath remained calm and guided it down the main straight. He brought it to a halt up out of the groove in the first turn, clambered out and walked toward the concrete retaining wall, as Sam Sessions (arrow 1) drives by on the track and the fire crew arrives. Standing on the wall (arrow 2) and seeing the fire extinguished with foam, he reaches up to remove his helmet. The fans applauded and cheered his actions as he walked back to the pits with helmet in hand, but for Jim McElreath (and for the #38 Adams Aircraft Special) it's the end of this year's "500."

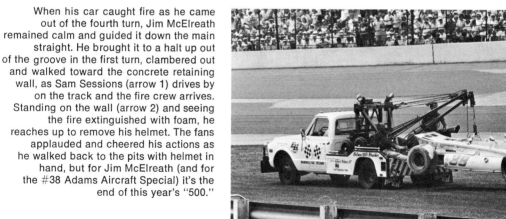

After so many years of hard work, tears, and heartbreaking near-misses (twenty-three for Andy Granatelli and four for Mario Andretti) these two men joined forces to make it an all-Italian victory and cause at least one writer to refer to Indy as "Italianapolis." Granatelli's enthusiasm was so boundless that he grabbed Andretti and planted a victory kiss on his cheek even before the beauty queen could get near him.

▲ Mark Donohue, twice United States Road Racing Champion, was a rookie at the Speedway, but throughout practice his times were very fast and many people expected him to outqualify some of the Indy veterans. Not only did he live up to their expectations, he astonished everyone with a qualifying average of 168.903 mph to capture the fourth starting position. Donohue ran a consistently fast race and was never out of the top ten from the 40-lap point onward. In fact, he had worked his way into second place during the closing stages of the race before magneto problems and a long pit stop dropped him to seventh. His fine performance netted him Rookie of the Year honors.

◄ Al Unser was considered to be one of the drivers with a real chance at victory this year before he broke his leg in a freak accident while riding a motorcycle around Gasoline Alley. Unser remained in good humor in spite of this, and could often be seen riding in an electric cart behind the pits.

▼ After qualifying in twenty-second place, Mike Mosley, in only his second year at the Speedway, drove a great race and had worked himself up to as high as second place late in the race before blowing his engine and retiring after 162 laps. He was awarded thirteenth finishing position.

▲ Rookie Bruce Walkup qualified in twenty-eighth position, but he did not complete a single lap in the race because the gearbox broke on the very first lap. This misfortune gave Walkup the dubious distinction of being the only driver in twenty years to drop out of the race with mechanical problems before completing a single lap.

▲ Wally Dallenbach (22) is closely pursued by Ruby (4) as they lap Bud Tingelstad (15) filling in for Al Unser, and Jim Malloy (10). Running in fourth place on lap 51, Dallenbach inherited the lead when the first three cars (Foyt, Andretti and Ruby) all made their first pit stops on lap 52. From this point on Dallenbach never dropped lower than sixth until his clutch went after 82 laps. He was awarded twenty-first place.

▼ As soon as the pace car had pulled off the track into the pits at the conclusion of the pace lap, and the starter waved the green flag to the accelerating field of screaming cars, Mario Andretti (2) jumped into the lead and began to pull away from pole-sitter A. J. Foyt (6) and last year's winner Bobby Unser (1), who also started with them on the front row. Andretti led for five laps before Foyt took over.

As the pre-race ceremonies draw to a close and the cars line up in their starting positions on the main straight in front of the pits, thousands of colorful balloons are released into the air. They drift across the track as the shattering explosions of aerial bombs announce that only a few minutes remain before Speedway owner Tony Hulman calls out those famous words: "Gentlemen, start your engines!"

▲ Eagle teammates Dan Gurney (48) and Denis Hulme (42) were running second and third at the 140-lap point in the race. Hulme dropped out with clutch troubles on the 146th lap, giving second place to Gurney, who held it all the way to the finish line. He placed second for the second consecutive year.

► At the start of the race, LeeRoy Yarbrough's engine refused to fire. As the rest of the field moved off behind the pace car, Yarbrough's crew pushed his car into the pits where they managed to get it running in time for him to speed around the track and slip into his starting position in the middle of the third row.

For the third year in a row, veteran Jim Hurtubise, a driver much favored by the fans, was trying to prove that a front-engined car could still get the job done at Indy. In 1967 he qualified but was bumped out of the field by a faster qualifier. In 1968 he qualified and finished thirtieth —out after only nine laps with a burned piston. This year he could not even qualify.

When a reporter asked Hurtubise what he would do if he could not qualify his turbocharged Offy-powered front-engined Mallard, Hurtubise replied: "I don't know. Maybe I'll go fishing." The day after qualifications had closed, everyone passing his locked garage could see this sign.

Three-time World Driving Champion Jack Brabham, *left,* came to the Speedway with two of his Brabham Repco racers, but had decided not to drive himself. Peter Revson, *right,* was to have his choice of the two cars and the other would remain as a backup. The old racing urge got to Brabham, however, and he qualified his car twenty-ninth. Revson was the last man to qualify, capturing the thirty-third place and finishing fifth.

◀ Since the first weekend of qualifications had been washed out by heavy rains—something that had never happened before in the memory of Indy followers—when qualifying opened on the following weekend there was a long line of cars waiting. Twenty-five cars qualified on Saturday, just short of the record of twenty-seven in one day set in 1963.

▶ In spite of the fact that rookie Jigger Sirois did not qualify for the "500" he will be remembered for as long as people think about this race. As a result of an odd, totally unpredictable set of circumstances, Sirois actually blew a chance at the pole position. The first in line to qualify on the first day, Sirois was on the track in his initial qualifying attempt when his crew decided his speed was not good enough and called him in to the pits. The next man on the track was prevented from qualifying when it started to rain. Had Sirois' crew allowed him to finish his attempt he would have been the fastest qualifier that day since nobody else got a chance to run.

◀ While waiting to qualify, former United States Road Racing Champion George Follmer—a rookie this year at Indy—seeks to break the tension by clowning around. Follmer climbed aboard the electrically powered cart used to push his race car to and from the garage area, saying, "If I can't qualify my race car, I'll qualify this."

▶ A. J. Foyt goes over proper refueling techniques with members of his pit crew during pit stop practice before the race. The pit stops take only seconds, but hours are spent in perfecting the procedures.

▲ Sam Sessions fractured his left kneecap when a universal joint broke as he started down the back straight while practicing. The car slid 480 feet, spun once, then hit the inner wall and spun twice more before sliding 560 feet onto the infield grass. Considered a highly unlikely qualifier, he hobbled around the pits on crutches after refusing a cast. Not only did he manage to qualify his car in twenty-third starting position, he drove a steady race to finish twelfth.

▲ If Colin Chapman and Andy Granatelli appear more than a little harrassed, perhaps it's because time is slipping away, and of their combined teams, the only member to qualify so far is Mario Andretti.

▼ Al Miller managed to qualify this Jack Adams Airplanes Special, the only turbine-powered car entered, but his speed was way too slow, and he was bumped. In addition, a later inspection by the USAC Technical Committee resulted in the car's disqualification.

◄ A dour Graham Hill leans on his Lotus. All efforts to make the car competitive were fruitless. Although his car was practically identical to Andretti's it was not nearly as fast. In fact, the entire Lotus crew seemed unable to extract competitive speeds from either Hill's or Jochen Rindt's turbocharged, Ford-powered, four-wheel-drive racer. The final blow came when it was learned that new wheels, ordered for Hill's and Rindt's cars, would not be ready in time for the qualifying deadline. (It had been decided after Andretti's accident to change all the Lotus wheels.) When it was determined they would not be ready, the cars were withdrawn from the race.

▲ As a rookie the year before, Billy Vukovich handled the excruciating pressures that go with competing in the "500" quite well for so inexperienced a driver. For some reason, this year the tension got to him.

◄ Totally immersed in the problems of getting team members Art Pollard and Carl Williams qualified, Andy Granatelli still finds time to joke with the fans. Moments after this picture was taken, Carl Williams came into the pits having failed to complete a qualifying attempt. A heckling spectator called out, "Hey, Andy, why don't you get another driver?" To which Andy replied with a big smile, "Do you want to come on down right now?" The fan wasn't heard from again.

▲ The entrance to Gasoline Alley draws racing fans like a magnet. Even in the rain they mill about hoping to get an autograph or a glimpse of their favorite driver.

▼ Joe Leonard, the man who almost won last year in an STP Turbocar, qualified this Smokey Yunick-prepared Eagle eleventh fastest. He was never out of the top ten positions in the first 120 laps of the race and was running in second place when forced to pit on lap 130 after a clamp from Arnie Knepper's wreck put a hole in his radiator. A member of the crew ran back to the garage, broke the lock on the door and brought out a new radiator. In spite of the fact that it took thirteen and a half minutes to replace it, Leonard worked his way back up to sixth place before the race was over.

May can be a hot time of the year in the Midwest—when it's not raining. The acres of light-colored concrete reflect a great deal of heat which can become intolerable, particularly to the drivers who wear fire-resistant uniforms over fire-resistant underwear, heavy flameproof driving gloves and tight helmets. The crews help the drivers beat the heat in many ways. Mike Mosley, *opposite page, top,* is being shaded with a pit signal board; LeeRoy Yarbrough, *opposite page, middle,* finds a colorful sun umbrella useful; Ronnie Bucknum, *opposite page, bottom,* lies down in the meager shadow cast by the low inner pit wall; Billy Vukovich, *top,* holds a lap chart board over his head, and Bobby Johns, *bottom,* hides under a mechanic's wipe cloth.

◀ Chris Economaki interviews Foyt's teammate Roger McCluskey after he failed to better Foyt's qualifying time. Since Foyt experienced problems with the waste gate on his turbocharger, his qualifying speed was considerably lower than what both he and McCluskey had been running in morning practice. It was assumed McCluskey would win the pole position, but he qualified a disappointing sixth. During the race, however, he ran the fastest single lap with a speed of 166.512 mph. Although he ran as high as second place, he dropped out after 157 laps with a broken manifold. He was awarded fourteenth finishing position.

◀ Noted mechanic and Indy car builder A. J. Watson succumbs to the exhausting pace. With no place else to go in Gasoline Alley, Watson climbed into Mike Mosley's car, hung a thick pad of wipe cloths over the windscreen and went to sleep.

▲ Shortly after the midway point in the race, George Snider (84) stalled his car in the fourth turn. A crew member came out from the pits and helped him push his car in. He got back into the race, but this lengthy stop dropped him from eighth to nineteenth place and he could only work his way back up to sixteenth before the race ended.

▶ Though no longer driving at Indy, Parnelli Jones still has a large following of devoted fans who seek his autograph wherever he goes. Now a car owner at Indy, Jones has not completely retired— he still drives other kinds of race cars.

◀ As Rodger Ward brings the pace car into t
pits at the completion of the pace lap, and as
the cars accelerate down the main straight for
start of the race, Jim Malloy spun as he was
coming out of the fourth turn and the cars beh
him braked and swerved to miss him. Instead
of giving the cars the green flag, Pat Vidan wa
the yellow and then the red to halt the race
before it got started.

▲ The fastest rookie qualifier in 1968, Jim Malloy
qualified in ninth spot this year—his best
starting position in three years of competition at
the Speedway—but never got a chance to take
the green flag. A broken suspension part sent him
sliding into the outer wall and then spinning
across the track, but due to the tremendous talents
of these drivers, not one car made contact
with Malloy's.

and the watch-setting precision of the pre-race and start was gone. Even though one line of a very popular song of the day tells us that it doesn't rain in Indianapolis in the summertime, it *does*—but not until moments before the start.

Until those final few moments, everything had gone on as usual, from the first of May when Al Unser began setting practice lap speeds far beyond the others, and veteran Lloyd Ruby began breaking engines in his annual attempt to win and retire.

It was obvious that Ruby's usual Indy luck was holding, and that Al Unser (Bobby Unser's kid brother) was going to be the driver to beat in his Ford-powered, Johnny Lightning "500" Special owned by Parnelli Jones. This magnificent blue and gold racer was beautiful on or off the track, perfectly prepared, and seemed ready to run on forever.

While other drivers, including champion Mario Andretti, sought speed, Al had found it and was enjoying it. Round and round he would go, faster and faster but, oddly, not quite as fast as last year. Although nearly every expert predicted all-time record lap speeds for the newly resurfaced track, the new surface seemed to be holding speeds down very slightly. Still, Unser was the fastest throughout the month, with even A. J. Foyt unable to match him. And this was supposed to be "Foyt's year." Every three years, since his first year of victory in 1961, Super Tex had won the "500" — '61, '64, '67 — and here it was 1970.

As expected, it was Al Unser on the pole on the first day of qualifications with a near-record speed of 170.221 mph. Johnny Rutherford,

surprised and very pleased, took the middle front row spot, and Foyt took the outside. Following these three, in order, were some of the other hot drivers of USAC: Roger McCluskey, Mark Donohue, Art Pollard, Bobby Unser, Mario Andretti, Jim Malloy, and on down the list. Crowd-favorite Ruby, after breaking his half-dozen engines, finally managed to qualify in the ninth row.

Rain threatened all morning on race day, and the ceremonies proceeded cautiously. Furtive glances skyward, however, only seemed to make matters worse, and just as the drivers were crawling into their cockpits, the shower started. Tarps were quickly tossed over poised racers as officials decided to await Tony Hulman's decision whether or not to allow the rain to continue.

"Gentlemen, start your engines," came the triumphant call from Hulman as the rain stopped, and the field moved away to thundering cheers and thundering engine noise. The parade lap — the pace lap — Rodger Ward hurtling the pace car down pit lane — and the start . . . NO! *No* start. Jim Malloy, who had heard something "pop" in his suspension, had hit the wall coming out of the fourth turn and the race was being stopped before it ever started. Amazingly, no other car had touched the spinning racer of a deeply disappointed Malloy.

Realigned, the racers waited as the track was cleared . . . and then the rain started again. But not for long, and with everything finally ready to go the decision was made by officials to allow an addition of fuel (2 gallons) before the start. This accomplished, Hulman once again stood in the back seat of the pace car and ordered engines "re-started."

▼ As the cars come to a halt on the main straightaway after getting the red flag, crew members scramble to learn if their cars were in any way involved in Malloy's mishap. Fuel consumption was a problem this year, and since the amount of fuel allotted each car is strictly regulated, officials allowed each car a few extra gallons before the restart on account of the delay.

▲ The restart went off without a hitch with the remaining thirty-two cars getting the green flag. Johnny Rutherford (18), who had surprised the racing world when he qualified only one one-hundredth of a second slower than pole-sitter Al Unser, surprised everyone again by beating Unser into the first turn. For the first time in seven years at the Speedway, Johnny was in the lead.

▲ Rutherford's glory was short-lived, however, as Unser sped by him on the back stretch and was several car lengths in front of him by the start of the second lap. Rutherford ran second for the first quarter of the race, but a lengthy pit stop eliminated him from contention for the lead and he finally dropped out of the race after 135 laps with a broken header.

The race was exciting, as always, but the 1970 first lap could have served as the last lap, as far as the winner was concerned. For although Johnny Rutherford grabbed the lead through the first turn, Al Unser took it from him on the backstretch, and that was that. Unser was never headed again except for brief times while he was in the pits. No man raced Al Unser, because no man really got that close. No man, perhaps, *could* have beaten the perfectly prepared, perfectly confident young Unser. He *knew* he was going to win, and he did.

There was excitement — Lloyd Ruby's dramatic charge to the front from his position in the back of the field, for example. By lap three he was in tenth place, by lap twenty-five in fifth place. He led the race during a Foyt/Unser pit stop, but on lap fifty-five the luckless Ruby dropped out with an engine failure. Few fans will forget the blazing engine as the car rushed down the backstretch, a dejected Ruby steering for the infield, shoulders slumping.

Foyt battled, but he couldn't catch the speeding Unser. Mario Andretti was never really in it,

his racer ill with suspension problems. Rutherford hung in second place for many laps until a flawed pit stop cost him whatever chances he might have had. Donohue made the best race of it for the lead, driving his usual carefully considered race. Other contenders in pre-race calculations didn't fare as well. Out early were Pollard, McCluskey (who later relieved Kenyon, with dramatic consequences), Follmer, Johncock, Bettenhausen, Joe Leonard (Al's partner in a similar car), and Revson. Al's brother Bobby sped along out of contention but was at least in the top ten.

In the last quarter of the race a spinout and crash at the end of the backstretch by McCluskey, in Kenyon's car, triggered a multi-car spin which removed Bucknum as well, and disabled several others by forcing them into the infield. Foyt, who was a certain second until then, slowed to freeway speeds and barely finished the long grind. Others fell back.

But not Al. In a race reminiscent of Jim Clark's in 1965, he thundered easily on to Victory Lane.

▼ Perhaps Lloyd Ruby (25) was filled with thoughts of a rain-shortened race or possibly he was frustrated with his poor starting position—but whatever the reason, Ruby thrilled the fans with his incredible charge to the front of the field, going from twenty-fifth to first in just fifty laps. Gordon Johncock (5). Joe Leonard (15) and Carl Williams (75) held starting positions seventeen through nineteen, but were no match for Ruby's determination.

▲ *Middle,* Rookie-of-the-Year honors for 1970 went to stock car ace Donnie Allison (83), who started twenty-third and finished fourth. Driving one of four cars entered by A. J. Foyt, Allison, the only rookie on the team, finished higher than any of his teammates. Peter Revson (73) joined the McLaren team following Denis Hulme's accident and was running as high as sixth place before mechanical problems eliminated him from the race shortly before the halfway mark.

▲ *Bottom,* Reigning USAC National Driving Champion Mario Andretti (1) fought handling problems all during the race but managed to hang on for a sixth-place finish, one lap behind Al Unser (2) who proved unbeatable, leading 190 of the 200 laps.

▼ Jack Brabham (32) is generally conceded to have begun the modern rear-engine trend at Indy when he drove a Cooper Climax here in 1961. He qualified one of his own Brabhams in twenty-sixth place and was awarded thirteenth finishing position after dropping out on the 176th lap with engine failure. Dan Gurney (48), a former teammate of Brabham's on the Grand Prix circuit, qualified eleventh and finished third after placing second the last two years in a row.

▲ *Middle,* George Follmer (20), teammate of Mario Andretti, was driving the car with which Mario won the previous year, but he lasted only eighteen laps before dropping out with engine failure. Gary Bettenhausen (16) was another fairly early dropout—he managed fifty-five laps before his engine blew. Follmer was awarded thirty-first and Bettenhausen twenty-sixth place, nearly duplicating their poor luck of the previous year.

▲ *Bottom,* Rookie Dick Simon (44) started on the last row and overcame five pit stops, totaling over half an hour, to finish fourteenth. He completed only 168 laps but was running at the end. Wally Dallenbach (22) in his fourth race at the Speedway was running in tenth place at the three-quarter mark when magneto failure sidelined him. He was awarded seventeenth place. Last year's Rookie of the Year, Mark Donohue, (66) drove a flawless race to finish second, just thirty-two seconds behind the winner.

▼ This was the unlucky thirteenth year at the Speedway for A. J. Foyt (7). Foyt, who qualified on the front row, led for two laps and was running second for half the race before he was forced to retire with transmission troubles with only five laps to go. Every three years since 1961 Foyt had been in Victory Lane—this year he was awarded tenth. And Roger McCluskey (11) certainly had more than his share of bad luck this year—his ninth at the Speedway. After qualifying fourth fastest he ran in the top ten until his first pit stop. One lap after rejoining the race, he was out with suspension failure. On lap 109 he took over as relief driver for Mel Kenyon. From eighteenth he worked his way up to fifteenth before crashing on lap 161. He was uninjured but out of the race for good. Andretti (partially hidden behind Foyt) drove into the infield to avoid the debris on the track caused by McCluskey's accident and, for reasons no one can explain, his car's handling, which had been poor up to now, began to improve.

▲ The Unser brothers: Al moves up to lap Bobby (3) who ran fifth from the halfway point in the race until the 171st lap, when he pitted and began dropping back with turbocharger problems. Bobby completed 192 laps and was awarded eleventh place.

◀ LeeRoy Yarbrough (27), George Snider (84) and Mike Mosley (9) were running nose to tail in the early stages of the race with no idea that they would finish in just this order (nineteenth, twentieth and twenty-first). About midway through the race all three retired with mechanical problems: Yarbrough with a faulty turbocharger, Snider with a broken right rear suspension, and Mosley with a radiator leak.

▼ Foyt made four pit stops instead of his planned three because teammate George Snider, whose pit just preceded Foyt's, was also in and was blocking Foyt's path when he came in for his second pit stop. A. J. was forced back out for another lap before he could make his scheduled stop which turned out to be the fastest of his three regular stops.

▲ Joe Leonard helps safety marshals push his car away from the track after he dropped out with an electrical problem. This was particularly frustrating to Leonard, who set the fastest lap of the day (lap fifty—167.785 mph), while charging from his eighteenth starting position to second place by the fiftieth lap. Joe was awarded twenty-fourth place.

◀ A dejected Lloyd Ruby takes the long walk back from the fourth turn as his Indy luck sours once again. In eleven years at the Speedway Lloyd has been unable to finish higher than third—and this was not the first time he had dropped out while leading the race.

► In his fifth race at the Speedway Al Unser wins the "big one"—to nobody's surprise. He had been considered the man to beat for the entire month of May. For Mom Unser, kissing Al, it's the second trip to Victory Lane. She was there in 1968 when older son Bobby won the "500."

◄ Billy Vukovich explains to *Auto Racing* photographer Major Baynes that his clutch has given out on him after seventy-eight laps. From his thirtieth starting spot Vukie had worked his way up to fourteenth place and was running in eighteenth when he was forced to retire.

▲ Rick Muther didn't make the race last year and this year he was forced to sell his Volkswagen in order to finance his trip from California to Indianapolis. He qualified fifteenth, ran smoothly all day, and finished eighth to collect a paycheck of $25,302.49. As he comes into the pits at the end of the race, members of his crew give him a big hand.

◄ Carl Williams joined the McLaren team when Chris Amon was unable to get up to qualifying speed. Williams qualified nineteenth, ran a steady race to overcome five pit stops, and finished ninth, his best in five years at the Speedway. Following the race Denis Hulme (with bandaged hand) and Bruce McLaren (dark glasses) offer their congratulations.

Bobby and Al Unser are the only brothers to have won the Indianapolis "500." Ralph DePalma (1915) and his nephew Peter DePaolo (1925) were the only other winners who were related.

Having starred in the film *Grand Prix,* James Garner developed an interest in auto racing and attends the Indy "500" every year. Moments before the start of the race he talks shop with A. J. Foyt, who hopes to become the only man who has won this race four times.

The efforts of Jim Hurtubise to compete against the modern rear-engined cars with his latest version of the Offy-powered roadster have often been criticized, but Jim is so universally liked and respected that inter-company rivalries are often ignored as racing people willingly come to his aid in any way possible. Tire temperatures are an important source of information in the search for peak performance and must be taken as soon as the car returns to the pits after a practice run. One day when Jim came in there were no Firestone racing engineers in the vicinity of his pit, but these Goodyear men gladly took the temperature readings.

New Zealander Chris Amon came to the Speedway in 1967, easily passed his driver's test, and was turning laps at better than 160 mph when the left rear suspension broke and he hit the wall in turn one. The car was repaired, but Chris was unable to attain qualifying speeds and decided not to make any attempt to qualify. This year he joined the McLaren team when Bruce McLaren decided not to drive either of his own cars. For some reason, Chris, an established Formula 1 star and one of the fastest drivers in Grand Prix racing, still could not get up to speed and left without attempting to qualify.

▲ Chief steward Harlan Fengler prepares to signal Jim McElreath out for his qualification run as car owner A. J. Foyt works the throttle to warm up the engine. Jimmy easily qualified in his first attempt in this car after it had been personally set up by A. J. himself who was on and off the track all afternoon. The only car to qualify on the last day, Jimmy started in last spot but moved up to finish fifth.

▲ No Indy driver works harder than A. J. Foyt, who would just as soon do the preparatory work as delegate it to a mechanic. With cars entered for three teammates in addition to one for himself, he was the busiest man at the track. All four cars qualified for the race, and three of them finished in the top ten.

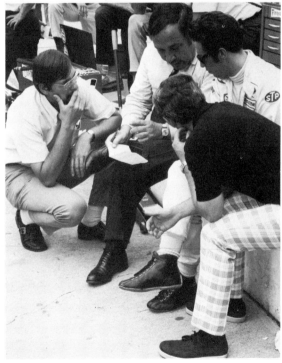

▲ This was to be Dan Gurney's last year at Indianapolis as a driver. Although he has never won the race, Dan has been building his own cars since 1966 and his influence has been felt. The Gurney-built Eagles were an immediate success. Six cars made the race that year and one of them led more laps than any other entrant in the field. Many of the top name drivers have driven Eagles, and Bobby Unser won the 1968 race in one of them.

▶ One of the most persistent problems plaguing the STP team during the entire month of May concerned the fuel system on Mario's new car. McNamara engineer Josef Karasek, team owner Andy Granatelli, number one driver Mario Andretti, and designer Frank McNamara spent much of their time at the track with their heads together, searching for an answer to proper fuel feed.

◄ Lloyd Ruby suffered his annual bout of rotten qualifying luck, destroying half a dozen engines in his attempts to make the race. Although his qualifying speed was one-and-a-half miles an hour slower than pole position winner Al Unser's, he did set a record of sorts—he blew three engines in one day. After blowing the second engine, Lloyd pitched in and helped the crew ready his third engine of the day, but the new engine didn't last as long as the others and Ruby had to wait until the following weekend to qualify.

▼ Talented, successful race drivers are a tremendous asset to racing-oriented manufacturers who depend upon them to promote their products. A. J. Foyt, in his constant search for perfection, has often switched back and forth between tire companies. He once changed from Goodyear to Firestone at the last minute, won the race, and hopped out of his car in Victory Lane still wearing a Goodyear driving suit. The following year just the reverse was true. Here, Goodyear's Herb Porter jokes, "This is what you'll get if you go back to Firestone."

▲ Could car owner Parnelli Jones be telling Al to stay away from motorcycles this year? Al had the fastest car at the Speedway and was the obvious favorite to win the race. Parnelli wouldn't want to chance a freak accident like the one that kept Al out of last year's race.

▼ A fuel breather cap vibrated loose on Denis Hulme's McLaren during the second week of practice. Fuel spilling from the tank was ignited by the exhaust header and Hulme was forced to bail out when every attempt to brake the car to a halt caused more fuel to spill out. The car continued down the track as he got to his feet with his fuel-soaked gloves burning. Unfortunately, the methanol fuel used in Indy cars burns without a visible flame and the crew on the fire truck, unable to see the fire, drove right past him as they chased after his car, causing Denny to run after them in search of aid.

◀ Suffering second- and third-degree burns of both hands, the heavily bandaged Hulme returned two weeks after his accident to watch the final weekend of qualifications. Surprisingly cheerful, Denny explained that his hands did not hurt too much now. He said the pain was so excruciating right after the fire that, "I wanted to smash my hands against something all the time I was in the ambulance— just to take the pain away." One month after the accident he was racing again with oversized gloves covering smaller bandages.

▼ Former ski-jumping and parachuting champion Dick Simon turned to Championship racing. He came to Indy with just two months' experience and quickly passed his driver's test. He qualified in thirty-first place with a speed of 165.548 mph and ran a steady, heads-up race to finish fourteenth in spite of five pit stops totaling over half an hour.

▼ Chief mechanic George Bignotti uses three hundredth-second stopwatches to record Al Unser's progress during shakedown runs on the new Colt he built for this season. In addition to winning the "500," Bignotti-prepared cars won ten other Championship races and carried Al to the USAC National Driving Championship with a record-breaking 5,130 points—2,870 points ahead of brother Bobby who finished second in the standings.

◄ With straightaway speeds in excess of 200 mph, getting a message across to your driver can be a problem, and misunderstandings are common. To help make communication easier this team switched to a metal pit board with large magnetized day-glo orange letters and numbers for signaling. Not only is the message easily changed, but the driver can read it better than one hastily scrawled in chalk on a blackboard.

◄ For those with even the slightest interest in numerology, 1970 certainly looked like Foyt's year. As these fans of his point out, his three previous wins had each been three years apart and this was the next three-year jump. In addition, Foyt's Indy victories followed years in which he had not done too well and in 1969 he had won only one race. Unfortunately, no matter how badly his fans wanted him to become the first four-time winner at Indy, A. J. was forced to settle for tenth place.

▼ Gary Bettenhausen (far left) engages in an impromptu motorcycle race on one of the Speedway's parking lots to help pass the tension-producing waiting period between qualifying and race day. Gary may have been enjoying himself, but memories of Al Unser's motorcycle accident of the year before would have destroyed the peace of mind of Bettenhausen's car owner, had he seen him.

▲ Jim Hurtubise poses for a snapshot with a young fan as the Gasoline Alley gates are opened at the end of the race. Jim may not have made the race for two years in a row, but his loyal fans never stop rooting for him.

▶ With a victory and two third-place finishes in the three races preceding Indy, Unser's fans are letting Al know they expect him to continue his winning ways. He didn't disappoint them as he completely dominated the entire race and was kept from setting a new race record average speed only by a lengthy yellow flag period at the three-quarter point of the race.

▲ There are many things about this year's front row that differ from the norm at Indy. The two fastest qualifiers—Peter Revson (86) and Mark Donohue (66)—had been rookies just two years ago; they are both known primarily as road racers with little oval racing experience; they are both at the wheel of a McLaren car (and this was only the second year that the McLarens have been at the Speedway); they are both college graduates; they were both born in the New York City area. The only thing that appeared normal was Indy winner Bobby Unser in a familiar-looking Eagle. This was the third time that Bobby had qualified third fastest since 1968.

IT WAS 1971

and the race started with a bang! The controversial decision had been made to allow an amateur to drive the pace car for the start of the race. This year, as the passenger car with three celebrities aboard rocketed down pit road, it skidded out of control. At the end of pit row it slammed into a stand loaded with photographers.

Twenty were injured, one critically.
In the race, which had started with a faster field than any in history, Mark Donohue in a sleek new McLaren sped into the lead. He was followed closely by Bobby Unser in an Eagle, pole-position winner Peter Revson in another McLaren, and Al Unser, last year's winner, in the car built by Parnelli Jones. Soon, though, Donohue was outrunning the field.

And almost immediately, on lap twelve in the third turn, the famous STP team of Mario Andretti and Steve Krisiloff was eliminated, along with veterans Mel Kenyon and Gordon Johncock. Krisiloff blew his engine, spun in his own oil, and took out the other three.

Unfortunately for Donohue, his record-setting pace took its toll, and after completing sixty-six laps he pulled down into the grass of the fourth turn safety apron with stripped gears. He was out, and Al Unser took firm command, with either Joe Leonard or brother Bobby Unser nipping at his heels from second place. Peter Revson was firmly in third, and A. J. Foyt in fourth, with perennial crowd-favorite Lloyd Ruby in contention and moving up.

Al Unser and Leonard put on a tremendous display of racing, exchanging the lead time after time for more than fifty laps, while in their pit

Jones shook his head. He owned both of these team cars.

On lap 112 fans along the main straightaway came screaming to their feet as David Hobbs blew his engine and dumped oil in the path of Rick Muther just behind. As Hobbs slowed, Muther spun and hit him broadside, then both cars disintegrated along a several hundred yard path down the stretch. Neither driver was injured.

Al Unser, the leader, barely missed disaster as he sped upon the scene. A flying part slammed into his helmet, stunning him momentarily, but he rushed on, still in the lead.

With the failure of Leonard's turbocharger, Bobby Unser was in second place . . . until lap 164. Closely following Mike Mosley, who had been suffering handling problems, Bobby was stunned to see Mike suddenly lose a wheel, skid violently, and explode against the wall of the fourth turn in a ball of flame. Bobby dodged and also skidded, slammed the wall, and then both cars spun down across the track. Bobby's car came to rest against the inside wall, but Mike crashed into the parked cars of Mark Donohue and Steve Krisiloff, destroying all three cars in another burst of flame.

Bobby crawled out, but Mosley, unconscious, was trapped in his car. He was finally removed to the hospital in serious condition.

Gary Bettenhausen, who had been coming around the inside with car problems, instantly stopped at the scene and rushed to help his buddy Mike. But the safety teams had already arrived and were doing their jobs. Re-entering the race, Bettenhausen eventually finished in tenth place.

Al Unser, receiving a sign from his pit that his brother Bobby was OK, sped on and near the end only Peter Revson was on the same lap with the leader. So they finished the wild, hectic 1971 Indianapolis 500-mile race. Unser was twenty-three seconds ahead of Revson, and A. J. Foyt was third.

Bettenhausen received a $1000 award and the "Extra Mile" trophy for his heroism, and Al Unser, who received $238,454.31 for his drive, became the first back-to-back winner since the great Bill Vukovich turned the trick in 1953-54.

And "The Mad Russian's" son, Bill, Jr., finished this 1971 race in fifth place, reminding many veteran fans just how many years have really slipped by.

▼ Donohue's performance had so demoralized all the other crews in Gasoline Alley that one waggish mechanic resorted to a little amateur voodoo in an attempt to slow Mark's incredible speeds. But Donohue just went faster and faster.

▲ As soon as the speed limit was lifted, Mark Donohue surprised the racing world by ripping off a lap that was a full six miles an hour faster than the previous record, which had stood since 1968. No one else was within shooting distance. Mark's speed kept climbing day by day and by the middle of the month car owner Roger Penske joyously put a 181 on Mark's board for all the world to see. The competition couldn't believe it.

▲ The only break in Donohue's domination of the Speedway came when Peter Revson, who had been unable to match Donohue's speeds all month in spite of the fact that he drove an identical McLaren Offy, put it all together and snatched the pole position from the man everyone knew would have it. It must have been a sweet victory indeed for Peter who agrees with all those who feel that he should have shared Rookie-of-the-Year honors with Mark in 1969.

This victory had a special meaning for the rest of the McLaren team as well. It was an affirmation that despite the death of Bruce McLaren, while testing a car in England a few days after last year's "500," the team would go on as top-flight competitors to be reckoned with wherever they choose to race.

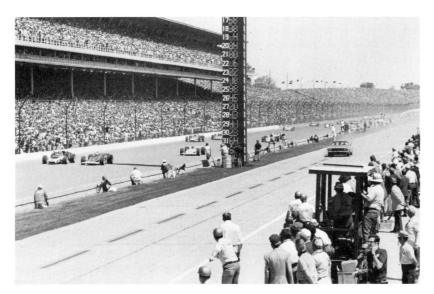

◄ Pole-sitter Peter Revson was first across the starting line, but Mark Donohue and Bobby Unser beat him going into the first turn. Then Donohue quickly began to build up a fantastic lead and no one could stay with him for the first quarter of the race.

▲ *Middle,* Lloyd Ruby (12) and A. J. Foyt (9) were the senior veterans in this year's "500." In his previous thirteen years at the Speedway, A. J. completed 4,760 miles in competition; Lloyd covered 4,300 miles in his eleven years of Indy racing.

▲ Denny Zimmerman, driving one of the two Vollstedts to qualify this year, worked his way up from his twenty-eighth starting position to finish eighth and capture the coveted Rookie-of-the-Year award.

▲ Mario Andretti (5) qualified ninth, right behind Foyt's (9) sixth-place starting spot. Mario stayed right on A. J.'s tail in the opening laps, passed him to move into eighth spot by lap ten, but then became involved in an accident on lap twelve. Andretti was awarded thirtieth spot while Foyt went on to finish third.

▼ On the twelfth lap, Steve Krisiloff (20) teammate to Mario Andretti, spun in the third turn and triggered a multiple car crash when his engine began leaking oil. Spinning to avoid Krisiloff, Mel Kenyon crashed into the wall and began climbing out of his car. As he was standing up and about to step out of the cockpit, he saw Gordon Johncock (7) sliding towards him. Kenyon slipped back down into his seat as Johncock's car went straight over the top, leaving tire marks on Kenyon's helmet. (Note track firemen, already on the scene to assist Kenyon, who are forced to return to the safety of the wall as Johncock comes through.)

▲ Although his right rear tire was torn from his car by the force of the collision, Johncock continued on, spinning about in midair as debris from the crash flew in all directions. When Mario Andretti (arrow) arrived at the third turn, he found the track blocked with cars and was forced to spin out to avoid them. All four cars were out of the race, but miraculously the only injury was a small puncture wound on Kenyon's leg that he received as he slid back into the cockpit.

▶ Art Pollard (64) was already out of the race, and Rick Muther (38) was making his fourth pit stop when Peter Revson (86) pitted on lap fifty-two for his first stop while running in sixth place. Revson's thirty-four-second stop was quick enough to get him back onto the track without losing a position. Some twenty laps later Muther was back in the pits and was a full twenty-two laps behind David Hobbs when they crashed midway through the race.

▶ After leading the first fifty laps of the race and then regaining the lead after his first pit stop, Donohue (66) was forced by a broken gear in the transmission to park his car on the infield grass at the exit of the fourth turn after completing sixty-six laps. As track personnel helped him from the cockpit, Mark could not have guessed that the slightly damaged car would be destroyed in a late race crash.

▲ With Donohue out, the race became a heated battle between Joe Leonard (15) and Al Unser (1). Their cars were painted different colors and had different company names on them, but nonetheless they were teammates, and car owner Parnelli Jones had many uneasy moments as he watched his two drivers trading positions as they battled wheel to wheel for fifty laps.

Leonard's fine drive came to an end after 123 laps when his turbocharger, which had been giving him problems the last few laps, just let go. Although Leonard would have to be considered the number two driver on the team, his car was in every way identical to Al's, and it was just racing luck that caused his car to break down while Al's kept running perfectly. Al reported later, "If Joe had been around at the end, it would have been something to see. We were both ready to run hard all the way."

▼ From a possible one-two finish for the Parnelli Jones team, the race turned to a possible Unser/Unser finish. Bobby, who was driving a Dan Gurney Eagle (2), was running smoothly in second place behind his younger brother until he pitted on lap 151.

▲ Lap 112 gave main stretch fans something to think about. With Al Unser solidly in front and rushing up to lap both David Hobbs and Rick Muther, Hobbs' engine blew. Immediately behind, Muther hit the Hobbs oil and skidded lightly into the wall. He caromed off and slammed into the side of the slowing Hobbs car, as parts flew everywhere. Rushing onto the scene of spinning cars and flying parts came leader Unser. It appeared impossible for him to squeeze through, but he did, with only one blow on the helmet from a flying part. He also picked up a piece of something which blocked the airflow to his radiator and caused his engine to start overheating, but a quick radio call to the pits (through his new car-to-pit communication system) and a quick stop corrected this problem. Neither Hobbs nor Muther was injured, but both racers were demolished, and another long caution period slowed the pace while the mess was being cleaned up.

Jim Malloy (42) and Gary Bettenhausen (16) had little trouble qualifying for this, their fourth race at Indy—both made the field on the first day with speeds of over 171 mph—but their luck in the race differed a great deal. Malloy completed the full 200 laps to finish fourth, while Bettenhausen nursed his sick car through eight pit stops in addition to a stop to assist Mike Mosley, and he could only manage to complete 178 laps to be awarded tenth place.

▲ Stock car ace Cale Yarborough (21) switched to USAC and was competing as Lloyd Ruby's teammate. After qualifying fourteenth he had worked his way up to seventh place by the halfway point before he was forced out with mechanical problems. Ruby (12) for the first time in years qualified on the first day without any of the many difficulties he usually suffers at Indy. In fact, things continued to go well for him for the first half of the race when he was in the lead, making him the only driver to have led each of the last four races. But once again his Indy luck turned sour and he was out of the race after 174 laps because his gearbox failed and the oil it contained burst into flame.

Mike Mosley had been having handling problems for many laps and had made several pit stops. Going into the fourth turn, his right front wheel flew off and he sped directly into the wall. A huge ball of flame rolled skyward. Directly behind, and skidding to miss the Mosley crash, came second-place runner Bobby Unser. He also slammed the wall, and then both cars skidded across the track to smash into and destroy the parked cars of Donohue and Krisiloff, which had not been moved behind the wall as had disabled cars in previous years. Groggy and suffering a severe headache, Bobby crawled out of his wrecked Eagle. Almost instantly, skilled Indianapolis fire fighters put out the flames, but Mike, seriously injured, could not crawl out.

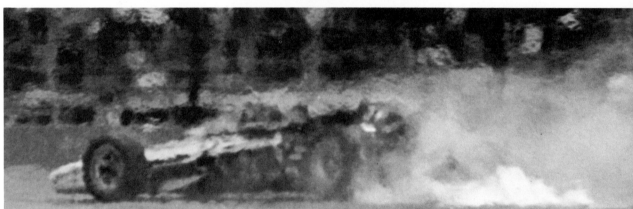

◀ Everyone in the pits after the conclusion of the race was horrified by the appearance of Mosley's car as it was carried back to its garage. It was one of the most thoroughly destroyed race cars they had ever seen. Mike might almost be considered lucky to have suffered "only" compound fractures of the right elbow and left leg and flash burns on the face and hands, for it took approximately a quarter of an hour—with the aid of a wrecker—to pry the crumpled cockpit far enough apart to get him out. Five weeks later to the day, Mike, in a wheelchair, was an interested spectator at the next 500-mile race on the USAC calendar.

▼ Mark Donohue, Roger Penske and another member of the crew walk back from the fourth turn where they had gone to check the condition of their car after Mosley's crash. When Mark left the car it only needed a few dollars worth of gears to be once again the finest car at the track, but now it was just a hundred-thousand-dollar pile of junk.

▲ Team manager Teddy Mayer races back to the McLaren pits from his vantage point alongside the track to prepare a signal board warning Revson that he was falling behind since Al Unser had not slowed down as much as Revson under the yellow flag. Revson, however, was stuck behind a slower car which he could not pass under the yellow and Mayer went to chief steward Harlan Fengler to get Unser slowed down and Revson back up where he belonged. With Revson less than twenty-three seconds behind at the end, one wonders if this yellow flag period could have affected the outcome. In a post-race interview, Revson admitted that during the closing stages of the race he was completely exhausted from fighting a steering which had gotten strangely heavy during the race, and he simply could not catch Unser.

▶ For the first time in his ten years at the Speedway, Roger McCluskey was still running at the end of the race. Said Roger: "It may only be ninth place, but at least I finished one." For McCluskey and the other thirty-one drivers that didn't win—there is always next year.

▼ Not since 1955 when the late Bill Vukovich scored his second consecutive "500" victory had another driver been able to put together back-to-back victories. Al Unser did it this year, making it three out of the last four wins at Indy for a driver named Unser. George Bignotti, Mom Unser and Parnelli Jones join Al in the pace car for a lap of honor around the track.

A

B

C

Qualifying is a time of tense determination
as drivers, owners and mechanics either
time their competitors or search their machines
and their minds for the speed and desire it
takes to be a winner. Larry Dickson qualified
Grant Kings' car (A) but only completed thirty-four
laps. Al Unser and Parnelli Jones (B) were
worried about the fantastic speeds displayed
by the McLarens. For Jim Hurtubise (C) it was
a time of fruitlessly searching for qualifying speed
while Mark Donohue (D) strained under
the mounting pressures as everyone expected him
to set a new record every day. As number one
driver on the McLaren team, former World
Champion Denis Hulme (E) seemed out of place
as the driver of the slowest McLaren entered.
The questions in everyone's minds were how
and why and what could be done about it.

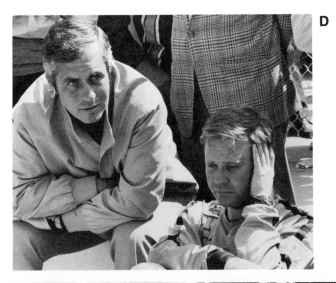

D

E

A

One of the key functions of Parnelli Jones, former Indy winner (now car owner), (A) is the task of keeping his number one driver loose and confident in the face of the blistering speeds shown by the McLarens, for winning takes confidence. For former winner and current driver A. J. Foyt, the problems are even greater as he works to impart experience gained in over a dozen years at the Speedway to his second-year teammate Donnie Allison (B) whose mind was also preoccupied with thoughts of an important stock car race just days away in Alabama. A. J. also works with Jim McElreath (C), who was in and out of the field three times this year, the last two at the wheel of Foyt-owned cars. This was the first field McElreath failed to qualify for since 1962.

B

C

▲ Since joining the All American Racers team (headed by Dan Gurney) for the last race of 1970, the Bobby Unser/Eagle combination has been one of the fastest at all of the USAC races. It is only a matter of time before they start winning. They weren't all that far off in this year's "500," with Bobby qualifying on the front row and leading the race twice for a total of twenty-one laps before Mosley's crash took him out of the race while he was in second place.

◀ Jerry Grant (right) worked all winter to ready a car of his own for this year's race, but he became a car owner when he was offered a good deal to drive Carroll Shelby's car. Although rookie Sam Posey had been unable to qualify the year before, Grant felt he showed promise and signed him as driver of his own car. Jerry qualified the first day but was bumped from the field the following weekend by none other than Sam Posey. Unfortunately, Sam was also bumped from the field, so Grant ended up as neither driver nor owner of a qualified car.

▲ It takes more than talented drivers and good equipment to be competitive in modern day auto racing. When Jud Phillips (chief mechanic for Bobby Unser when he won the "500") joined the team of car owner Jerry O'Connor, he completely revamped the cars and made the team competitive, as illustrated by their performance this year. Not only did both cars qualify the first weekend, but Billy Vukovich (32) finished fifth and Bud Tingelstad (58) finished seventh.

▶ Dick Simon's teammate John Mahler qualified at a speed of 170.164 mph to make him the fastest rookie in the field. But, as Simon appears to be explaining to him here, when Simon's first weekend qualifying speed of 168.903 mph proved too slow to make the race and he was bumped from the field, the team's sponsor insisted that their contract was with Simon and that they wanted their number one driver in the race. Mahler had qualified the car in twenty-seventh position, but when track officials approved the driver change, they also decided to make the car start in the last spot.

◀ Swede Savage, the most promising new driver scheduled to be at the Speedway this year was reduced to the role of spectator as he continued to recover from a very bad road racing crash in March. Since winning his first USAC race (the last race of the previous year and the first oval race he had ever entered), Swede has been looked upon as the greatest all-around new driver of the decade.

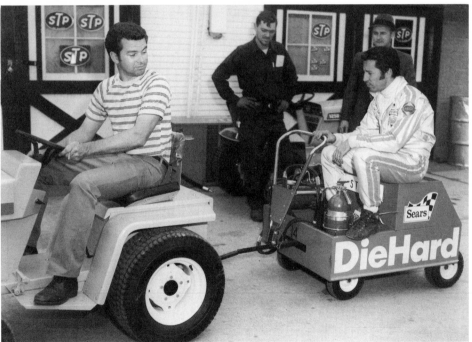

▲ As Jim McGee gives him a lift through Gasoline Alley, Mario Andretti seems to be pondering the vagaries of racing. Jim had been his co-chief mechanic back in the "good days" of the late 1960's when Mario put together three USAC national driving titles, was runner-up twice and won the "500." This year's ninth-place starting position was his worst in all seven years at the Speedway, and even then he didn't last a dozen laps in the race.

► Since children are barred from Gasoline Alley, Johnny Rutherford has to talk to his son Johnny IV through the fence during working hours. Young Johnny won't be driving for a few years yet; besides, his dad isn't finished making a name for himself in the sport. Rutherford, who was USAC Sprint Car Champion in 1965, broke both his arms during a spectacular flip over the guardrail at Eldora, Ohio, in April, 1966. Healing slowly, his injuries kept him out of racing for over a year. In April, 1968 he suffered badly burned hands in a crash at Phoenix, Arizona, but still managed to qualify for Indy the following month. He set the fastest single lap during qualifying last year, but problems this year forced him to accept a twenty-fourth-place starting position. By the twentieth lap he had moved into seventh place, but then eight pit stops—totaling over an hour in a vain effort to cure persistent mechanical problems—prevented him from completing more than 128 laps for an assigned final position of eighteenth.

▲ The rumors of the future existence of a Porsche Indy car took on added credence as Porsche racing director Baron Huschke von Hanstein takes notes during a conversation with Denis Hulme in the pits. The Ferrari factory has also had thoughts of building an Indy car and their interest would undoubtedly be increased at the appearance of their arch rival. The international flavor of the "500" would be greatly enhanced by the participation of these fiercely competitive companies.

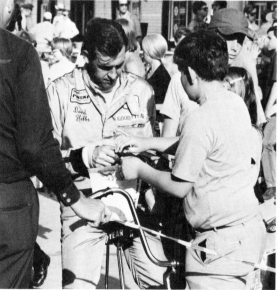

► Although a rookie at the Speedway, Englishman David Hobbs is certainly known to American racing fans through his participation in Can-Am, Trans-Am and Continental road racing in the United States. Indy was not the first time that Hobbs appeared as teammate to Mark Donohue—he had already started out the 1971 racing season by finishing third in the Daytona 24-hour race as Donohue's co-driver.

◀ The effects of the women's liberation movement were apparent in the heretofore "men only" pits at the Speedway. A court ruling declared that the new laws against sex discrimination meant that track personnel could no longer refuse to issue press credentials to qualified women journalists. Women, allowed in the pits for the first time since the track opened, were the subject of many a stare and photograph.

▼ George Bignotti, Al Unser and Parnelli Jones, the most powerful and successful team in USAC racing today, put their heads together to seek the impossible goal of all racing teams: perfection. When you're number one, everyone wants to beat you or see you get beaten, and there were many who were happy at the ease with which the McLarens outran Unser's Colt. But it takes more than just speed to win races, and this team showed the world that they deserved to be number one.

1911

FIN	START	QUAL.* SPEED	NUMBER, TYPE, CYLINDERS			DRIVER	CAR NAME	CHASSIS	FIN
1	28	—	32	MN	6	Ray Harroun	Marmon Wasp	Marmon	1
2	29	—	33	L	4	Ralph Mulford	Lozier	Lozier	2
3	25	—	28	F	4	David Bruce-Brown	Fiat	Fiat	3
4	11	—	11	MS	4	Spencer Wishart	Mercedes	Mercedes	4
5	27	—	31	MN	4	Joe Dawson	Marmon	Marmon	5
6	2	—	2	SX	4	Ralph DePalma	Simplex	Simplex	6
7	18	—	20	N	4	Charlie Merz	National	National	7
8	12	—	12	AX	4	W. H. Turner	Amplex	Amplex	8
9	13	—	15	K	6	Fred Belcher	Knox	Knox	9
10	22	—	25	J	4	Harry Cobe	Jackson	Jackson	10
11	10	—	10	SZ	4	Gil Anderson	Stutz	Stutz	11
12	32	—	36	MR	4	Hughie Hughes	Mercer	Mercer	12
13	26	—	30	FC	4	Lee Frayer	Firestone-Columbus	Firestone-Columbus	13
14	19	—	21	N	4	Howdy Wilcox	National	National	14
15	33	—	37	MR	4	Charley Bigelow	Mercer	Mercer	15
16	3	—	3	IS	4	Harry Endicott	Inter-state	Inter-state	16
17	36	—	41	V	4	Howard Hall	Velie	Velie	17
18	40	—	46	BZ	4	Billy Knipper	Benz	Benz	18
19	39	—	45	BZ	4	Bob Burman	Benz	Benz	19
20	34	—	38	SX	4	Ralph Beardsley	Simplex	Simplex	20
21	16	—	18	F	4	Eddie Hearne	Fiat	Fiat	21
22	6	—	6	PH	4	Frank Fox	Pope-Hartford	Pope-Hartford	22
23	24	—	27	CU	4	Ernest Delaney	Cutting	Cutting	23
24	23	—	26	J	4	Jack Tower	Jackson	Jackson	24
25	20	—	23	McF	6	Bert Adams	McFarlan	McFarlan	25
26	37	—	42	CO	4	Bill Endicott	Cole	Cole	26
27	4	—	4	N	4	Johnny Aitken	National	National	27
28	9	—	9	CA	4	Will Jones	Case	Case	28
29	1	—	1	CA	4	Lewis Strang	Case	Case	29
30	7	—	7	W	6	Harry Knight	Westcott	Westcott	30
31	8	—	8	CA	4	Joe Jagersberger	Case	Case	31
32	31	—	35	APP	4	Herb Lytle	Apperson	Apperson	32
33	17	—	19	AL	6	Harry Grant	Alco	Alco	33
34	15	—	17	BU	4	Charles Basle	Buick Super 100	Buick	34
35	5	—	5	PH	4	Louis Disbrow	Pope-Hartford	Pope-Hartford	35
36	14	—	16	BU	4	Arthur Chevrolet	Buick Super 100	Buick	36
37	35	—	39	F	4	Caleb Bragg	Fiat	Fiat	37
38	21	—	24	J	4	Fred Ellis	Jackson	Jackson	38
39	30	—	34	L	4	Teddy Tetzlaff	Lozier	Lozier	39
40	38	—	44	AX	4	Art Greiner	Amplex	Amplex	40

Qualified too slow: Rupert Jeffkins, Velie, #40, V, (Below 75 MPH)*
Louis Edmonds, Cole, #43, CO, (Below 75 MPH)*

Total entries: 46

Qualifying: Minimum of 75 MPH over quarter mile on main straight. Lined up in order of entry date.

*No times available

FIN	ENTRANT	LAPS	SPEED, REASON OUT	RELIEF DRIVER	FIN
1	Nordyke & Marmon Co.	200	74.59	Cy Patschke	1
2	Lozier Motor Co.	200	74.29	—	2
3	E. E. Hewlett	200	72.73	—	3
4	Spencer Wishart	200	72.65	Dave Murphy	4
5	Nordyke & Marmon Co.	200	72.34	Cy Patschke	5
6	Simplex Automobile Co.	200	71.13	—	6
7	National Motor Vehicle Co.	200	70.37	—	7
8	Simplex Automobile Co.	200	68.82	Walter Jones	8
9	Knox Automobile Co.	200	68.63	Jim Coffey	9
10	Jackson Automobile Co.	200	67.90	—	10
11	Ideal Motor Car Co.	200	67.73	—	11
12	Mercer Motors Co.	200	67.73	—	12
13	Columbus Buggy Co.		Flagged	Eddie Rickenbacker	13
14	National Motor Vehicle Co.		Flagged	—	14
15	Mercer Motors Co.		Flagged	E. H. Sherwood, Howard Frey	15
16	Interstate Automobile Co.		Flagged	—	16
17	Velie Motors Corp.		Flagged	Rupert Jeffkins	17
18	E. A. Moross		Flagged	—	18
19	E. A. Moross		Flagged	—	19
20	Simplex Automobile Co.		Flagged	Frank Goode	20
21	Edward A. Hearne		Flagged	Ed Parker	21
22	Pope Manufacturing Co.		Flagged	Jap Clemons	22
23	Clark-Carter Auto Co.		Flagged	—	23
24	Jackson Automobile Co.		Flagged	Bob Evans	24
25	Speed Motors Co.		Flagged	Mel Marquette	25
26	Cole Motor Car Co.		Flagged	John Jenkins	26
27	National Motor Vehicle Co.	125	Con. rod	—	27
28	J. I. Case T. M. Co.	122	Steering	—	28
29	J. I. Case T. M. Co.	109	Steering	Elmer Ray	29
30	Westcott Motor Car Co.	90	Wreck	—	30
31	J. I. Case T. M. Co.	87	Wreck	—	31
32	Apperson Bros. Automobile Co.	82	Wreck	—	32
33	American Locomotive Co.	51	Bearings	—	33
34	Buick Motor Co.	46	Mechanical	—	34
35	Pope Manufacturing Co.	45	Wreck	—	35
36	Buick Motor Co.	30	Mechanical	—	36
37	Caleb S. Bragg	24	Wreck	—	37
38	Jackson Automobile Co.	22	Fire damage	—	38
39	Lozier Motor Co.	20	Wreck	—	39
40	Simplex Motor Car Co.	12	Wreck	—	40

AL = Alco	BZ = Benz	F = Fiat	K = Knox	MR = Mercer	SX = Simplex
APP = Apperson	CA = Case	FC = Firestone-Columbus	L = Lozier	MS = Mercedes	SZ = Stutz
AX = Amplex	CO = Cole	IS = Interstate	McF = McFarlan	N = National	V = Velie
BU = Buick	CU = Cutting	J = Jackson	MN = Marmon	PH = Pope Hartford	W = Westcott

1912

FIN	START	QUAL. SPEED	NUMBER, TYPE, CYLINDERS			DRIVER	CAR NAME	CHASSIS	FIN
1	7	86.13	8	N	4	Joe Dawson	National	National	1
2	3	84.24	3	F	4	Teddy Tetzlaff	Fiat	Fiat	2
3	17	81.81	21	MR	4	Hughie Hughes	Mercer	Mercer	3
4	22	78.88	28	SZ	4	Charlie Merz	Stutz	Stutz	4
5	15	80.57	18	SC	4	Bill Endicott	Schacht	Schacht	5
6	2	78.85	2	SZ	4	Len Zengel	Stutz	Stutz	6
7	11	80.82	14	W	6	John Jenkins	White	White	7
8	18	80.48	22	L	4	Joe Moran	Lozier	Lozier	8
9	8	87.20	9	N	4	Howdy Wilcox	National	National	9
10	16	87.88	19	K	6	Ralph Mulford	Knox	Knox	10
11	4	86.02	4	MS	4	Ralph DePalma	Mercedes	Mercedes	11
12	12	84.11	15	CU	4	Bob Burman	Cutting	Cutting	12
13	10	80.77	12	SX	4	Bert Dingley	Simplex	Simplex	13
14	21	79.90	25	L	4	Joe Matson	Lozier	Lozier	14
15	6	83.95	7	MS	4	Spencer Wishart	Mercedes	Mercedes	15
16	1	80.93	1	SZ	4	Gil Anderson	Stutz	Stutz	16
17	14	77.51	17	BU	4	Billy Liesaw	Marquette-Buick	Marquette	17
18	24	76.54	5	CA	6	Louis Disbrow	Case	Case	18
19	19	78.08	23	McF	6	Mel Marquette	McFarlan	McFarlan	19
20	5	81.85	6	CA	6	Eddie Hearne	Case	Case	20
21	13	77.30*	16	FC	4	Eddie Rickenbacker*	Firestone-Columbus	Firestone-Columbus	21
22	23	88.45	29	N	4	David Bruce-Brown	National	National	22
23	9	75.92	10	LX	6	Harry Knight	Lexington	Lexington	23
24	20	84.09	24	OP	4	Len Ormsby	Opel	Opel	24

Qualified too slow: Albert Romine, Continental, #27, CL, 74.227, Below 75 MPH minimum
Jimmy Hill, Continental, #27, CL, 68.182, Below 75 MPH minimum
Lee Oldfield, Mason, #31, MA, Below 75 MPH minimum

Total entries: 29

Qualifying: Minimum of 75 MPH for 1 lap. Line up in order of entry date, 3 tries.

*Rickenbacker's car qualified by Lee Frayer

FIN	ENTRANT	LAPS	SPEED, REASON OUT	RELIEF DRIVER	FIN
1	National Motor Vehicle Co.	200	78.72	Don Herr	1
2	E. E. Hewlett	200	76.75	Caleb Bragg	2
3	Mercer Motors Co.	200	76.13	—	3
4	Ideal Motor Car Co.	200	76.00	Billy Knipper	4
5	Schacht Motor Car Co.	200	74.25	Harry Endicott	5
6	Ideal Motor Car Co.	200	73.83	Billy Knipper	6
7	White Indianapolis Co.	200	73.25	Charles Arnold	7
8	Dr. W. H. Chambers	200	71.50	George Ainslee	8
9	National Motor Vehicle Co.	200	69.30	Bill Rader	9
10	Ralph Mulford	200	56.29	—	10
11	E. J. Schroeder	198	Con. rod	—	11
12	Clark-Carter Auto Co.	157	Wreck	—	12
13	Bert Dingley	116	Con. rod	—	13
14	O. Applegate	110	Crankshaft	—	14
15	Spencer Wishart	82	Water connection	—	15
16	Ideal Motor Car Co.	80	Wreck	—	16
17	Will Thomson	72	Carb. fire	W. H. Farr	17
18	J. I. Case T. M. Co.	67	Differential pin	Neil Whalen	18
19	Speed Motors Co.	63	Broken wheels	—	19
20	J. I. Case T. M. Co.	55	Burned bearing	Neil Whalen	20
21	Columbus Buggy Co.	43	Intake valve	—	21
22	National Motor Vehicle Co.	25	Valve	—	22
23	Lexington Motor Car Co.	6	Engine	—	23
24	I. C. Stern & B. C. Noble	5	Con. rod	—	24

BU = Buick
CA = Case
CL = Continental
CU = Cutting

F = Fiat
FC = Firestone-Columbus
K = Knox

L = Lozier
LX = Lexington
McF = McFarlan

MA = Mason
MR = Mercer
MS = Mercedes

N = National
OP = Opel
SC = Schacht

SX = Simplex
SZ = Stutz
W = White

1913

FIN	START	QUAL. SPEED	NUMBER, TYPE, CYLINDERS			DRIVER	CAR NAME	CHASSIS	FIN
1	7	86.03	16	P	4	Jules Goux, France	Peugeot	Peugeot	1
2	19	81.99	22	MR	4	Spencer Wishart	Mercer	Mercer	2
3	16	84.46	2	SZ	4	Charlie Merz	Stutz	Stutz	3
4	2	80.75	9	SB	6	Albert Guyot, France	Sunbeam	Sunbeam	4
5	13	75.52	23	KT	4	Theodore Pilette, Belgium	Mercedes-Knight	Mercedes	5
6	20	81.46	12	PH	4	Howdy Wilcox	Gray Fox	Pope-Hartford	6
7	22	80.79	29	MS	4	Ralph Mulford	Mercedes	Mercedes	7
8	23	82.76	31	CA	4	Louis Disbrow	Case	Case	8
9	15	80.72	35	DU	4	Willie Haupt	Mason	Duesenberg	9
10	27	75.91	25	TL	4	George Clark	Tulsa	Tulsa	10
11	21	84.17	4	KE	4	Bob Burman	Keeton	Keeton	11
12	14	82.63	3	SZ	4	Gil Anderson	Stutz	Stutz	12
13	4	82.01	5	DU	4	Bob Evans	Mason	Duesenberg	13
14	3	78.02	17	BU	4	Billy Liesaw	Anel	Buick	14
15	1	87.34	19	MR	4	Caleb Bragg	Mercer	Mercer	15
16	11	80.26	10	DU	4	Billy Knipper	Henderson	Knipper	16
17	8	81.30	27	IF	4	Teddy Tetzlaff	Isotta-Fraschini	Isotta	17
18	24	78.89	32	CA	4	Joe Nikrent	Case	Case	18
19	25	88.23	6	DU	4	Jack Tower	Mason	Duesenberg	19
20	18	81.94	28	IF	4	Vincenzo Trucco, Italy	Isotta-Fraschini	Isotta	20
21	10	76.35	1	NY	6	Harry Endicott	Nyberg	Nyberg	21
22	26	85.83	15	P	4	Paul Zuccarelli, France	Peugeot	Peugeot	22
23	12	76.30	21	MR	4	Ralph DePalma	Mercer	Mercer	23
24	6	75.96	26	IF	4	Harry Grant	Isotta-Fraschini	Isotta	24
25	17	82.84	18	SC	4	John Jenkins	Schacht	Schacht	25
26	5	82.84	8	SZ	4	Don Herr	Stutz	Stutz	26
27	9	85.70	33	CA	6	Bill Endicott	Case	Case	27

Total entries: 31

Qualifying: Minimum of 75 MPH for 1 lap. Starting positions by draw, 3 tries.

FIN	ENTRANT	LAPS	SPEED, REASON OUT	RELIEF DRIVER	FIN
1	Peugeot	200	75.933	—	1
2	Mercer Motors Co.	200	73.49	Ralph DePalma	2
3	Ideal Motor Car Co.	200	73.38	Earl Cooper	3
4	Sunbeam Motor Car Co.	200	70.92	—	4
5	E. C. Patterson	200	68.15	—	5
6	Frank Fox	200	67.65	Frank Fox	6
7	E. J. Schroeder	200	66.95	—	7
8	J. I. Case T. M. Co.	200	66.80	I. J. Kilpatrick	8
9	Mason Motor Co.	200	63.48	Lee Oldfield	9
10	Tulsa Auto Manufacturing Co.	200	62.99	Tom Alley	10
11	Keeton Motor Co.		Flagged	Hughie Hughes	11
12	Ideal Motor Car Co.	187	Camshaft gears	Earl Cooper	12
13	Mason Motor Co.	158	Clutch	Lee Oldfield	13
14	Will Thomson	148	Loose rods	Lee Oldfield	14
15	Mercer Motors Co.	128	Pump shaft	Ralph DePalma	15
16	Henderson Motor Car Co.	125	Clutch	Harry Grant	16
17	Isotta	118	Drive chain	—	17
18	J. I. Case T. M. Co.	67	Bearing	Eddie Hearne	18
19	Mason Motor Co.	51	Wreck	—	19
20	Isotta	39	Loose gas tank	—	20
21	Nyberg Auto Co.	23	Transmission	Ed Madden	21
22	Peugeot	18	Main bearing	—	22
23	Mercer Motors Co.	15	Bearing	—	23
24	Isotta	14	Gas tank	—	24
25	Schacht Motor Car Co.	13	Crankshaft	—	25
26	Ideal Motor Car Co.	7	Clutch shaft	—	26
27	J. I. Case T. M. Co.	1	Drive shaft	—	27

BU = Buick	IF = Isotta	MR = Mercer	P = Peugeot	SC = Schacht
CA = Case	KE = Keeton	MS = Mercedes	PH = Pope-Hartford	SZ = Stutz
DU = Duesenberg	KT = Knight	NY = Nyberg	SB = Sunbeam	TL = Tulsa

1914

FIN	START	QUAL. SPEED	NUMBER, TYPE, CYLINDERS			DRIVER	CAR NAME	CHASSIS	FIN
1	15	94.54	16	D	4	Rene Thomas, France	Delage	Delage	1
2	10	90.00	14	P	4	Arthur Duray, France	Peugeot	Peugeot	2
3	11	89.15	10	D	4	Albert Guyot, France	Delage	Delage	3
4	19	98.13	6	P	4	Jules Goux, France	Peugeot	Peugeot	4
5	30	87.25	3	SZ	4	Barney Oldfield	Stutz	Stutz	5
6	7	91.21	9	E	6	Josef Christiaens, Belgium	Excelsior	Excelsior	6
7	26	86.46	27	SB	6	Harry Grant	Sunbeam	Sunbeam	7
8	27	86.87	5	CA	4	Charley Keene	Beaver Bullet	Keene	8
9	5	93.36	25	MX	4	Billy Carlson	Maxwell	Maxwell	9
10	23	88.14	42	DU	4	Eddie Rickenbacker	Duesenberg	Duesenberg	10
11	6	88.21	23	P	4	Ralph Mulford	Mercedes	Mercedes	11
12	28	89.39	43	DU	4	Willie Haupt	Duesenberg	Duesenberg	12
13	12	89.57	31	CA	4	Billy Knipper	Keeton	Keeton	13
14	29	99.86	7	P	4	Georges Boillot, France	Peugeot	Peugeot	14
15	18	87.73	34	BG	4	Ernst Friedrich, Germany	Bugatti	Bugatti	15
16	24	86.79*	1	CA	4	Louis Disbrow*	Burman	Burman	16
17	25	92.69	19	MR	4	Spencer Wishart	Mercer	Mercer	17
18	14	88.02	2	SZ	4	Earl Cooper	Stutz	Stutz	18
19	9	92.97	21	MR	4	Caleb Bragg	Mercer	Mercer	19
20	8	86.87	15	CA	4	Art Klein	King	King	20
21	4	87.54	38	DU	4	Willie Chandler	Braender Bulldog	Duesenberg	21
22	3	90.76	4	PH	4	Howdy Wilcox	Gray Fox	Fox	22
23	13	87.10	13	DU	4	George Mason	Mason	Duesenberg	23
24	22	90.41	17	CA	4	Bob Burman	Burman	Burman	24
25	17	93.55	26	MN	4	Joe Dawson	Marmon	Marmon	25
26	16	90.49	24	SZ	4	Gil Anderson	Stutz	Stutz	26
27	20	84.20	49	IF	4	Ray Gilhooley	Isotta-Fraschini	Isotta	27
28	2	96.36	8	MX	4	Teddy Tetzlaff	Maxwell	Maxwell	28
29	1	88.31	12	SB	6	Jean Chassagne, France	Sunbeam	Sunbeam	29
30	21	87.83	48	CA	4	S. F. Brock	Ray	Ray	30

Qualified, did not start: Ralph DePalma, Mercedes, #18, MS, 88.132, Qualified but withdrew
Eddie Pullen, Mercer, #22, MR, 84.587, Withdrew
Mort Roberts, Pope Bullet, #39, PB, 76.930, Too slow
DePalma withdrew and Pullen as first alternate also withdrew
Gilhooley as second alternate filled the spot

Total entries: 45

Qualifying: Minimum of 75 MPH for 1 lap. 3 tries, fastest 30. Starting positions by draw.

*Disbrow's car qualified by Bob Burman

FIN	ENTRANT	LAPS	SPEED, REASON OUT	RELIEF DRIVER	FIN
1	L. Delage Co.	200	82.47	—	1
2	Jacques Munier	200	80.99	—	2
3	Albert Guyot	200	80.20	—	3
4	Jules Goux	200	79.49	—	4
5	Stutz Motor Car Co.	200	78.15	Gil Anderson	5
6	Josef Christiaens	200	77.44	—	6
7	Sunbeam Motor Car Co.	200	75.69	—	7
8	Charles Keene	200	74.82	C. L. Rogers	8
9	United States Motor Co.	200	70.97	Jack LeCain	9
10	Duesenberg Bros.	200	70.83	—	10
11	E. J. Schroeder	200	69.55	—	11
12	Duesenberg Bros.	200	66.66	—	12
13	Keeton Motor Co.	200	65.79	Bob Burman	13
14	Georges Boillot	141	Broken frame	—	14
15	Ettore Bugatti	134	Drive pinion	—	15
16	Bob Burman	128	Con. rod	—	16
17	Mercer Motors Co.	122	Camshaft	—	17
18	Stutz Motor Car Co.	118	Broken wheel	Bill Rader	18
19	Mercer Motors Co.	117	Camshaft	Eddie Pullen	19
20	Arthur H. Klein	87	Valve	—	20
21	Braender Rubber Co.	69	Con. rod	—	21
22	Frank Fox	67	Valve	—	22
23	Mason Motor Co.	66	Piston	Lee Oldfield	23
24	Bob Burman	47	Con. rod	—	24
25	Charles E. Erbstein	45	Wreck	—	25
26	Stutz Motor Car Co.	42	Loose cylinder bolts	—	26
27	G. M. Heckschew	41	Wreck	—	27
28	United States Motor Co.	33	Rocker arm	—	28
29	Sunbeam Motor Car Co.	20	Wreck	—	29
30	S. F. Brock	5	Camshaft	—	30

BG = Bugatti   DU = Duesenberg   MN = Marmon   P = Peugeot   SB = Sunbeam
CA = Case   E = Excelsior   MR = Mercer   PB = Pope Bullet   SZ = Stutz
D = Delage   IF = Isotta   MX = Maxwell   PH = Pope-Hartford

1915

FIN	START	QUAL. SPEED	NUMBER, TYPE, CYLINDERS			DRIVER	CAR NAME	CHASSIS	FIN
1	2	98.58	2	MS	4	Ralph DePalma	Mercedes	Mercedes	1
2	3	98.47	3	P	4	Dario Resta, France	Peugeot	Peugeot	2
3	5	95.14	5	SZ	4	Gil Anderson	Stutz	Stutz	3
4	4	96.77	4	SZ	4	Earl Cooper	Stutz	Stutz	4
5	11	88.93	15	DU	4	Eddie O'Donnell	Duesenberg	Duesenberg	5
6	7	92.40	8	P	4	Bob Burman	Peugeot	Peugeot	6
7	1	98.90	1	SZ	4	Howdy Wilcox	Stutz	Stutz	7
8	9	90.00	10	DU	4	Tom Alley	Duesenberg	Duesenberg	8
9	16	84.11	19	MX	4	Billy Carlson	Maxwell	Maxwell	9
10	14	86.87[a]	7	SB	4	Noel Van Raalte,[a] England	Sunbeam	Sunbeam	10
11	24	80.36[b]	28	E	4	Willie Haupt[b]	Emden	Emden	11
12	10	89.29	14	SB	6	Harry Grant	Sunbeam	Sunbeam	12
13	17	83.55	21	MX	4	Tom Orr	Maxwell	Maxwell	13
14	6	94.74	6	SB	4	Jean Porporato, France	Sunbeam	Sunbeam	14
15	15	85.55	18	DU	4	Joe Cooper	Sebring	Duesenberg	15
16	18	82.72	22	DU	4	Ralph Mulford	Duesenberg	Duesenberg	16
17	12	89.46	12	P	4	George Babcock	Peugeot	Peugeot	17
18	8	90.45	9	DU	4	Art Klein	Kleinart	Duesenberg	18
19	19	81.97	23	MX	4	Eddie Rickenbacker	Maxwell	Maxwell	19
20	23	81.01[c]	27	C	4	Louis Chevrolet[c]	Cornelian	Cornelian	20
21	13	87.04	17	D	4	John DePalma	Delage	Delage	21
22	20	81.97	24	MR	4	John Mais	Mais	Mais	22
23	22	81.52[a]	26	B	4	George Hill[a]	Bugatti	Bugatti	23
24	21	81.52	25	MR	4	C. C. Cox	Cino-Purcell	Cino	24

Qualified, did not start: Jack LeCain, Peugeot, 89.463, Withdrawn*
Carl Limberg, Sunbeam, 86.124, Withdrawn*
Grover Ruckstell, Mercer, 83.799, Withdrew
Jimmy Hill, Bals Spl., 79.3, Below 80 MPH minimum
Earl DeVore, F.R.P., 79.156, Below 80 MPH minimum
Willie Haupt, Bergdoll, 76.078, Below 80 MPH minimum

Total entries: 41

Qualifying: Minimum of 80 MPH for 1 lap. 3 tries, fastest 33, in order of speed.

[a]Van Raalte's car and Hill's car both qualified by Barney Oldfield
[b]Haupt's car qualified by Harry Donaldson
[c]Chevrolet's car qualified by Joe Boyer
*LeCain and Limberg withdrew because of the rule stating that no more than three cars in one team could start.

FIN	ENTRANT	LAPS	SPEED, REASON OUT	RELIEF DRIVER	FIN
1	E. C. Patterson	200	89.84	—	1
2	Peugeot Auto Import Co.	200	88.91	—	2
3	Stutz Motor Car Co.	200	87.60	Johnny Aitken	3
4	Stutz Motor Car Co.	200	87.11	Johnny Aitken	4
5	Duesenberg Bros.	200	81.47	—	5
6	Bob Burman	200	80.36	—	6
7	Stutz Motor Car Co.	200	80.11	—	7
8	Duesenberg Bros.	200	79.33	—	8
9	United States Motor Co.	200	78.96	Hughie Hughes	9
10	Sunbeam Motor Car Co.	200	75.87	—	10
11	R. E. Donaldson	200	70.75	—	11
12	Fortuna Racing Team, Inc.	184	Loose mud apron	Carl Limberg	12
13	United States Motor Co.	168	Axle bearing	—	13
14	Sunbeam Motor Car Co.	164	Piston	—	14
15	E. E. Miles & J. W. Gwin	154	Wreck	—	15
16	Duesenberg Bros.	124	Con. rod	Willie Chandler	16
17	Peugeot Auto Import Co.	117	Broken cylinder	—	17
18	Art Klein	111	Disqualified—smoke	Willie Chandler	18
19	United States Motor Co.	103	Con. rod	—	19
20	Louis Chevrolet	76	Valve	—	20
21	James E. Wilson	41	Loose flywheel	—	21
22	John A. Mais	23	Left course	—	22
23	C. W. Fuller	20	Water pump gear	—	23
24	Edward D. McNay	12	Timing gears	—	24

B = Bugatti	E = Emden	P = Peugeot
C = Cornelian	MR = Mercer	SB = Sunbeam
D = Delage	MS = Mercedes	SZ = Stutz
DU = Duesenberg	MX = Maxwell	

1916

FIN	START	QUAL. SPEED	NUMBER, TYPE, CYLINDERS			DRIVER	CAR NAME	CHASSIS	FIN
1	4	94.40	17	P	4	Dario Resta, France	Peugeot	Peugeot	1
2	10	90.87	1	DU	4	Wilbur D'Alene	Duesenberg	Duesenberg	2
3	20	91.09	10	P	4	Ralph Mulford	Peugeot	Peugeot	3
4	14	86.08	14	SB	6	Josef Christiaens, Belgium	Sunbeam	Sunbeam	4
5	5	94.33	15	D	4	Barney Oldfield	Delage	Delage	5
6	9	91.33	4	MX	4	Pete Henderson	Maxwell	Maxwell	6
7	6	93.81	29	PR	4	Howdy Wilcox	Premier	Premier	7
8	17	83.69	26	DU	4	Art Johnson	Crawford	Crawford	8
9	15	84.84	24	DU	4	Willie Chandler	Crawford	Crawford	9
10	13	87.08	9	W	4	Ora Haibe	Osteweg	Osteweg	10
11	19	82.04	12	DU	4	Tom Alley	Ogren	Duesenberg	11
12	21	87.69*	8	F	4	Louis Chevrolet*	Frontenac	Frontenac	12
13	3	95.94	28	PR	4	Gil Anderson	Premier	Premier	13
14	18	83.12	25	DU	4	Dave Lewis	Crawford	Crawford	14
15	1	96.69	18	P	4	Johnny Aitken	Peugeot	Peugeot	15
16	12	87.17	21	D	4	Jules DeVigne, France	Delage	Delage	16
17	7	93.39	27	PR	4	Tom Rooney	Premier	Premier	17
18	11	87.74	7	F	4	Arthur Chevrolet	Frontenac	Frontenac	18
19	8	93.33	19	P	4	Charlie Merz	Peugeot	Peugeot	19
20	2	96.44	5	MX	4	Eddie Rickenbacker	Maxwell	Maxwell	20
21	16	84.12	23	SB	4	Aldo Franchi	Peusun	Peugeot	21

Qualified, did not start: Louis Chevrolet, Frontenac, #6, 87.69, Broke crankshaft
Eddie O'Donnell, Duesenberg, 86.71, Broke brake drum
Jack LeCain, Delage, #22, 82.48, Broke crankshaft
*Gaston Chevrolet, Frontenac, #8, 73.85, Below minimum
Robert Delno, Richards, Below minimum—withdrew—overweight

Total entries: 30

Qualifying: Minimum of 80 MPH for 1 lap. 3 tries, fastest 33 in order of speed.

*Louis Chevrolet's car qualified by Joe Boyer after Gaston Chevrolet failed to reach 80 MPH minimum.

FIN	ENTRANT	LAPS	SPEED, REASON OUT	RELIEF DRIVER	FIN
1	Peugeot Auto Racing Co.	120	83.26	—	1
2	Duesenberg Bros.	120	83.15	—	2
3	Ralph Mulford	120	82.60	—	3
4	Sunbeam Motor Car Co.	120	79.96	—	4
5	Barney Oldfield	120	79.20	—	5
6	Prest-O-Lite Racing Team	120	78.30	Eddie Rickenbacker	6
7	Indianapolis Speedway Team Co.	120	76.80	Gil Anderson	7
8	William Chandler	120	74.40	—	8
9	William Chandler	120	74.20	Frank Elliott	9
10	S. Osteweg	120	74.00	—	10
11	Ogren Motor Car Co.	120	73.55	—	11
12	Chevrolet Bros.	82	Con. rod	—	12
13	Indianapolis Speedway Team Co.	75	Oil line	—	13
14	William Chandler	71	Loose gas tank	—	14
15	Indianapolis Speedway Team Co.	69	Valve	—	15
16	Harry Harkness	61	Wreck	Jack LeCain	16
17	Indianapolis Speedway Team Co.	48	Wreck	—	17
18	Chevrolet Bros.	35	Magneto	—	18
19	Indianapolis Speedway Team Co.	25	Lubrication	—	19
20	Prest-O-Lite Racing Team	9	Steering	—	20
21	Aldo Franchi	9	Engine trouble	—	21

D = Delage
DU = Duesenberg
F = Frontenac
MX = Maxwell

P = Peugeot
PR = Premier
S = Sunbeam
W = Wisconsin

1919

FIN	START	QUAL. SPEED	NUMBER, TYPE, CYLINDERS			DRIVER	CAR NAME	CHASSIS	FIN
1	2	100.01	3	P	4	Howdy Wilcox	Peugeot	Peugeot	1
2	8	94.50	14	SZ	4	Eddie Hearne	Durant Spl.	Stutz	2
3	22	95.00	6	PM	4	Jules Goux, France	Peugeot	Peugeot	3
4	3	98.30	32	B	8	Albert Guyot, France	Ballot	Ballot	4
5	28	92.20	26	BR	4	Tom Alley	Bender Spl.	Bender	5
6	4	98.20	4	PK	12	Ralph DePalma	Packard Spl.	Packard	6
7	12	103.10	7	F	4	Louis Chevrolet	Frontenac Spl.	Frontenac	7
8	10	94.10	27	H	6	Ira Vail	Hudson Super-six	Hudson	8
9	27	92.50	21	H	6	Denny Hickey	Stickle Spl.	Hudson	9
10	16	100.40	41	F	4	Gaston Chevrolet	Frontenac Spl.	Frontenac	10
11	1	104.70	31	B	8	Rene Thomas, France	Ballot	Ballot	11
12	9	94.25	8	SZ	4	Earl Cooper	Stutz Spl.	Stutz	12
13	29	91.70	23	DU	4	Elmer Shannon	Shannon Spl.	Duesenberg	13
14	26	92.80	17	H	6	Ora Haibe	Hudson Super-six	Hudson	14
15	32	89.50	37	P	4	Andre Boillot, France	Baby Peugeot	Peugeot	15
16	21	95.00	48	P	4	Ray Howard	Peugeot	Peugeot	16
17	23	94.20	22	DU	4	Wilbur D'Alene	Duesenberg Spl.	Duesenberg	17
18	25	92.90	15	DU	4	Louis LeCocq, France	Roamer	Duesenberg	18
19	7	94.90	29	P	4	Art Klein	Peugeot	Peugeot	19
20	11	90.00	19	MC	4	Charles Kirkpatrick	Detroit Spl.	Mercedes Copy	20
21	6	94.90	33	B	8	Paul Bablot, France	Ballot	Ballot	21
22	5	97.30	10	DU	4	Eddie O'Donnell	Duesenberg Spl.	Duesenberg	22
23	24	93.50	12	DU	4	Kurt Hitke	Roamer	Duesenberg	23
24	20	96.50	1	SZ	4	Cliff Durant	Chevrolet Spl.	Stutz	24
25	31	89.90	9	DU	4	Tommy Milton	Duesenberg Spl.	Duesenberg	25
26	13	101.70	34	B	8	Louis Wagner, Germany	Ballot	Ballot	26
27	18	98.00	18	DU	4	Arthur Thurman	Thurman Spl.	Duesenberg	27
28	30	91.50	43	M	4	Omar Toft	Toft Spl.	Miller	28
29	15	100.50	2	F	4	Ralph Mulford	Frontenac Spl.	Frontenac	29
30	33	86.50	36		4	J. J. McCoy	McCoy Spl.		30
31	14	100.90	39	F	4	Joe Boyer	Frontenac Spl.	Frontenac	31
32	17	99.80	5	B-B	6	W. W. Brown	Richards Spl.	Brown	32
33	19	97.70	28	M	4	Roscoe Sarles	Oldfield Spl.	Miller	33

Qualified, did not start: Jim Reynolds, Hudson Super-six, #24, H, 83.5, Bumped
Al Cotey, Ogren Spl., #35, DU, 82.9, Too slow

Total entries: 42

Qualifying: Minimum of 80 MPH for 1 lap. 3 tries, fastest 33.

FIN	ENTRANT	LAPS	SPEED, REASON OUT	RELIEF DRIVER	FIN
1	Indianapolis Motor Speedway	200	88.05	—	1
2	R. Cliff Durant	200	87.09	—	2
3	Indianapolis Motor Speedway	200	85.93	—	3
4	Ernest Ballot	200	84.44	—	4
5	Ahlberg Bearing Co.	200	82.18	—	5
6	Packard Motor Car Co.	200	81.04	—	6
7	Frontenac Motors	200	81.03	Joe Boyer	7
8	Hudson Motor Car Co.	200	80.49	—	8
9	A. C. Stickle	200	80.22	—	9
10	Frontenac Motors	200	79.50	Louis Chevrolet	10
11	Ernest Ballot	200	78.75	—	11
12	Earl Cooper	200	78.60	Reeves Dutton	12
13	Elmer T. Shannon	200	76.75	E. Rawlings	13
14	Hudson Motor Car Co.	200		—	14
15	Jules Goux	195	Wreck	—	15
16	A. G. Kaufman	130	Lost oil pressure	—	16
17	Duesenberg Bros.	120	Axle	—	17
18	Roscoe Sarles	96	Wreck	—	18
19	Arthur H. Klein	70	Oil line	—	19
20	Frank P. Book	69	Con. rod	—	20
21	Ernest Ballot	63	Wreck	Jean Chassagne	21
22	Duesenberg Bros.	60	Piston	—	22
23	Roscoe Sarles	56	Rod bearing	—	23
24	R. Cliff Durant	54	Steering	—	24
25	Duesenberg Bros.	50	Con. rod	—	25
26	Ernest Ballot	44	Broken wheel	—	26
27	Arthur Thurman	44	Wreck	—	27
28	Omar Toft	44	Con. rod	—	28
29	Ralph Mulford	37	Drive shaft	—	29
30	J. J. McCoy	36	Oil line	—	30
31	Frontenac Motors	30	Rear axle	—	31
32	C. L. Richards	14	Con. rod	—	32
33	Barney Oldfield	8	Rocker arm	—	33

B = Ballot
B-B = Brown & Brett
BR = Bender
DU = Duesenberg
F = Frontenac
H = Hudson
M = Miller
MC = Mercedes Copy
P = Peugeot
PK = Packard
PM = Premier
SZ = Stutz

1920

FIN	START	QUAL. SPEED	NUMBER, TYPE, CYLINDERS			DRIVER	CAR NAME	CHASSIS	FIN
1	6	91.55	4	F	4	Gaston Chevrolet	Monroe Spl.	Frontenac	1
2	18	93.95	25	B	8	Rene Thomas, France	Ballot	Ballot	2
3	11	90.20	10	DU	8	Tommy Milton	Duesenberg Spl.	Duesenberg	3
4	15	88.70	12	DU	8	Jimmy Murphy	Duesenberg Spl.	Duesenberg	4
5	1	99.15	2	B	8	Ralph DePalma	Ballot	Ballot	5
6	9	88.05	31	DU	8	Eddie Hearne	Duesenberg Spl.	Duesenberg	6
7	4	95.45	26	B	8	Jean Chassagne, France	Ballot	Ballot	7
8	19	92.80	28	F	4	Joe Thomas	Monroe Spl.	Frontenac	8
9	23	NT	33	DU	8	Ralph Mulford	Mulford	Mulford	9
10	17	81.15	15	DU	4	Pete Henderson	Revere Spl.	Duesenberg	10
11	14	81.85	32	BT	6	John Boling	Richards Spl.	Brett	11
12	2	96.90	6	F	4	Joe Boyer	Frontenac Spl.	Frontenac	12
13	10	84.60	9	P	4	Ray Howard	Peugeot	Peugeot	13
14	12	88.20	29	DU	8	Eddie O'Donnell	Duesenberg Spl.	Duesenberg	14
15	21	84.30	16	P	4	Jules Goux, France	Peugeot	Peugeot	15
16	13	85.48	34	DU	8	Willie Haupt	Meteor	Duesenberg	16
17	8	90.55	7	F	4	Bennie Hill	Frontenac Spl.	Frontenac	17
18	3	96.30	3	F	4	Louis Chevrolet	Monroe Spl.	Frontenac	18
19	20	88.82	18	P	4	Howdy Wilcox	Peugeot	Peugeot	19
20	7	90.75	5	F	4	Roscoe Sarles	Monroe Spl.	Frontenac	20
21	5	92.70	8	F	4	Art Klein	Frontenac Spl.	Frontenac	21
22	22	79.98*	19	GR	4	Jean Porporato,* France	Gregoire	Gregoire	22
23	16	85.40	17	P	4	Andre Boillot, France	Peugeot	Peugeot	23

Total entries: 32

Qualifying: Minimum of 80 MPH for 4 laps. Fastest 33.

*Jean Porporato started after barely missing minimum qualifying speed.
 Mulford allowed to start with no attempt.

FIN	ENTRANT	LAPS	SPEED, REASON OUT	RELIEF DRIVER	FIN
1	William Small Co.	200	88.16	—	1
2	Ernest Ballot	200	87.47	—	2
3	Duesenberg Bros.	200	86.52	—	3
4	Duesenberg Bros.	200	85.10	—	4
5	Ralph DePalma	200	82.12	—	5
6	Duesenberg Bros.	200	80.15	—	6
7	Ernest Ballot	200	79.94	—	7
8	William Small Co.	200	78.60	Art Klein, Harry Thicksten	8
9	Ralph Mulford	200	68.33	—	9
10	Revere Motor Car Corp.	200	67.93	Tom Alley	10
11	C. L. Richards	199	Flagged	Riley Brett	11
12	Frontenac Motor Co.	192	Wreck	Ira Vail	12
13	Peugeot Auto Racing Co.	150	Camshaft	Aldo Franchi	13
14	Duesenberg Bros.	149	Oil line	—	14
15	Jules Goux	148	Engine trouble	—	15
16	Meteor Motors Co.	146	Con. rod	Wade Morton	16
17	Frontenac Motor Co.	115	Wreck	Roscoe Sarles	17
18	William Small Co.	94	Steering	Salvatore Barbarino	18
19	Jules Goux	65	Engine trouble	—	19
20	William Small Co.	58	Wreck	—	20
21	Frontenac Motor Co.	40	Wreck	—	21
22	Jean Porporato	23	Ruled off	—	22
23	Jules Goux	16	Engine trouble	—	23

B = Ballot   F = Frontenac
BT = Brett   GR = Gregoire
DU = Duesenberg   P = Peugeot

1921

FIN	START	QUAL. SPEED	NUMBER, TYPE, CYLINDERS			DRIVER	CAR NAME	CHASSIS	FIN
1	20	93.05	2	F	8	Tommy Milton	Frontenac Spl.	Frontenac	1
2	2	98.35	6	DU	8	Roscoe Sarles	Duesenberg Spl.	Duesenberg	2
3	8	87.00	23	F	4	Percy Ford	Chicago-Frontenac Spl.	Frontenac	3
4	9	83.85	5	DU	8	Eddie Miller	Duesenberg Spl.	Duesenberg	4
5	13	93.50	16	SB	8	Ora Haibe	Sunbeam	Sunbeam	5
6	14	87.78	9	DU	8	Albert Guyot, France	Duesenberg Spl.	Duesenberg	6
7	10	82.35	3	M	8	Ira Vail	Leach Spl.	Leach	7
8	15	87.75	21	DU	8	Benny Hill	Duesenberg Spl.	Duesenberg	8
9	21	91.70	8	F	8	Ralph Mulford	Frontenac	Frontenac	9
10	17	83.75	15	SB	8	Rene Thomas, France	Sunbeam	Sunbeam	10
11	18	80.50[a]	27	F	4	Tom Alley[a]	Frontenac Spl.	Frontenac	11
12	1	100.75	4	B	8	Ralph DePalma	Ballot	Ballot	12
13	4	96.18	1	DU	8	Eddie Hearne	Revere Spl.	Duesenberg	13
14	19	93.60	24	DU	8	Jimmy Murphy	Duesenberg Spl.	Duesenberg	14
15	16	87.70	17	BT	6	Riley Brett	Junior Spl.	Brett	15
16	23	88.35	28	F	4	C. W. Van Ranst	Frontenac Spl.	Frontenac	16
17	3	96.65	7	DU	8	Joe Boyer	Duesenberg Spl.	Duesenberg	17
18	6	91.00	19	P	4	Jean Chassagne, France	Peugeot	Peugeot	18
19	5	95.40	22	F	4	Jules Ellingboe	Frontenac Spl.	Frontenac	19
20	11	97.60	14	SB	8	Andre Boillot, France	Talbot-Darracq	Sunbeam	20
21	7	88.30[b]	18	BT	6	Louis Fontaine[b]	Junior Spl.	Brett	21
22	22	96.25[c]	25	DU	8	Joe Thomas[c]	Duesenberg Spl.	Duesenberg	22
23	12	96.00	10	P	4	Howdy Wilcox	Peugeot	Peugeot	23

Total entries: 25

Qualifying: Minimum 80 MPH for 4 laps. Fastest 33.

[a]Alley's car qualified by Lora Corum
[b]Fontaine's car qualified by Joe Thomas
[c]Thomas' car qualified by Joe Boyer

FIN	ENTRANT	LAPS	SPEED, REASON OUT	RELIEF DRIVER	FIN
1	Louis Chevrolet	200	89.62	—	1
2	Duesenberg Bros.	200	88.61	—	2
3	Stanley Kandul	200	85.02	Andy Burt, Jules Ellingboe	3
4	Duesenberg Bros.	200	84.65	Jimmy Murphy	4
5	Sunbeam Motor Car Co.	200	84.28	—	5
6	Duesenberg Bros.	200	83.03	Joe Boyer, Eddie Miller	6
7	Ira Vail	200	80.15	—	7
8	John Thiele	200	79.13	Jerry Wonderlich	8
9	Louis Chevrolet	177	Flagged	—	9
10	Sunbeam Motor Car Co.	144	Water connection	—	10
11	L. L. Corum	133	Con. rod	—	11
12	Ralph DePalma	112	Con. rod	—	12
13	E. A. Hearne	111	Oil line	—	13
14	Duesenberg Bros.	107	Wreck	Eddie Pullen	14
15	George L. Wade	91	Hit wall	Harry Thicksten	15
16	C. W. Van Ranst	87	Water connection	—	16
17	Duesenberg Bros.	74	Rear axle	—	17
18	Jean Chassagne	65	Lost hood	—	18
19	Jules Ellingboe	49	Steering	—	19
20	Louis Coatalen	41	Con. rod	—	20
21	George L. Wade	33	Wreck	—	21
22	Duesenberg Bros.	25	Steering	—	22
23	Jules Goux	22	Con. rod	—	23

B = Ballot   M = Miller

BT = Brett   P = Peugeot

DU = Duesenberg   SB = Sunbeam

F = Frontenac

1922

FIN	START	QUAL. SPEED	NUMBER,	TYPE,	CYLINDERS	DRIVER	CAR NAME	CHASSIS	FIN
1	1	100.50	35	M	8	Jimmy Murphy	Murphy Spl.	Duesenberg	1
2	2	99.97	12	DU	8	Harry Hartz	Duesenberg Spl.	Duesenberg	2
3	23	95.60	15	B	8	Eddie Hearne	Ballot	Ballot	3
4	3	99.55	17	DU	8	Ralph DePalma	Duesenberg Spl.	Duesenberg	4
5	14	92.90	31	DU	8	Ora Haibe	Duesenberg Spl.	Duesenberg	5
6	7	97.76	24	DU	8	Jerry Wonderlich	Duesenberg Spl.	Duesenberg	6
7	13	93.28	21	DU	8	I. P. Fetterman	Duesenberg Spl.	Duesenberg	7
8	9	96.75	1	DU	8	Ira Vail	Disteel-Duesenberg Spl.	Duesenberg	8
9	12	94.05	26	F	4	Tom Alley	Monroe Spl.	Frontenac	9
10	17	88.80	10	DU	8	Joe Thomas	Duesenberg Spl.	Duesenberg	10
11	16	89.60	3	F	8	E. G. "Cannonball" Baker	Frontenac Spl.	Frontenac	11
12	11	95.85	34	M	8	Cliff Durant	Durant Spl.	Miller	12
13	19	81.90	22	BY	4	Douglas Hawkes, England	Bentley	Bentley	13
14	21	NT*	18	FF	4	Jack Curtner*	Fronty Ford Spl.	Ford T	14
15	18	87.80	25	F	4	Wilbur D'Alene	Monroe Spl.	Frontenac	15
16	8	97.75	9	M	8	Frank Elliott	Leach Spl.	Miller	16
17	15	89.65	27	F	4	Lora Corum	Monroe	Frontenac	17
18	27	83.90	19	FF	4	Glenn Howard	Fronty Ford Spl.	Ford T	18
19	5	99.20	5	F	4	Ralph Mulford	Frontenac Spl.	Frontenac	19
20	10	96.20	7	F	8	Pete DePaolo	Frontenac Spl.	Frontenac	20
21	25	87.15	6	F	4	Art Klein	Frontenac Spl.	Frontenac	21
22	4	99.25	4	F	4	Leon Duray	Frontenac Spl.	Frontenac	22
23	6	98.00	2	F	4	Roscoe Sarles	Frontenac Spl.	Frontenac	23
24	24	94.40	8	M	8	Tommy Milton	Leach Spl.	Milton	24
25	22	96.95	14	B	8	Jules Goux, France	Ballot	Ballot	25
26	20	95.50	23	DU	8	Jules Ellingboe	Duesenberg Spl.	Duesenberg	26
27	26	86.10	16	P	8	Howdy Wilcox	Peugeot	Peugeot	27

Total entries: 32

Qualifying: Minimum 80 MPH for 4 laps. Fastest 33.

*Allowed to start without qualifying

FIN	ENTRANT	LAPS	SPEED, REASON OUT	RELIEF DRIVER	FIN
1	Jimmy Murphy	200	94.48	—	1
2	Duesenberg Bros.	200	93.53	—	2
3	Jules Goux	200	93.04	—	3
4	Ralph DePalma	200	90.61	—	4
5	Duesenberg Bros.	200	90.58	Jules Ellingboe	5
6	Duesenberg Bros.	200	88.79	Jules Ellingboe	6
7	Duesenberg Bros.	200	87.99	Phil Shafer	7
8	Disteel Flyers, Inc.	200	86.15	Dave Koetzla	8
9	William Small Co.	200	84.20	—	9
10	Duesenberg Bros.	200	82.50	Wade Morton, Pete DePaolo	10
11	Louis Chevrolet	200	79.25	—	11
12	R. Cliff Durant	200	77.75	Dave Lewis	12
13	Bentley Motor Car Co.	200	74.95	—	13
14	Jack Curtner	160	Flagged	—	14
15	William Small Co.	160	Flagged	—	15
16	Ira Vail	195	Axle	Art Klein	16
17	William Small Co.	169	Engine trouble	—	17
18	Chevrolet Bros. Mfg. Co.	165	Engine trouble	Homer Ormsby	18
19	Louis Chevrolet	161	Con. rod	—	19
20	Louis Chevrolet	110	Wreck	—	20
21	Louis Chevrolet	105	Con. rod	—	21
22	Louis Chevrolet	94	Broken axle	—	22
23	Louis Chevrolet	88	Con. rod	—	23
24	Tommy Milton	44	Loose gas tank	—	24
25	Jules Goux	25	Broken axle	—	25
26	Duesenberg	25	Wreck	—	26
27	Howdy Wilcox	7	Valve spring	—	27

B = Ballot
BY = Bentley
DU = Duesenberg
F = Frontenac

FF = Fronty Ford
M = Miller
P = Peugeot

1923

FIN	START	QUAL. SPEED	NUMBER, TYPE, CYLINDERS			DRIVER	CAR NAME	CHASSIS	FIN
1	1	108.17	1	M	8	Tommy Milton	H.C.S. Spl.	Miller	1
2	2	103.70	7	M	8	Harry Hartz	Durant Spl.	Miller	2
3	9	104.05	5	M	8	Jimmy Murphy	Durant Spl.	Miller	3
4	14	97.30	6	M	8	Eddie Hearne	Durant Spl.	Miller	4
5	7	86.65	23	FF	4	Lora Corum	Barber-Warnock Fronty Ford Spl.	Ford T	5
6	16	93.25	31	M	8	Frank Elliott	Durant Spl.	Miller	6
7	10	102.65	8	M	8	Cliff Durant	Durant Spl.	Miller	7
8	20	90.55	15	MS	4	Max Sailer	Mercedes	Mercedes	8
9	22	88.90	19	BG	8	Prince de Cystria, France	Bugatti	Bugatti	9
10	24	88.00*	34	DU	8	Wade Morton*	Duesenberg Spl.	Duesenberg	10
11	15	95.20	16	MS	4	Christian Werner, Germany	Mercedes	Mercedes	11
12	6	90.30	18	BG	8	Pierre de Viscaya, France	Bugatti	Bugatti	12
13	21	89.90	28	M	8	Leon Duray	Durant Spl.	Miller	13
14	3	98.02	4	PK	6	Dario Resta, France	Packard Spl.	Packard	14
15	11	100.42	2	PK	6	Ralph DePalma	Packard Spl.	Packard	15
16	19	90.75	26	M	8	Harlan Fengler	Durant Spl.	Miller	16
17	8	81.00	25	M	8	Howdy Wilcox	H.C.S. Spl.	Miller	17
18	13	98.80	3	PK	6	Joe Boyer	Packard Spl.	Packard	18
19	18	91.20	35	M	8	Benny Hill	Miller Spl.	Miller	19
20	5	91.80	27	BG	8	Count Louis Zbrowski, France	Bugatti	Bugatti	20
21	12	99.40	29	M	8	Earl Cooper	Durant Spl.	Miller	21
22	23	95.30	22	BG	8	Raoul Riganti, Argentina	Bugatti	Bugatti	22
23	17	93.20	14	MS	4	Christian Lautenschlager, Germany	Mercedes	Mercedes	23
24	4	92.90	21	BG	8	Martin de Alsaga, France	Bugatti	Bugatti	24

Total entries: 35

Qualifying: Minimum 80 MPH for 4 laps. Fastest 33.

*Qualified by Phil Shafer on the morning of the race

FIN	ENTRANT	LAPS	SPEED, REASON OUT	RELIEF DRIVER	FIN
1	H.C.S. Motor Co.	200	90.95	Howdy Wilcox	1
2	R. Cliff Durant	200	90.06	—	2
3	R. Cliff Durant	200	88.08	—	3
4	R. Cliff Durant	200	86.65	Earl Cooper	4
5	Barber-Warnock	200	82.58	—	5
6	R. Cliff Durant	200	82.22	Dave Lewis	6
7	R. Cliff Durant	200	82.17	Eddie Hearne	7
8	Daimler Motoren Gesellschaft	200	80.68	Karl Sailer	8
9	Prince de Cystria	200	77.64	—	9
10	Duesenberg Bros.	200	74.98	Phil Shafer, Ora Haibe, Jerry Wonderlich	10
11	Daimler Motoren Gesellschaft	200	74.65	Max Sailer	11
12	Martin de Alsaga	166	Con. rod	—	12
13	R. Cliff Durant	136	Con. rod	—	13
14	Packard Motor Car Co.	88	Head gasket	Ernie Ansterberg, Joe Boyer	14
15	Packard Motor Car Co.	69	Head gasket	Ernie Ansterberg	15
16	R. Cliff Durant	69	Gas tank	Lou Wilson	16
17	H.C.S. Motor Co.	60	Clutch	—	17
18	Packard Motor Car Co.	59	Differential	—	18
19	Harry A. Miller	44	Crankshaft	Martin de Alsaga	19
20	Count Louis Zbrowski	41	Con. rod	—	20
21	R. Cliff Durant	21	Wreck	Tom Alley	21
22	Martin de Alsaga	19	Gas leak	—	22
23	Daimler Motoren Gesellschaft	14	Wreck	—	23
24	Martin de Alsaga	6	Con. rod	—	24

BG = Bugatti   M = Miller
DU = Duesenberg   MS = Mercedes
FF = Fronty Ford   PK = Packard

1926

FIN	START	QUAL. SPEED	NUMBER, TYPE, CYLINDERS			DRIVER	CAR NAME	CHASSIS	FIN
1	20	95.780	15	M	8	Frank Lockhart	Miller Spl.	Miller	1
2	2	109.542	3	M	8	Harry Hartz	Miller Spl.	Miller	2
3	14	105.109	36	M	8	Cliff Woodbury	Boyle Valve Spl.	Miller	3
4	13	100.612	8	M	8	Fred Comer	Miller Spl.	Miller	4
5	27	96.709	12	DU	8	Pete DePaolo	Duesenberg Spl.	Duesenberg	5
6	8	105.873	6	M	8	Frank Elliott	Miller Spl.	Miller	6
7	16	101.428	14	M	8	Norman Batten	Miller Spl.	Miller	7
8	15	102.517	19	M	8	Ralph Hepburn	Miller Spl.	Miller	8
9	28	95.546	18	M	8	John Duff, England	Elcar Spl.	Miller	9
10	5	106.647	4	M	8	Phil Shafer	Miller Spl.	Miller	10
11	12	102.789	31	M	8	Tony Gulotta	Miller Spl.	Miller	11
12	7	105.876	16	M	8	Benny Hill	Miller Spl.	Miller	12
13	21	93.672	33	M	8	Thane Houser	Abell Spl.	Miller	13
14	17	94.977	27	EL	4	Douglas Hawkes, England	Eldridge Spl.	Eldridge	14
15	4	107.009	1	M	8	Dave Lewis	Miller Spl.	Miller	15
16	1	111.735	5	M	8	Earl Cooper	Miller Spl.	Miller	16
17	11	104.855	9	LC	8	Cliff Durant	Locomobile Junior 8 Spl.	Fengler	17
18	18	92.142	29	DU	8	Ben Jones	Duesenberg Two Cycle Spl.	Duesenberg	18
19	23	89.777	26	EL	4	Ernest Eldridge, England	Eldridge Spl.	Eldridge	19
20	24	88.849	23	AG	6	Lora Corum	Schmidt Spl.	Schmidt	20
21	22	92.937	24	AG	6	Steve Nemish	Schmidt Spl.	Schmidt	21
22	6	106.376	7	M	8	Jules Ellingboe	Miller Spl.	Miller	22
23	3	109.186	10	LC	8	Leon Duray	Locomobile Junior 8 Spl.	Fengler	23
24	26	100.398	17	M	8	Fred Lecklider	Nickel Plate Spl.	Miller	24
25	25	86.418	28	FF	4	Jack McCarver	Hamlin Front Drive Spl.	Ford T	25
26	9	105.180	34	M	8	Bon McDougall	Miller Spl.	Miller	26
27	10	104.977	22	M	8	Doc Shattuc	Miller Spl.	Miller	27
28	19	88.580	39	AG	6	Albert Guyot, France	Guyot Spl.	Schmidt	28

Qualified, did not start: Dan Cain, K & M Spl., #37, KM-S, 70.358 MPH (below 80 MPH minimum)

Total entries: 39

Qualifying: Minimum 80 MPH for 4 laps. Fastest 33.

FIN	ENTRANT	LAPS	SPEED, REASON OUT	RELIEF DRIVER	FIN
1	Duesenberg Bros.	200	98.23	Joe Boyer	1
2	Earl Cooper	200	97.79	—	2
3	Jimmy Murphy	200	97.27	—	3
4	R. Cliff Durant	200	96.55	—	4
5	Harry A. Miller	200	96.46	—	5
6	Duesenberg Bros.	200	94.30	—	6
7	R. Cliff Durant	200	93.43	Wade Morton	7
8	Ira Vail	200	92.45	C. W. Van Ranst	8
9	Antoine Mourre	200	91.76	—	9
10	Harry A. Miller	200	90.51	—	10
11	Harry A. Miller	200	90.47	—	11
12	R. Cliff Durant	200	85.48	Wade Morton	12
13	R. Cliff Durant	199	Out of gas	Phil Shafer, Eddie Hearne	13
14	Barber-Warnock	191	Flagged	—	14
15	Albert Schmidt	182	Flagged	Elmer Dempsey	15
16	Barber-Warnock	177	Flagged	—	16
17	Barber-Warnock	177	Flagged	—	17
18	Duesenberg Bros.	176	Hit wall	Ernie Ansterberg, Fred Comer, Lora Corum, Thane Houser	18
19	R. Cliff Durant	151	Fuel line	—	19
20	Frank R. Elliott	149	Gas tank	—	20
21	Tommy Milton	110	Gas tank	—	21
22	Duesenberg Bros.	2	Wreck	—	22

DU = Duesenberg
FF = Fronty Ford
M = Miller
MS = Mercedes

1925

FIN	START	QUAL. SPEED	NUMBER, TYPE, CYLINDERS			DRIVER	CAR NAME	CHASSIS	FIN
1	2	113.083	12	DU-S	8	Pete DePaolo	Duesenberg Spl.	Duesenberg	1
2	5	109.061	1	M-S	8	Dave Lewis	Junior 8 Spl.	Miller	2
3	22	103.523	9	DU-S	8	Phil Shafer	Duesenberg Spl.	Duesenberg	3
4	3	112.433	6	M-S	8	Harry Hartz	Miller Spl.	Miller	4
5	11	104.366	4	M-S	8	Tommy Milton	Miller Spl.	Miller	5
6	1	113.196	28	M-S	8	Leon Duray	Miller Spl.	Miller	6
7	18	108.607	8	M-S	8	Ralph DePalma	Miller Spl.	Miller	7
8	9	106.338	35	DU-S	8	Peter Kreis	Duesenberg Spl.	Duesenberg	8
9	14	102.070	15	M-S	8	Doc Shattuc	Miller Spl.	Miller	9
10	8	107.661	22	FT-S	8	Pietro Bordino, Italy	Fiat Spl.	Fiat	10
11	12	104.296	5	M-S	8	Fred Comer	Miller Spl.	Miller	11
12	10	104.910	27	M-S	8	Frank Elliott	Miller Spl.	Miller	12
13	15	97.799	24	M-S	8	Earl DeVore	Miller Spl.	Miller	13
14	20	101.931	14	M-S	8	Bob McDonough	Miller Spl.	Miller	14
15	16	95.821[a]	23	DU-S	8	Wade Morton[a]	Duesenberg Spl.	Duesenberg	15
16	6	108.489	17	M	8	Ralph Hepburn	Miller Spl.	Miller	16
17	4	110.487	2	M	8	Earl Cooper	Junior 8 Spl.	Miller	17
18	13	104.167[b]	3	M-S	8	Benny Hill[b]	Miller Spl.	Miller	18
19	17	89.401	29	M	8	Herb Jones	Jones-Whitaker Spl.	Miller	19
20	19	104.785	19	M	8	Ira Vail	R. J. Spl.	Miller	20
21	21	88.478[c]	7	FF	4	Milt Jones[c]	Skelly Spl.	Ford T	21
22	7	107.832	10	M	8	Jules Ellingboe	Miller Spl.	Miller	22

Qualified, did not start: Benny Hill, Miller Spl., #21, M-S, 105.708, Withdrew
Lora Corum, Miller Spl., #16, M, 103.535, Wrecked day before race

Total entries: 34

Qualifying: Minimum 80 MPH for 4 laps. 33 fastest.

[a]Qualified by Ray Cariens
[b]Qualified by Antoine Mourre
[c]Qualified by Harold Skelly

FIN	ENTRANT	LAPS	SPEED, REASON OUT	RELIEF DRIVER	FIN
1	Duesenberg Bros.	200	101.13	Norman Batten	1
2	R. Cliff Durant	200	100.82	Benny Hill	2
3	Duesenberg Bros.	200	100.18	Wade Morton	3
4	Harry Hartz	200	98.89	—	4
5	Tommy Milton	200	97.26	—	5
6	Harry Hartz	200	96.91	Fred Comer	6
7	Ralph DePalma	200	96.85	Lora Corum	7
8	Duesenberg Bros.	200	96.32	Norman Batten	8
9	Dr. W. E. Shattuc	200	95.74	—	9
10	Pietro Bordino	200	94.75	Antoine Mourre	10
11	Harry Hartz	200	93.67	Wade Morton	11
12	Richard G. Doyle	200	92.23	Ora Haibe	12
13	Bancroft & Pope	198	Flagged	Glen Schultz	13
14	Tommy Milton	188	Truss rod	Benny Hill	14
15	Duesenberg Bros.	156	Wrecked	Antoine Mourre, Jimmy Gleason	15
16	Earl Cooper	144	Gas tank	—	16
17	R. Cliff Durant	127	Wrecked	—	17
18	Harry A. Miller	69	Rear spring	Ray Cariens, Jules Ellingboe, Jerry Wonderlich	18
19	Herbert Jones	69	Wrecked	Alfred Moss	19
20	R. J. Johnson	63	Con. rod	—	20
21	H. J. Skelly	33	Transmission	Fred Harder	21
22	Jerry Wonderlich	24	Steering key	—	22

DU = Duesenberg   M = Miller
FF = Fronty Ford   -S = Supercharged
FT = Fiat

1924

FIN	START	QUAL. SPEED	NUMBER, TYPE, CYLINDERS			DRIVER	CAR NAME	CHASSIS	FIN
1	21	93.333	15	DU	8	Lora Corum	Duesenberg Spl.	Duesenberg	1
2	6	103.900	8	M	8	Earl Cooper	Studebaker Spl.	Miller	2
3	1	108.037	2	M	8	Jimmy Murphy	Miller Spl.	Miller	3
4	2	107.130	4	M	8	Harry Hartz	Durant Spl.	Miller	4
5	5	104.840	3	M	8	Benny Hill	Miller Spl.	Miller	5
6	13	99.280	12	DU	8	Pete DePaolo	Duesenberg Spl.	Duesenberg	6
7	16	92.880	14	M	8	Fred Comer	Durant Spl.	Miller	7
8	15	96.400	6	M	8	Ira Vail	Vail Spl.	Miller	8
9	9	99.490	32	M	8	Antoine Mourre, France	Mourre Spl.	Miller	9
10	18	91.550	19	M	8	Bob McDonough	Miller Spl.	Miller	10
11	7	102.600	18	M	8	Jules Ellingboe	Miller Spl.	Miller	11
12	11	99.360	7	M	8	Jerry Wonderlich	Durant Spl.	Miller	12
13	8	101.610	16	M	8	Cliff Durant	Durant Spl.	Miller	13
14	19	85.040	26	FF	4	Bill Hunt	Barber-Warnock Fronty Ford Spl.	Ford T	14
15	17	92.810	31	MS	4	Ora Haibe	Schmidt Spl.	Mercedes	15
16	20	85.270	28	FF	4	Alfred Moss, England	Barber-Warnock Fronty Ford Spl.	Ford T	16
17	22	82.770	27	FF	4	Fred Harder	Barber-Warnock Fronty Ford Spl.	Ford T	17
18	4	104.840	9	DU	8	Joe Boyer	Duesenberg Spl.	Duesenberg	18
19	14	99.230	1	M	8	Eddie Hearne	Durant Spl.	Miller	19
20	12	99.310	21	M	8	Frank Elliott	Miller Spl.	Miller	20
21	3	105.200	5	M	8	Tommy Milton	Miller Spl.	Miller	21
22	10	99.400	10	DU	8	Ernie Ansterberg	Duesenberg Spl.	Duesenberg	22

Qualified, did not start: F. H. Wells, Wells Hornet Spl., #17, 75 MPH (below 80 MPH minimum)

Total entries: 32

Qualifying: Minimum 80 MPH for 4 laps. Fastest 33.

FIN	ENTRANT	LAPS	SPEED, REASON OUT	RELIEF DRIVER	FIN
1	Peter Kreis	160	95.885	—	1
2	Harry Hartz	158	94.481	—	2
3	Cliff R. Woodbury	158	94.131	—	3
4	Harry Hartz	155	92.323	Wade Morton	4
5	Duesenberg Bros.	153	91.544	—	5
6	Frank Elliott	152	90.917	Leon Duray	6
7	Norman Batten	151	90.275	—	7
8	Ralph Hepburn	151	89.882	Bob McDonough	8
9	Al Cotey	147	87.551	—	9
10	Phil Shafer	146	87.096	Fred Lecklider	10
11	Harry Hartz	142	Flagged	—	11
12	Harry A. Miller	136	Flagged	Jules Ellingboe	12
13	George G. Abell	102	Flagged	—	13
14	E. A. D. Eldridge	91	Frozen camshaft	Ernest Eldridge	14
15	Harry A. Miller	91	Broken valve	Earl Cooper	15
16	Harry A. Miller	73	Transmission	—	16
17	R. Cliff Durant	60	Gas tank leak	Eddie Hearne	17
18	Duesenberg Bros.	54	Wreck	—	18
19	E. A. D. Eldridge	45	Tie rod	Hershell McKee	19
20	Albert Schmidt	44	Shock absorber	—	20
21	Albert Schmidt	41	Transmission	—	21
22	F. P. Cramer	39	Supercharger	—	22
23	R. Cliff Durant	33	Broken axle	—	23
24	Earl DeVore	24	Con. rod	—	24
25	Chevrolet Bros.	23	Con. rod	—	25
26	R. G. McDougall	19	Valve	—	26
27	Dr. W. E. Shattuc	15	Valve	—	27
28	Albert Guyot	8	Steering knuckle	—	28

AG = Argyle   KM = K & M
DU = Duesenberg   LC = Locomobile
EL = Eldridge   M = Miller
FF = Fronty Ford

NOTE: All engines were supercharged.

1927

FIN	START	QUAL. SPEED	NUMBER, TYPE, CYLINDERS			DRIVER	CAR NAME	CHASSIS	FIN
1	22	111.551	32	DU	8	George Souders	Duesenberg Spl.	Duesenberg	1
2	15	107.497	10	M	8	Earl DeVore	Miller Spl.	Miller	2
3	27	107.765	27	M	8	Tony Gulotta	Miller Spl.	Miller	3
4	19	104.465	29	M	8	Wilbur Shaw	Jynx Spl.	Miller	4
5	28	107.360	21	DU	8	Dave Evans	Duesenberg Spl.	Duesenberg	5
6	7	113.175	14	M	8	Bob McDonough	Cooper Spl.	Cooper	6
7	18	105.115	16	M	8	Eddie Hearne	Miller Spl.	Miller	7
8	25	108.758	6	M	8	Tommy Milton	Detroit Front Drive Spl.	Detroit	8
9	14	108.820	25	M	8	Cliff Bergere	Miller Spl.	Miller	9
10	13	109.682	5	M	8	Frank Elliott	Junior 8 Spl.	Miller	10
11	33	106.859	31	M	8	Fred Frame	Miller Spl.	Miller	11
12	32	107.392	42	M	8	Jimmy Hill	Nickel Plate Spl.	Miller	12
13	31	110.152	24	DU	8	Bennie Shoaff	Perfect Circle Duesenberg Spl.	Duesenberg	13
14	26	108.075	41	DU	8	Wade Morton	Thompson Valve Spl.	Duesenberg	14
15	20	102.918	44	M	8	Al Melcher	Miller Spl.	Miller	15
16	23	109.910	43	M	8	Louis Schneider	Miller Spl.	Miller	16
17	12	109.900	9	M	8	Peter Kreis	Cooper Spl.	Cooper	17
18	1	120.100	2	M	8	Frank Lockhart	Perfect Circle Spl.	Miller	18
19	6	113.200	15	M	8	Cliff Woodbury	Boyle Valve Spl.	Miller	19
20	17	106.078	26	M	8	Dutch Bauman	Miller Spl.	Miller	20
21	29	106.295	35	M	8	Al Cotey	Elcar Spl.	Miller	21
22	16	107.060	17	M	8	Doc Shattuc	Miller Spl.	Miller	22
23	30	105.729	23	M	8	Fred Lecklider	Elgin Piston Pin Spl.	Miller	23
24	5	114.209	19	M	8	Ralph Hepburn	Boyle Valve Spl.	Miller	24
25	4	116.739	1	M	8	Harry Hartz	Erskine Spl.	Miller	25
26	2	119.510	3	M	8	Pete DePaolo	Perfect Circle Spl.	Miller	26
27	3	118.788	12	M	8	Leon Duray	Miller Front Drive Spl.	Miller	27
28	9	112.013	4	M	8	Benny Hill	Cooper Spl.	Miller	28
29	21	113.239	18	M	8	Jules Ellingboe	Cooper Spl.	Miller	29
30	10	111.940	8	M	8	Norman Batten	Miller Spl.	Fengler	30
31	24	109.555	38	DU	8	Babe Stapp	Duesenberg Spl.	Duesenberg	31
32	11	109.920	22	M	8	Jack Petticord	Boyle Valve Spl.	Miller	32
33	8	112.275	7	M	8	Dave Lewis	Miller Front Drive Spl.	Miller	33

Qualified, did not start: Lora Corum, Duesenberg Spl., #28, DU, 94.604 MPH—Bumped

Total entries: 41

Qualifying: Minimum 90 MPH for 4 laps. 33 fastest.

FIN	ENTRANT	LAPS	SPEED, REASON OUT	RELIEF DRIVER	FIN
1	Wm. S. White	200	97.545	—	1
2	F. P. Cramer	200	93.868	Zeke Meyer	2
3	Anthony Gulotta	200	93.139	Pete DePaolo	3
4	Fred Clemons	200	93.110	Louis Meyer	4
5	David E. Evans	200	90.782	Steve Nemish	5
6	Cooper Engineering	200	90.410	Pete DePaolo	6
7	Harry Hartz	200	90.064	Harry Hartz, Leon Duray, Ira Vail	7
8	Tommy Milton	200	85.081	Leon Duray, C. W. Van Ranst, Ralph Hepburn	8
9	Muller Bros.	200	79.929	Wesley Crawford	9
10	Frank Elliott	200	78.244	Fred Frame	10
11	O. B. Dolfinger	199	Flagged	George Fernic, George Abell	11
12	Earl DeVore	197	Flagged	Don Orstrander	12
13	Duesenberg Bros.	198	Rear end gears	Babe Stapp	13
14	Duesenberg Bros.	152	Wrecked	Ralph Holmes, Fred Winnai	14
15	Chas. Haase	144	Supercharger	Jack Petticord, Fred Lecklider	15
16	Fred Lecklider	137	Timing gears	Lora Corum, Dutch Bauman	16
17	Cooper Engineering	123	Bent front axle	Benny Hill, Harry Hartz	17
18	Frank S. Lockhart	120	Con. rod	—	18
19	Cliff Woodbury	108	Supercharger	Ralph Hepburn	19
20	Harry. A. Miller	90	Pinion shaft	—	20
21	Al Cotey	87	Universal	Eddie Burbach	21
22	Doc Shattuc	83	Valve	—	22
23	Henry Kohlert	49	Wrecked	Henry Kohlert	23
24	Cliff Woodbury	39	Leaking fuel	—	24
25	Harry Hartz	38	Crankshaft	—	25
26	Peter DePaolo	31	Supercharger gears	—	26
27	Leon Duray	26	Leaking fuel	—	27
28	Cooper Engineering	26	Rear spring shackle bolt	—	28
29	Earl Cooper	25	Wrecked	—	29
30	Norman K. Batten	24	Caught fire	—	30
31	Duesenberg Bros.	24	Universal	—	31
32	Cliff Woodbury	22	Supercharger	—	32
33	Dave Lewis	21	Front spring pad	—	33

DU = Duesenberg   M = Miller

NOTE: All engines were supercharged.

1928

FIN	START	QUAL. SPEED	NUMBER, TYPE, CYLINDERS			DRIVER	CAR NAME	CHASSIS	FIN
1	13	111.352	14	M	8	Louis Meyer	Miller Spl.	Miller	1
2	8	113.826	28	M	8	Lou Moore	Miller Spl.	Miller	2
3	12	111.444	3	M	8	George Souders	State Auto Insurance Spl.	Miller	3
4	10	113.421	15	M	8	Ray Keech	Simplex Piston Ring Spl.	Miller	4
5	15	106.585	22	M	8	Norman Batten	Miller Spl.	Fengler	5
6	5	116.887	7	M	8	Babe Stapp	Miller Spl.	Miller	6
7	20	111.926	43	M	8	Billy Arnold	Boyle Valve Spl.	Miller	7
8	14	107.501	27	DU	8	Fred Frame	State Auto Mutual Insurance Spl.	Duesenberg	8
9	9	113.690	25	M	8	Fred Comer	Boyle Valve Spl.	Miller	9
10	4	117.031	8	M	8	Tony Gulotta	Stutz Spl.	Miller	10
11	7	114.036	24	M	8	Louis Schneider	Armacost Spl.	Miller	11
12	23	108.264	12	M	8	Dave Evans	Boyle Valve Spl.	Miller	12
13	28	93.545	29	M	8	Henry Kohlert	Elgin Piston Pin Spl.	Miller	13
14	17	106.213	23	M	8	Deacon Litz	Miller Spl.	Miller	14
15	21	111.708	39	DU	8	Jimmy Gleason	Duesenberg Spl.	Duesenberg	15
16	18	99.990	5	M	8	Cliff Durant	Detroit Front Drive Spl.	Detroit	16
17	11	111.673	33	M	8	Johnny Seymour	Marmon Spl.	Cooper	17
18	24	109.810	6	M	8	Earl DeVore	Chromolite Spl.	Miller	18
19	1	122.391	4	M	8	Leon Duray	Miller Spl.	Miller	19
20	16	106.572	38	M	8	Sam Ross	Aranem Spl.	Miller	20
21	27	96.886	26	DU	8	Ira Hall	Duesenberg Spl.	Duesenberg	21
22	19	112.906	32	M	8	Peter Kreis	Marmon Spl.	Cooper	22
23	2	120.418	10	M	8	Cliff Woodbury	Boyle Valve Spl.	Miller	23
24	6	116.354	16	M	8	Ralph Hepburn	Miller Spl.	Miller	24
25	29	100.956	1	M	8	Wilbur Shaw	Flying Cloud Spl.	Miller	25
26	26	102.409	18	DU	8	Benny Shoaff	Duesenberg Spl.	Duesenberg	26
27	25	96.026	41	GR	8	Clarence Belt	Green Super Ford Spl.	Green	27
28	3	119.956	21	M	8	Cliff Bergere	Miller Spl.	Miller	28
29	22	111.618	34	M	8	Russ Snowberger	Marmon Spl.	Cooper	29

Qualified, did not start: Buddy Marr, B. W. Cooke Spl., #35, M. 109.685, Wrecked in practice by Chet Miller
Dutch Bauman, Duesenberg Spl., #19, DU, 106.226, Wrecked morning of race
Lora Corum, Duesenberg Spl., #17, DU, 96.172, Wrecked morning of race

Total entries: 36

Qualifying: Minimum 90 MPH for 4 laps. Fastest 33.

FIN	ENTRANT	LAPS	SPEED, REASON OUT	RELIEF DRIVER	FIN
1	Alden Sampson II	200	99.482	—	1
2	Charles Haase	200	99.241	Louis Schneider	2
3	William S. White	200	98.034	—	3
4	M. A. Yagle	200	93.320	Wilbur Shaw	4
5	Norman K. Batten	200	93.228	Zeke Meyer	5
6	Phil Shafer	200	92.638	Ralph Hepburn	6
7	Boyle Valve Co.	200	91.111	Bill Spence	7
8	William S. White	200	90.079	Ralph Hepburn, Benny Shoaff	8
9	Boyle Valve Co.	200	88.889	Cliff Woodbury	9
10	J. R. Burgamy	200	88.888	Dutch Bauman	10
11	Louis F. Schneider	200	87.964	Lou Wilson	11
12	Boyle Valve Co.	200	87.401	—	12
13	Elgin Piston Pin Co.	180	Flagged	Shorty Cantlon, Doc Shattuc	13
14	A. B. Litz	161	Flagged	Wesley Crawford	14
15	H. C. Henning	195	Magneto	Russ Snowberger	15
16	Tommy Milton	175	Supercharger	Bob McDonough	16
17	Cooper Engineering Co.	170	Supercharger	—	17
18	Metals Protection Co.	161	Wrecked	Cy Marshall	18
19	Leon Duray	133	Overheating	Cliff Bergere	19
20	Reed & Mulligan	132	Timing gears	—	20
21	Henry Maley	115	Wrecked	Jack Petticord	21
22	Cooper Engineering Co.	73	Rod bearings	—	22
23	Boyle Valve Co.	55	Timing gears	—	23
24	Harry A. Miller	48	Timing gears	—	24
25	Peter DePaolo	42	Timing gears	—	25
26	Duesenberg Bros.	35	Wrecked	—	26
27	Green Engineering Co.	32	Valve	Harry Nichols	27
28	Cliff Bergere	7	Supercharger	—	28
29	Cooper Engineering Co.	4	Supercharger	—	29

DU = Duesenberg
GR = Green
M = Miller

Note: All engines were supercharged.

1929

FIN	START	QUAL. SPEED	NUMBER, TYPE, CYLINDERS			DRIVER	CAR NAME	CHASSIS	FIN
1	6	114.905	2	M	8	Ray Keech	Simplex Piston Ring Spl.	Miller	1
2	8	114.704	1	M	8	Louis Meyer	Miller Spl.	Miller	2
3	23	110.345	53	DU	8	Jimmy Gleason	Duesenberg Spl.	Duesenberg	3
4	25	108.440	43	M	8	Carl Marchese	Marchese Spl.	Miller	4
5	21	113.892	42	DU	8	Fred Winnai	Duesenberg Spl.	Duesenberg	5
6	28	105.985	48	M	8	Speed Gardner	Chromolite Spl.	Miller	6
7	14	107.351	6	DEL	8	Louis Chiron, Monaco	Delage	Delage	7
8	7	114.752	9	M	8	Billy Arnold	Boyle Valve Spl.	Miller	8
9	32	103.687	25	M	8	Cliff Bergere	Armacost Spl.	Miller	9
10	22	111.328	34	M	8	Fred Frame	Cooper Spl.	Cooper	10
11	29	105.857	28	M	8	Frank Brisko	Burbach Spl.	Miller	11
12	18	111.628	17	M	8	Phil Shafer	Miller Spl.	Miller	12
13	13	110.677	3	M	8	Lou Moore	Miller-Majestic Spl.	Miller	13
14	26	107.972	36	M	8	Frank Farmer	Miller Spl.	Miller	14
15	24	108.607	49	M	8	Wesley Crawford	Miller Spl.	Fengler	15
16	17	112.528	4	M	8	Peter Kreis	Detroit Front Drive Spl.	Detroit	16
17	11	112.146	23	M	8	Tony Gulotta	Packard Cable Spl.	Miller	17
18	19	111.614	5	M	8	Bob McDonough	Miller Spl.	Miller	18
19	33	102.509*	46	M	8	Bill Lindau*	Pittsburg Spl.	Miller	19
20	27	107.477	31	M	8	Herman Schurch	Armacost Spl.	Miller	20
21	16	114.307	38	M	8	Johnny Seymour	Cooper Spl.	Cooper	21
22	2	119.087	21	M	8	Leon Duray	Packard Cable Spl.	Miller	22
23	30	105.288	29	M	8	Rick Decker	Miller Spl.	Miller	23
24	9	114.526	26	M	8	Deacon Litz	Rusco-Durac Brake Spl.	Miller	24
25	31	104.749	27	M	8	Bert Karnatz	Richard Bros. Spl.	Miller	25
26	20	114.789	47	DU	8	Ernie Triplett	Buckeye Spl.	Duesenberg	26
27	10	113.622	12	M	8	Russ Snowberger	Cooper Spl.	Cooper	27
28	4	115.618	32	M	8	Babe Stapp	Spindler Spl.	Duesenberg	28
29	15	105.609	35	AM	6	Jules Moriceau, France	Thompson Products Spl.	Amilcar	29
30	5	115.093	37	M	8	Pete DePaolo	Boyle Valve Spl.	Miller	30
31	3	116.543	18	M	8	Ralph Hepburn	Packard Cable Spl.	Miller	31
32	12	111.649	10	DU	8	Bill Spence	Duesenberg Spl.	Duesenberg	32
33	1	120.599	8	M	8	Cliff Woodbury	Boyle Valve Spl.	Miller	33

Qualified, did not start: Phil Pardee, Miller Spl., #44, M, 111.211 MPH, Wrecked day before race
Frank Sweigert, Duesenberg Spl., #54, DU, 99.585 MPH, Too slow

Total entries: 44

Qualifying: Minimum of 90 MPH for 4 laps. Fastest 33.

*Originally first alternate; started because of Pardee's wreck

FIN	ENTRANT	LAPS	SPEED, REASON OUT	RELIEF DRIVER	FIN
1	M. A. Yagle	200	97.585	—	1
2	Alden Sampson II	200	95.596	—	2
3	A. S. Duesenberg	200	93.699	Thane Houser, Ernie Triplett	3
4	Marchese Bros.	200	93.541	—	4
5	A. S. Duesenberg	200	88.792	Lora Corum, Roscoe Ford	5
6	F. P. Cramer	200	88.390	Chet Gardner	6
7	Louis Chiron	200	87.728	—	7
8	Cliff R. Woodbury	200	83.909	Cliff Woodbury, Red Roberts	8
9	Cliff Bergere	200	80.703	Peter Kreis	9
10	Cooper Engineering	193	Flagged	Johnny Seymour	10
11	Frank Brisko	180	Flagged	—	11
12	Phil Shafer	150	Flagged	Cliff Woodbury, Russ Snowberger	12
13	Charles Haase	198	Con. rod	Barney Kloepfer	13
14	William Albertson	140	Supercharger	Bill Albertson	14
25	Marian Batten	127	Carburetor	Ted Simpson, Zeke Meyer, Dave Evans	15
16	Tommy Milton	91	Engine seized	—	16
17	Leon Duray	91	Supercharger	—	17
18	M. R. Dodds	74	Oil tank	Cliff Woodbury	18
19	Painter & Hufnagle	70	Valve	—	19
20	Fred Schneider	70	Gas tank split	Jack Buxton, Bert Karnatz	20
21	Cooper Engineering	65	Rear axle	—	21
22	Leon Duray	65	Carburetor	Ralph Hepburn	22
23	Rickliffe Decker	61	Supercharger	Jimmy Rossi	23
24	A. B. Litz	56	Con. rod	—	24
25	Reed & Mulligan	50	Gas leak	—	25
26	C. H. Cunard	48	Con. rod	—	26
27	Cooper Engineering	45	Supercharger	—	27
28	William S. White	40	Universal	—	28
29	Thompson Products	30	Wrecked	—	29
30	Cliff R. Woodbury	25	Steering	—	30
31	Leon Duray	14	Transmission	—	31
32	A. S. Duesenberg	14	Wrecked	—	32
33	Cliff R. Woodbury	3	Wrecked	—	33

AM = Amilcar
DEL = Delage
DU = Duesenberg
M = Miller

1930

FIN	START	QUAL. SPEED	NUMBER, TYPE, CYLINDERS			DRIVER	CAR NAME	CHASSIS	FIN
1	1	113.263	4	M	8	Billy Arnold	Miller-Hartz Spl.	Summers	1
2	3	109.810	16	M	4	Shorty Cantlon	Miller-Schofield Spl.	Stevens	2
3	4	106.107	23	M	8	Louis Schneider	Bowes Seal Fast Spl.	Stevens	3
4	2	111.290	1	M	16	Louis Meyer	Sampson Spl.	Stevens	4
5	22	106.173	6	DU	8	Bill Cummings	Duesenberg Spl.	Stevens	5
6	33	97.342	24	M	8	Dave Evans	Jones & Maley Spl.	Stevens	6
7	8	102.279	15	M	4	Phil Shafer	Coleman Front Drive Spl.	Coleman	7
8	7	104.577	22	S	8	Russ Snowberger	Russell 8 Spl.	Snowberger	8
9	9	101.919	25	M	4	Les Allen	Allen Miller Products Spl.	Miller	9
10	17	94.130	27	SZ	8	Lora Corum	Jones Stutz Spl.	Stutz	10
11	16	95.087	38	OK	8	Claude Burton	V8 Spl.	Oakland	11
12	30	91.584	42	MAS	8	Letterio Cucinotta, Italy	Maserati Spl.	Maserati	12
13	15	97.360	41	FF	4	Chet Miller	Fronty Ford Spl.	Ford T	13
14	38	87.003	46	BU	6	Harry Butcher	Butcher Bros. Spl.	Buick	14
15	6	105.618	17	M	4	Ernie Triplett	Guiberson Spl.	Whippet	15
16	34	95.357	21	M	8	Zeke Meyer	Miller Spl.	Miller	16
17	23	103.327	10	M	4	Mel Keneally	MAVV Spl.	Whippet	17
18	13	98.953	35	S	8	J. C. McDonald	Romthe Spl.	Studebaker	18
19	20	100.033	9	M	4	Tony Gulotta	MAVV Spl.	Whippet	19
20	37	89.639	28	CR	6	Roland Free	Slade Spl.	Chrysler	20
21	11	100.615	33	M	8	Frank Farmer	Betholine Spl.	Miller	21
22	25	106.132	3	M	8	Wilbur Shaw	Empire State Spl.	Smith	22
23	26	101.178	34	M	8	Joe Huff	Guass Spl.	Cooper	23
24	14	97.606	29	DU	8	Joe Caccia	Alberti Spl.	Duesenberg	24
25	35	90.650	44	DU	8	Bill Denver	Nardi Spl.	Duesenberg	25
26	10	100.846	36	DU	8	Cy Marshall	Duesenberg Spl.	Duesenberg	26
27	19	89.733	32	DP	8	Charles Moran, Jr.	Du Pont Spl.	Du Pont	27
28	24	93.709	7	M	8	Jimmy Gleason	Waverly Oil Spl.	Miller	28
29	12	99.867	14	M	4	Lou Moore	Coleman Front Drive Spl.	Coleman	29
30	31	105.755	12	DU	8	Deacon Litz	Duesenberg Spl.	Duesenberg	30
31	32	104.950	8	DU	8	Babe Stapp	Duesenberg Spl.	Duesenberg	31
32	18	93.376	39	M	8	Johnny Seymour	Guass Spl.	Cooper	32
33	21	99.956	5	DU	8	Pete DePaolo	Duesenberg Spl.	Stevens	33
34	29	92.978	45	LY	8	Marion Trexler	Trexler Spl.	Auburn	34
35	27	95.585	19	M	8	Speed Gardner	Miller Spl.	Miller	35
36	36	92.293	48	CL	4	Rick Decker	Hoosier Pete Spl.	Mercedes	36
37	28	95.213	26	MAS	16	Baconi Borzachini, Italy	Maserati Spl.	Maserati	37
38	5	105.811	18	DU	8	Chet Gardner	Buckeye Spl.	Duesenberg	38

Total entries: 46

Qualifying: Minimum of 80 MPH for 4 laps. Fastest 40.

FIN	ENTRANT	LAPS	SPEED, REASON OUT	RELIEF DRIVER	FIN
1	Harry Hartz	200	100.448	—	1
2	William S. White	200	98.054	Herman Schurch	2
3	Louis F. Schneider	200	96.752	—	3
4	Alden Sampson II	200	95.253	—	4
5	Peter DePaolo	200	93.579	Fred Winnai	5
6	David E. Evans	200	92.571	—	6
7	Coleman Motor Corp.	200	90.921	—	7
8	Russell Snowberger	200	89.166	—	8
9	Leslie Allen	200	85.749	Stubby Stubblefield, Fred Lecklider	9
10	Milton Jones	200	85.340	—	10
11	Ira Vail	196	Flagged	—	11
12	Letterio Piccolo Cucinotta	185	Flagged	—	12
13	Thomas J. Mulligan	161	Flagged	Paul Bost	13
14	Harry M. Butcher	127	Flagged	—	14
15	Allen Guiberson	125	Piston	—	15
16	Zeke Meyer	115	Con. rod	—	16
17	James Talbot, Jr.	114	Valve	—	17
18	William H. Richards	112	Leaking gas tank	Johnny Kreiger	18
19	James Talbot, Jr.	79	Valve	—	19
20	Julius Claude Slade	69	Clutch	—	20
21	M. A. Yagle	69	Wreck	—	21
22	Empire State Motors	54	Wrist pin	—	22
23	Herman N. Guass	48	Valve	Ted Chamberlain, Speed Gardner	23
24	William Alberti	43	Wreck	Rick Decker	24
25	Gabriel Nardi	41	Con. rod	—	25
26	George A. Henry	29	Wreck	—	26
27	Du Pont Motors, Inc.	22	Wreck	—	27
28	Thomas J. Mulligan	22	Wreck	—	28
29	Coleman Motors Corp.	23	Wreck	—	29
30	Henry W. Maley	22	Wreck	—	30
31	A. S. Duesenberg	18	Wreck	—	31
32	Herman N. Guass	21	Wreck	—	32
33	Peter DePaolo	19	Wreck	Red Roberts	33
34	M. M. Lain, Jr.	19	Wreck	—	34
35	W. H. Gardner	14	Loose main bearing	—	35
36	Clemons Motors, Inc.	8	Oil tank	—	36
37	Alfieri Maserati	7	Magneto, plugs	Jimmy Rossi	37
38	James H. Booth	1	Spun out	—	38

BU = Buick	DP = Du Pont	LY = Lycoming	OK = Oakland
CL = Clemons	DU = Duesenberg	MAS = Maserati	S = Studebaker
CR = Chrysler	FF = Fronty Ford	M = Miller	SZ = Stutz

1931

FIN	START	QUAL. SPEED	NUMBER, TYPE, CYLINDERS			DRIVER	CAR NAME	CHASSIS	FIN
1	13	107.210	23	M	8	Louis Schneider	Bowes Seal Fast Spl.	Stevens	1
2	8	109.273	34	DU	8	Fred Frame	Hartz Duesenberg Spl.	Duesenberg	2
3	10	107.933	19	M	8	Ralph Hepburn	Miller Spl.	Miller	3
4	35	107.463	21	M	8	Myron Stevens	Jadson Spl.	Stevens	4
5	1	112.796	4	STU	8	Russ Snowberger	Russell 8 Spl.	Snowberger	5
6	20	111.400	33	DU	8	Jimmy Gleason	Duesenberg Spl.	Duesenberg	6
7	5	111.034	25	DU	8	Ernie Triplett	Buckeye Spl.	Duesenberg	7
8	9	108.797	36	M	4	Stubby Stubblefield	Milt Jones Spl.	Whippet	8
9	14	106.781	28	REO	8	Cliff Bergere	Elco Royale Spl.	Reo	9
10	15	106.185	27	HUD	8	Chet Miller	Marr Spl.	Hudson	10
11	30	102.844	44	CHR	8	George Howie	G.N.H. Spl.	Chrysler	11
12	23	105.103	12	BU	8	Phil Shafer	Shafer Buick 8 Spl.	Rigling	12
13	17	96.871	8	CU	4	Dave Evans	Cummins Diesel Spl.	Duesenberg	13
14	31	102.509	72	DU	8	Al Aspen	Alberti Spl.	Duesenberg	14
15	37	104.642	59	M	4	Sam Ross	Yahr Bros. Spl.	Smith	15
16	40	102.386	69	M	8	Joe Huff	Goldberg Bros. Spl.	Cooper	16
17	4	111.531	5	DU	8	Deacon Litz	Maley Spl.	Duesenberg	17
18	19	111.725	37	STU	8	Tony Gulotta	Hunt Spl.	Rigling	18
19	18	116.080	1	M	8	Billy Arnold	Miller-Hartz Spl.	Summers	19
20	12	107.652	57	STU	8	Luther Johnson	Bill Richards Spl.	Studebaker	20
21	36	105.405	55	CL	8	Billy Winn	Hoosier Pete Spl.	Rigling	21
22	27	106.286	16	M	8	Frank Brisko	Brisko-Atkinson Spl.	Stevens	22
23	34	108.395	26	FF	4	Gene Haustein	Fronty Ford Spl.	Ford T	23
24	16	104.822	41	DU	8	Joe Russo	Russo Spl.	Rigling	24
25	7	109.820	17	M	8	Speed Gardner	Nutmeg State Spl.	Miller	25
26	38	103.725	14	M	8	Lou Moore	Boyle Valve Spl.	Miller	26
27	26	110.372	2	M	16	Shorty Cantlon	Harry Miller Spl.	Miller	27
28	2	112.563	3	M	8	Bill Cummings	Empire State Spl.	Cooper	28
29	28	105.899	24	M	8	Fred Winnai	Bowes Seal Fast Spl.	Stevens	29
30	11	107.772	32	DU	8	Phil Pardee	Duesenberg Spl.	Duesenberg	30
31	3	112.125	31	M	8	Paul Bost	Empire State Spl.	Smith	31
32	22	108.303	35	M	4	Frank Farmer	Milt Jones Spl.	Whippet	32
33	32	100.139	58	DU	8	George Wingerter	Wingerter Spl.	Duesenberg	33
34	25	113.953	7	M	16	Louis Meyer	Sampson Spl.	Stevens	34
35	6	110.125	39	DU	8	Babe Stapp	Rigling-Henning Spl.	Rigling	35
36	24	102.860	48	M & B	8	John Boling	Grapho Metal Spl.	M & B	36
37	29	103.134	54	DUR	16	Leon Duray	Leon Duray Spl.	Stevens	37
38	33	99.343	49	BU	8	Harry Butcher	Butcher Bros. Spl.	Buick	38
39	39	102.845	10	CL	8	Herman Schurch	Hoosier Pete Spl.	Rigling	39
40	21	111.321	67	F	4	Francis Quinn	Tucker Tappet Spl.	Miller	40

Qualified, did not start: Peter Kreis, Coleman Spl., #22, M, 102.860, Qualified—withdrew
Ted Chamberlain, Miller SL Spl., #68, M, 99.182, Bumped
Rick Decker, Miller Spl., #46, M, 98.061
Lora Corum, Stutz Bearcat Spl. #29, SZ, 97.389
Bill Denver, Brady & Nardi Spl., #42, DU, 96.085, Bumped
C. C. Reeder, Copper Spl., #45, LY, 95.643
Joe Thomas, Finneran Spl., #53, M, 91.403
Benny Brandfon, Duesenberg Spl., #66, DU, 88.561, Below minimum of 90 MPH
Carl Smith, C. C. Smith Spl., #73, MR, 79.782, Below minimum of 90 MPH

Total entries: 70   Qualifying: Minimum of 90 MPH for 4 laps. Fastest 40.

FIN	ENTRANT	LAPS	SPEED, REASON OUT	RELIEF DRIVER	FIN
1	B. L. Schneider	200	96.629	—	1
2	Harry Hartz	200	96.406	—	2
3	Ralph Hepburn	200	94.224	Peter Kreis	3
4	Louis Meyer	200	94.142	Louis Meyer	4
5	Russ Snowberger	200	94.090	—	5
6	Denny Duesenberg	200	93.605	Wilbur Shaw	6
7	James H. Booth	200	93.041	—	7
8	Milton Jones	200	92.424	—	8
9	Elco Grease & Oil	200	91.839	—	9
10	R. G. "Buddy" Marr	200	89.580	Bryan Saulpaugh	10
11	George N. Howie	200	87.651	Lora Corum, Herman Schurch	11
12	Phil Shafer	200	86.391	—	12
13	Cummins Engine Co.	200	86.107	—	13
14	William Alberti	200	85.764	Bill Denver	14
15	William M. Yahr	200	85.139	—	15
16	S. C. Goldberg	180	Flagged	Speed Gardner	16
17	Henry Maley	177	Wrecked	Bill Cummings	17
18	D. A. "Ab" Jenkins	167	Wrecked	—	18
19	Harry Hartz	162	Wrecked	—	19
20	William H. Richards	156	Wrecked	—	20
21	F. E. Clemons	138	Flagged	Jimmy Patterson	21
22	Frank Brisko	138	Steering arm	—	22
23	Fronty-Ford Sales	117	Lost wheel	—	23
24	George A. Henry	109	Oil leak	—	24
25	C. E. Ricketts	107	Frame	Wesley Crawford	25
26	M. J. Boyle	103	Differential	—	26
27	William S. White	88	Con. rod	—	27
28	Empire State Gas Motors	70	Oil line	—	28
29	B. L. Schneider	60	Wrecked	—	29
30	Phil Pardee	60	Wrecked	Wilbur Shaw	30
31	Empire State Gas Motors	35	Crankshaft	—	31
32	Milton Jones	32	Rod bearing	—	32
33	George Wingerter	29	Fuel tank	—	33
34	Alden Sampson II	28	Oil leak	—	34
35	Rigling & Henning	9	Oil leak, clutch	—	35
36	Grapho Metal Packing	7	Con. rod	—	36
37	Leon Duray	6	Overheating	—	37
38	Harry H. Butcher	6	Wrecked	—	38
39	F. E. Clemons	5	Transmission	—	39
40	James H. Wade	3	Rear Axle	—	40

BU = Buick
CHR = Chrysler
CL = Clemons
CU = Cummins

DU = Duesenberg
DUR = Duray
F = Ford

FF = Fronty Ford
HUD = Hudson
LY = Lycoming

M = Miller
MR = Mercer
M&B = Morton & Brett

REO = Reo
STU = Studebaker
SZ = Stutz

1932

FIN	START	QUAL. SPEED	NUMBER, TYPE, CYLINDERS			DRIVER	CAR NAME	CHASSIS	FIN
1	27	113.856	34	M	8	Fred Frame	Miller-Hartz Spl.	Wetteroth	1
2	6	113.468	6	M	4	Howdy Wilcox II	Lion Head Spl.	Stevens	2
3	10	111.503	22	STU	8	Cliff Bergere	Studebaker Spl.	Rigling	3
4	14	111.070	61	M	8	Bob Carey	Meyer Spl.	Stevens	4
5	4	114.326	4	HUP	8	Russ Snowberger	Hupp Comet Spl.	Snowberger	5
6	38	110.745	37	STU	8	Zeke Meyer	Studebaker Spl.	Rigling	6
7	5	114.206	35	DU	8	Ira Hall	Duesenberg Spl.	Stevens	7
8	35	108.755	65	DU	8	Fred Winnai	Forman Axle Shaft Spl.	Duesenberg	8
9	9	111.801	2	DU	8	Billy Winn	Duesenberg Spl.	Duesenberg	9
10	15	110.402	55	COO	16	Joe Huff	Highway Truck Parts Spl.	Cooper	10
11	26	110.708	33	BU	8	Phil Shafer	Shafer Buick Spl.	Rigling	11
12	40	104.465	36	M	4	Kelly Petillo	Milt Jones Spl.	Whippet	12
13	20	108.896	25	STU	8	Tony Gulotta	Studebaker Spl.	Rigling	13
14	25	112.899	15	M	4	Stubby Stubblefield	Gilmore Spl.	Adams	14
15	17	110.270	18	STU	8	Peter Kreis	Studebaker Spl.	Rigling	15
16	11	111.218	46	STU	8	Luther Johnson	Studebaker Spl.	Rigling	16
17	22	114.326	3	M	8	Wilbur Shaw	Veedol Spl.	Miller	17
18	19	109.546	24	DU	8	Deacon Litz	Bowes Seal Fast Spl.	Duesenberg	18
19	12	111.204	10	M	8	Bill Cummings	Bowes Seal Fast Spl.	Stevens	19
20	32	111.149	57	STU	8	Malcolm Fox	Bill Richards Spl.	Studebaker	20
21	29	111.053	9	HUD	8	Chet Miller	Hudson Spl.	Hudson	21
22	31	114.935	7	M	4	Ernie Triplett	Floating Power Spl.	Miller	22
23	30	110.681	1	M	8	Louis Schneider	Bowes Seal Fast Spl.	Stevens	23
24	21	108.791	41	DU	8	Joe Russo	Art Rose Spl.	Rigling	24
25	1	117.363	8	M	8	Lou Moore	Boyle Valve Spl.	Miller	25
26	36	107.466	14	CHR	8	Juan Guadino, Argentina	Golden Seal Spl.	Chrysler	26
27	18	110.129	29	HUD	8	Al Miller	Hudson Spl	Hudson	27
28	39	108.154	42	STU	8	Doc Mackenzie	Brady Spl.	Studebaker	28
29	13	111.149	32	M	8	Frank Brisko	Brisko-Atkinson Spl.	Stevens	29
30	34	108.969	72	GR	8	Ray Campbell	Folly Farm Spl.	Graham	30
31	2	116.290	5	M	8	Billy Arnold	Miller-Hartz Spl.	Summers	31
32	3	114.369	27	M	16	Bryan Saulpaugh	Harry Miller Spl.	Miller	32
33	7	112.471	16	M	16	Louis Meyer	Sampson Spl.	Stevens	33
34	23	108.008	21	DU	8	Al Aspen	Brady & Nardi Spl.	Duesenberg	34
35	33	109.276	49	DU	8	Johnny Kreiger	Consumers Petroleum Oil Spl.	Duesenberg	35
36	16	110.396	48	M	8	Wesley Crawford	Boyle Valve Spl.	Miller	36
37	8	111.885	17	M	8	Paul Bost	Empire State Spl.	Cooper	37
38	24	113.276	58	M	8	Bob McDonough	F.W.D. Spl.	Miller	38
39	28	112.003	45	M	8	Gus Schrader	Harry Miller Spl.	Miller	39
40	37	111.290	26	M	4	Al Gordon	Lion Tamer Spl.	Miller	40

Qualified, did not start: George Howie, Howie Spl., #47, CHR, 103.490, MPH Bumped
Jimmy Patterson, Duesenberg Spl., #75, DU, 101.246 , MPH Too slow

Total entries: 72

Qualifying: Minimum of 100 MPH for 4 laps. Fastest 40.

FIN	ENTRANT	LAPS	SPEED, REASON OUT	RELIEF DRIVER	FIN
1	Harry Hartz	200	104.144	—	1
2	William Cantlon	200	103.881	—	2
3	Studebaker Corp.	200	102.662	—	3
4	Louis Meyer	200	101.363	—	4
5	Russell Snowberger	200	100.791	—	5
6	Studebaker Corp.	200	98.476	—	6
7	G. B. Hall	200	98.207	Ned Meyers	7
8	Henry Maley	200	97.437	—	8
9	Fred Frame	200	97.421	Jimmy Patterson	9
10	S. C. Goldberg	200	87.586	Dusty Fahrnow	10
11	Phil Shafer	197	Flagged	—	11
12	Milton Jones	189	Flagged	—	12
13	Studebaker Corp.	184	Flagged	—	13
14	Sparks & Weirick	178	Flagged	—	14
15	Studebaker Corp.	178	Wrecked	—	15
16	Studebaker Corp.	164	Lost wheel	—	16
17	Ralph Hepburn	157	Rear axle	—	17
18	John Rutner	152	Con. rod	—	18
19	B. L. Schneider	151	Crankshaft	Frank Brisko	19
20	William H. Richards	132	Spring	—	20
21	R. G. "Buddy" Marr	125	Engine trouble	Al Miller	21
22	William S. White	125	Clutch	—	22
23	B. L. Schneider	125	Frame	Bill Cummings	23
24	George A. Henry	107	Con. rod	—	24
25	M. J. Boyle	79	Timing gear	—	25
26	Juan Guadino	71	Clutch	Joe Bonadeo	26
27	R. G. "Buddy" Marr	66	Engine trouble	—	27
28	Ray T. Brady	65	Engine trouble	—	28
29	F. Brisko & D. Atkinson	61	Clutch	—	29
30	E. D. Stairs, Jr.	60	Crankshaft	—	30
31	Harry Hartz	59	Wrecked	—	31
32	William S. White	55	Oil line	—	32
33	Alden Sampson II	50	Crankshaft	—	33
34	G. Nardi & Ray Brady	31	Con. rod	—	34
35	Fred Duesenberg	30	Con. rod	—	35
36	M. J. Boyle	28	Crankshaft	—	36
37	Paul B. Bost	18	Crankshaft	—	37
38	Four Wheel Drive Auto Co.	17	Oil line	—	38
39	William Burden	7	Wrecked	—	39
40	G. D. Harrison	3	Wrecked	—	40

BU = Buick   DU = Duesenberg   HUP = Hupmobile
COO = Cooper   GR = Graham   M = Miller
CHR = Chrysler   HUD = Hudson   STU = Studebaker

1933

FIN	START	QUAL. SPEED	NUMBER, TYPE, CYLINDERS			DRIVER	CAR NAME	CHASSIS	FIN
1	6	116.977	36	M	8	Louis Meyer	Tydol Spl.	Miller	1
2	23	115.497	17	M	4	Wilbur Shaw	Mallory Spl.	Stevens	2
3	4	117.843	37	M	4	Lou Moore	Forman Axle Shaft Spl.	Duesenberg	3
4	15	112.319	21	M	16	Chet Gardner	Sampson Radio Spl.	Stevens	4
5	10	114.784	8	BU	8	Stubby Stubblefield	Abels & Fink Auto Spl.	Rigling	5
6	36	109.448	38	STU	8	Dave Evans	Art Rose Spl.	Cooper	6
7	12	113.578	34	STU	8	Tony Gulotta	Studebaker Spl.	Rigling	7
8	17	110.769	4	STU	8	Russ Snowberger	Russell 8 Spl.	Snowberger	8
9	16	111.099	9	STU	8	Zeke Meyer	Studebaker Spl.	Rigling	9
10	20	110.097	46	STU	8	Luther Johnson	Studebaker Spl.	Rigling	10
11	9	115.643	6	STU	8	Cliff Bergere	Studebaker Spl.	Rigling	11
12	18	110.465	47	STU	8	Lora Corum	Studebaker Spl.	Rigling	12
13	40	107.776	49	DU	8	Willard Prentiss	Jack C. Carr Spl.	Rigling	13
14	27	108.081	14	CHR	8	Raoul Riganti, Argentina	Golden Seal Spl.	Chrysler	14
15	28	107.603	29	HUD	8	Gene Haustein	Martz Spl.	Hudson	15
16	14	113.138	26	M	4	Deacon Litz	Bowes Seal Fast Spl.	Miller	16
17	31	112.531	18	DU	8	Joe Russo	Wonderbread Spl.	Duesenberg	17
18	39	108.073	51	STU	8	Doc MacKenzie	Brady Spl.	Duesenberg	18
19	25	113.037	27	M	4	Kelly Petillo	Sacks Bros. Spl.	Smith	19
20	32	112.025	28	HUD	8	Chet Miller	Marr Spl.	Hudson	20
21	24	109.799	19	HUD	8	Al Miller	Marr Spl.	Hudson	21
22	19	110.264	68	COO	16	Benny Hill	Goldberg Bros. Spl.	Cooper	22
23	29	116.626	45	M	4	Babe Stapp	Boyle Products Spl.	Miller	23
24	26	109.862	32	M	8	Wesley Crawford	Boyle Valve Spl.	Stevens	24
25	1	118.521	5	M	8	Bill Cummings	Boyle Products Spl.	Miller	25
26	7	116.903	15	M	4	Les Spangler	Miller Spl.	Miller	26
27	35	110.018	65	DU	8	Fred Winnai	Kemp Spl.	Duesenberg	27
28	30	112.922	57	STU	8	Malcolm Fox	Universal Service Garage Spl.	Studebaker	28
29	3	117.864	12	M	8	Fred Frame	Miller-Hartz Spl.	Wetteroth	29
30	22	112.410	64	DU	8	Mark Billman	Kemp-Mannix Spl.	Duesenberg	30
31	34	110.590	53	M	4	Johnny Sawyer	Lencki-Madis Spl.	Miller	31
32	11	114.370	2	M	8	Peter Kreis	Frame-Miller Spl.	Summers	32
33	5	117.685	16	M	4	Ernie Triplett	Floating Power Spl.	Weil	33
34	13	113.384	25	M	4	Shorty Cantlon	Sullivan & O'Brien Spl.	Stevens	34
35	42	117.649*	3	M	8	Mauri Rose*	Gilmore Spl.	Stevens	35
36	2	118.388	58	M	8	Frank Brisko	F.W.D. Spl.	Miller	36
37	8	115.739	10	DU	8	Ira Hall	Denny Duesenberg Spl.	Stevens	37
38	41	110.001	23	COO	16	Ralph Hepburn	Highway Truck Parts Spl.	Cooper	38
39	37	108.650	59	HUD	8	Ray Campbell	G. & D. Spl.	Hudson	39
40	33	111.330	24	M	4	Paul Bost	Frame-Miller Spl.	Duesenberg	40
41	38	108.280	61	M	8	Rick Decker	Miller Spl.	Miller	41
42	21	109.850	22	M	8	Louis Schneider	Edelweiss Spl.	Stevens	42

Qualified, did not start: Phil Shafer, Abels & Fink Auto Spl., #7, BU, 107.972 MPH
Sam Palmer, R & W Cam Co. Spl., #41, DU, 105.998 MPH, Bumped
Doc Williams, C. O. Warnock Spl., #66, FV8, 104.538 MPH, Bumped

Total entries: 63

Qualifying: Minimum of 100 MPH for 10 laps. Fastest 42.   *Car qualified by Howdy Wilcox II who was declared physically unfit to drive.

FIN	ENTRANT	LAPS	SPEED, REASON OUT	RELIEF DRIVER	FIN
1	Lou Meyer	200	104.162	—	1
2	Leon Duray	200	101.795	—	2
3	Maley & Scully	200	101.599	—	3
4	Alden Sampson II	200	101.182	—	4
5	Phil Shafer	200	100.762	—	5
6	Arthur E. Rose	200	100.425	—	6
7	Studebaker Corp.	200	99.071	—	7
8	Russell Snowberger	200	99.011	George Howie, Mauri Rose	8
9	Studebaker Corp.	200	98.122	—	9
10	Studebaker Corp.	200	97.393	Ralph Hepburn, Sam Palmer	10
11	Studebaker Corp.	200	97.286	Sam Palmer	11
12	Studebaker Corp.	200	96.458	—	12
13	J. W. Kleinschmidt	200	93.595	Harold Shaw	13
14	Raoul Riganti	200	93.244	Juan Gaudino	14
15	Lawrence J. Martz	197	Flagged	—	15
16	A. B. Litz	197	Flagged	Louis Schneider	16
17	F. P. Duesenberg	192	Flagged	—	17
18	Ray T. Brady	192	Rear axle	—	18
19	William M. Yahr	168	Spun, stalled	Sam Hoffman	19
20	R. G. "Buddy" Marr	163	Con. rod	Shorty Cantlon	20
21	R. G. "Buddy" Marr	161	Con. rod	—	21
22	S. C. Goldberg	158	Con. rod	Frank Brisko	22
23	M. J. Boyle	156	Out of gas	—	23
24	Frank Brisko	147	Wrecked	Billy Winn	24
25	M. J. Boyle	136	Leaking radiator	Frank Brisko	25
26	Harry Hartz	132	Wrecked	—	26
27	James Kemp	125	Engine trouble	Terry Curley	27
28	William Richards	121	Wrecked	—	28
29	Harry Hartz	85	Valve	—	29
30	James Kemp	79	Wrecked	—	30
31	Lencki & Unger	77	Clutch	—	31
32	Fred Frame	63	Universal	—	32
33	William S. White	61	Piston	—	33
34	William Cantlon	50	Con. rod	—	34
35	Joe Marks	48	Timing gears	—	35
36	F.W.D. Auto Co.	47	Oil too hot	—	36
37	Denny Duesenberg	37	Piston	—	37
38	S. C. Goldberg	33	Con. rod bearing	—	38
39	Tulio Gulotta	24	Oil lead	—	39
40	Fred Frame	13	Oil line	—	40
41	Bessie Decker	13	Manifold	—	41
42	W. R. Blackburn	1	Stalled	—	42

BU = Buick
CHR = Chrysler
COO = Cooper
DU = Duesenberg
FV8 = Ford V8
HUD = Hudson
M = Miller
STU = Studebaker

1934

FIN	START	QUAL. SPEED	NUMBER, TYPE, CYLINDERS			DRIVER	CAR NAME	CHASSIS	FIN
1	10	116.116	7	M	4	Bill Cummings	Boyle Products Spl.	Miller	1
2	4	116.044	9	M	4	Mauri Rose	Leon Duray Spl.	Stevens	2
3	20	113.442	2	M	4	Lou Moore	Foreman Axle Shaft Spl.	Miller	3
4	19	113.731	12	M	4	Deacon Litz	Stokely Food Products Spl.	Miller	4
5	24	113.115	16	DU	8	Joe Russo	Duesenberg Spl.	Duesenberg	5
6	8	113.307	36	BU	8	Al Miller	Shafer Buick 8 Spl.	Rigling	6
7	18	115.243	22	M	4	Cliff Bergere	Floating Power Spl.	Weil	7
8	9	111.428	10	STU	8	Russ Snowberger	Russell 8 Spl.	Snowberger	8
9	3	116.894	32	M	4	Frank Brisko	F.W.D. Spl.	Miller	9
10	14	111.722	24	GR	8	Herb Ardinger	Lucenti Spl.	Graham	10
11	1	119.329	17	M	4	Kelly Petillo	Red Lion Spl.	Adams	11
12	29	105.921	5	CU	4	Stubby Stubblefield	Cummins Diesel Spl.	Duesenberg	12
13	11	114.321	31	M	8	Ralph Hepburn	Art Rose Spl.	Miller	13
14	12	113.859	18	M	8	George Barringer	Boyle Products Spl.	Miller	14
15	6	113.816	26	BU	8	Phil Shafer	Shafer Buick 8 Spl.	Rigling	15
16	28	108.784	49	FV8	8	Charlie Crawford	Detroit Gasket Spl.	Ford	16
17	7	113.733	8	STU	8	Tony Gulotta	Schroeder Spl.	Cooper	17
18	13	112.332	1	M	4	Louis Meyer	Ring Free Spl.	Stevens	18
19	22	102.414	6	CU	4	Dave Evans	Cummins Diesel Spl.	Duesenberg	19
20	15	117.875	15	M	4	Shorty Cantlon	Sullivan & O'Brien Spl.	Stevens	20
21	5	114.786	4	M	16	Chet Gardner	Sampson Radio Spl.	Stevens	21
22	17	116.273	51	M	4	Al Gordon	Abels-Fink Auto Spl.	Adams	22
23	23	113.639	35	M	4	Rex Mays	Frame Miller Duesenberg Spl.	Duesenberg	23
24	25	113.070	42	COO	16	Dusty Fahrnow	Superior Trailer Spl.	Cooper	24
25	21	109.808	41	LN	4	Johnny Sawyer	Burd Piston Ring Spl.	Miller	25
26	33	108.591	33	M	4	Johnny Seymour	Miller-Streamline Spl.	Adams	26
27	27	110.895	45	M	8	Rick Decker	Carter Carburetor Spl.	Miller	27
28	2	117.647	3	M	8	Wilbur Shaw	Lion Head Spl.	Stevens	28
29	26	111.933	73	STU	8	Doc McKenzie	Cresco Spl.	Mikan-Carson	29
30	31	109.426	29	HUD	8	Gene Haustein	Martz Spl.	Hudson	30
31	30	111.067	63	M	4	Harry McQuinn	DeBaets Spl.	Rigling	31
32	16	111.063	58	STU	8	George Bailey	Scott Spl.	Snowberger	32
33	32	109.252	46	FV8	8	Chet Miller	Bohnalite Spl.	Ford	33

Qualified, did not start: Willard Prentiss, G & D Spl., #59, HUD, 107.797 MPH, Too slow
Harry Lewis, Don Hulbert Spl., #52, FV8, 101.524 MPH, Too slow
Babe Stapp, Leon Duray Spl., #54, DUR, 109.648 MPH, Disqualified, too much gas
Charles Tramison, Economy Gas Spl., #72, GR, 104.434 MPH, Disqualified, too much gas and too slow

Total entries: 54

Qualifying: Minimum of 100 MPH for 10 laps. Fastest 33.

FIN	ENTRANT	LAPS	SPEED, REASON OUT	RELIEF DRIVER	FIN
1	H. C. Henning	200	104.863	—	1
2	Leon Duray	200	104.697	—	2
3	California Racers	200	103.625	Wilbur Shaw	3
4	A. B. Litz	200	100.749	Babe Stapp	4
5	Joe E. Russo	200	99.893	—	5
6	Phil Shafer	200	98.264	Zeke Meyer	6
7	William S. White	200	97.818	Tony Gulotta, Billy Winn	7
8	Russell Snowberger	200	97.297	—	8
9	F.W.D. Auto Co.	200	96.787	Rex Mays	9
10	Angelo Lucenti	200	95.936	Dany Day	10
11	Joe Marks	200	93.432	—	11
12	Cummins Engine Co.	200	88.566	Dave Evans	12
13	Ralph Hepburn	164	Con. rod	Louis Meyer	13
14	H. C. Henning	161	Bent front axle	Chet Gardner	14
15	Phil Shafer	130	Camshaft drive	Zeke Meyer	15
16	Detroit Gasket & Mfg.	110	Head gasket	—	16
17	Floyd Smith	94	Con. rod	—	17
18	Lou Meyer	92	Oil tank	—	18
19	Cummins Engine Co.	81	Transmission	—	19
20	William J. Cantlon	76	Crankshaft	Billy Winn	20
21	Alden Sampson II	72	Con. rod	—	21
22	Paul Weirick	66	Wrecked	—	22
23	Fred Frame	53	Front axle	—	23
24	Irving Goldberg	28	Con. rod	—	24
25	Lencki & Unger	27	Con. rod	—	25
26	Fred Frame	22	Pinion gear	—	26
27	Rickliffe Decker	17	Clutch	—	27
28	Joe Marks	15	Lost oil	—	28
29	Mikan & Carson	15	Wrecked	—	29
30	Lawrence J. Martz	13	Wrecked	—	30
31	Michael DeBaets	13	Con. rod	—	31
32	Roy Scott	12	Wrecked	—	32
33	Bohn Aluminum & Brass	11	Over SW wall	—	33

BU = Buick
COO = Cooper
CU = Cummins
DU = Duesenberg
DUR = Duray
FV8 = Ford V8
GR = Graham
HÜD = Hudson
LN = Lencki
M = Miller
STU = Studebaker

1935

FIN	START	QUAL. SPEED	NUMBER, TYPE, CYLINDERS			DRIVER	CAR NAME	CHASSIS	FIN
1	22	115.095	5	O	4	Kelly Petillo	Gilmore Speedway Spl.	Wetteroth	1
2	20	116.854	14	O	4	Wilbur Shaw	Pirrung Spl.	Shaw	2
3	5	116.901	1	M	4	Bill Cummings	Boyle Products Spl.	Miller	3
4	3	118.671	22	M	4	Floyd Roberts	Abels & Fink Auto Spl.	Miller	4
5	7	115.156	21	M	8	Ralph Hepburn	Veedol Spl.	Miller	5
6	19	118.205	9	M	4	Shorty Cantlon	Sullivan & O'Brien Spl.	Stevens	6
7	9	114.556	18	M	4	Chet Gardner	Sampson Radio Spl.	Stevens	7
8	13	114.488	16	M	4	Deacon Litz	Sha-Litz Spl.	Miller	8
9	15	114.294	8	M	4	Doc McKenzie	Pirrung Spl.	Rigling	9
10	17	113.552	34	M	8	Chet Miller	Milac Spl.	Summers	10
11	8	114.701	19	M	8	Fred Frame	Miller-Hartz Spl.	Wetteroth	11
12	4	117.938	36	M	4	Louis Meyer	Ring Free Spl.	Stevens	12
13	16	114.162	15	BU	8	Cliff Bergere	Victor Gasket Spl.	Rigling	13
14	31	111.729	62	STU	8	Harris Insinger	Cresco Spl.	Mikan-Carson	14
15	21	115.303	4	M	4	Al Miller	Boyle Products Spl.	Smith	15
16	26	113.213	43	FV8	8	Ted Horn	Ford V8 Miller Spl.	Miller-Ford	16
17	1	120.736	33	M	4	Rex Mays	Gilmore Spl.	Adams	17
18	23	114.180	7	M	4	Lou Moore	Foreman Axle Shaft Spl.	Miller	18
19	14	114.321	37	M	8	George Connor	Marks Spl.	Stevens	19
20	10	116.470	2	M	4	Mauri Rose	F.W.D. Spl.	Miller	20
21	6	115.459	44	M	4	Tony Gulotta	Bowes Seal Fast Spl.	Stevens	21
22	30	112.249	39	STU	8	Jimmy Snyder	Blue Prelude Spl.	Snowberger	22
23	24	113.307	41	STU	8	Frank Brisko	Art Rose Spl.	Cooper	23
24	27	112.696	42	FV8	8	Johnny Seymour	Ford V8 Miller Spl.	Miller-Ford	24
25	12	116.736	17	M	4	Babe Stapp	Marks Spl.	Adams	25
26	29	113.432	35	FV8	8	George Bailey	Ford V8 Miller Spl.	Miller-Ford	26
27	11	114.209	3	M	8	Russ Snowberger	Boyle Products Spl.	Miller	27
28	32	110.794	26	LN	8	Louis Tomei	Burd Piston Ring Spl.	Miller	28
29	33	110.519	46	FV8	8	Bob Sall	Ford V8 Miller Spl.	Miller-Ford	29
30	2	119.481	6	M	4	Al Gordon	Cocktail Hour Cigarette Spl.	Weil	30
31	28	115.138	27	M	4	Fred Winnai	Gyro Duesenberg Spl.	Duesenberg	31
32	25	115.902	45	M	4	Clay Weatherly	Bowes Seal Fast Spl.	Stevens	32
33	18	111.111	66	M	4	Harry McQuinn	DeBaets Spl.	Rigling	33

Qualified, did not start: Dave Evans, Ford V8 Miller Spl., #32, FV8, 109.937 MPH, Too slow
Emil Andres, Cresco Spl., #56, M, 109.068 MPH, Too slow
Dusty Fahrnow, Superior Trailer Spl., #53, COO, 109.138 MPH, Too slow; too much fuel
Roy Painter, Frigenor Spl., #51, GR, 106.638 MPH, Too slow; mechanical
Overton Snell, Snell Bros. Spl., #58, FV8, 99.669 MPH, Below 100 MPH minimum

Total entries: 59

Qualifying: Minimum of 100 MPH for 10 laps. Fastest 33.

FIN	ENTRANT	LAPS	SPEED, REASON OUT	RELIEF DRIVER	FIN
1	Kelly Petillo	200	106.240	—	1
2	Gil Pirrung	200	105.990	—	2
3	H. C. Henning	200	104.758	—	3
4	Earl Haskell	200	103.228	—	4
5	Ralph Hepburn	200	103.177	Gene Haustein	5
6	William J. Cantlon	200	101.140	Billy Winn	6
7	Alden Sampson II	200	101.129	—	7
8	A. B. Litz	200	100.907	Johnny Sawyer, Babe Stapp	8
9	Gil Pirrung	200	100.598	—	9
10	Fred Frame	200	100.474	—	10
11	Harry Hartz	200	100.436	Frank Brisko	11
12	Lou Meyer	200	100.256	—	12
13	Phil Shafer	196	Out of gas	—	13
14	Mikan & Carson	185	Flagged	—	14
15	H. C. Henning	178	Magneto	—	15
16	Harry A. Miller	145	Steering	—	16
17	Paul Weirick	123	Spring shackle	—	17
18	Lou Moore	116	Con. rod	Tony Gulotta	18
19	Joe Marks	112	Transmission	—	19
20	Four Wheel Drive Auto Co.	103	Mechanical failure	Paul Bost	20
21	Leon Duray	102	Magneto	—	21
22	Joel Thorne	97	Spring	—	22
23	Kenneth Schroeder	79	Universal	—	23
24	Harry A. Miller	71	Grease leak	George Barringer	24
25	Joe Marks	70	Radiator	—	25
26	Harry A. Miller	65	Steering	—	26
27	H. C. Henning	59	Exhaust pipe	—	27
28	Joe Lencki	47	Valve	—	28
29	Harry A. Miller	47	Steering	—	29
30	William S. White	17	Wrecked	—	30
31	Harry Hartz	16	Con. rod	—	31
32	Leon Duray	9	Wrecked	—	32
33	Michael DeBaets	4	Con. rod	—	33

BU = Buick   LN = Lencki
COO = Cooper   M = Miller
FV8 = Ford V8   O = Offenhauser
GR = Graham   STU = Studebaker

1936

FIN	START	QUAL. SPEED	NUMBER, TYPE, CYLINDERS			DRIVER	CAR NAME	CHASSIS	FIN
1	28	114.171	8	M	4	Louis Meyer	Ring Free Spl.	Stevens	1
2	11	116.564	22	M	8	Ted Horn	Miller-Hartz Spl.	Wetteroth	2
3	4	116.961	10	O	4	Doc MacKenzie	Gilmore Speedway Spl.	Wetteroth	3
4	30	113.890	36	M	4	Mauri Rose	F.W.D. Spl.	Miller	4
5	3	117.675	18	M	4	Chet Miller	Boyle Products Spl.	Summers	5
6	25	116.703	41	M	4	Ray Pixley	Fink Auto Spl.	Miller	6
7	9	117.503	3	O	4	Wilbur Shaw	Gilmore Spl.	Shaw	7
8	14	112.700	17	O	4	George Barringer	Kennedy Tank Spl.	Rigling	8
9	32	111.476	53	STU	8	Zeke Meyer	Boyle Products Spl.	Cooper	9
10	5	116.269	38	M	4	George Connor	Marks Spl.	Adams	10
11	12	116.221	35	O	4	Freddie Winnai	Midwest Red Lion Spl.	Stevens	11
12	24	112.673	9	O	4	Ralph Hepburn	Art Rose Spl.	Miller	12
13	27	114.118	28	M	4	Harry McQuinn	Sampson Radio Spl.	Stevens	13
14	10	116.912	7	M	4	Shorty Cantlon	Hamilton-Harris Spl.	Weil	14
15	1	119.644	33	SP	4	Rex Mays	Gilmore Spl.	Adams	15
16	23	112.837	54	M	4	Doc Williams	Superior Trailer Spl.	Cooper	16
17	29	113.996	32	O	4	Lou Moore	Burd Piston Ring Spl.	Miller	17
18	33	111.455	19	CR	4	Emil Andres	Carew Spl.	Rigling	18
19	15	112.403	4	O	4	Floyd Roberts	Burd Piston Ring Spl.	Stevens	19
20	20	114.213	14	BR	4	Frank Brisko	Elgin Piston Pin Spl.	Miller	20
21	17	116.138	12	M	4	Al Miller	Boyle Products Spl.	Smith	21
22	7	113.377	42	M	4	Cliff Bergere	Bowes Seal Fast Spl.	Stevens	22
23	26	115.997	15	M	4	Deacon Litz	Deacon Litz Spl.	Miller	23
24	2	118.945	21	O	4	Babe Stapp	Pirrung Spl.	Shaw	24
25	19	114.648	5	M	4	Billy Winn	Harry A. Miller Spl.	Miller	25
26	22	113.102	52	CR	4	Frank McGurk	Abel's Auto Ford Spl.	Adams	26
27	8	111.078	27	M	4	Louis Tomei	Wheeler's Spl.	Wetteroth	27
28	6	115.082	44	M	4	Herb Ardinger	Bowes Seal Fast Spl.	Stevens	28
29	18	116.000	6	O	4	Chet Gardner	Gardner Spl.	Duesenberg	29
30	16	111.291	43	M	8	Jimmy Snyder	Belanger Spl.	Stevens	30
31	21	113.169	47	M	4	Johnny Seymour	Sullivan & O'Brien Spl.	Stevens	31
32	31	112.877	46	M	4	Fred Frame	Burd Piston Ring Spl.	Miller	32
33	13	115.939	2	O	4	Bill Cummings	Boyle Products Spl.	Miller	33

Qualified, did not start: Al Putnam, Kennedy Tank Spl., #26, BU, 110.485 MPH
Henry Banks, DePalma-Miller Spl., #29, M, 110.277 MPH
Roy Painter, American Twist Drill Spl., #34, STU, 109.867 MPH
Overton Snell, Snell Bros. Spl., #24, M, 109.561 MPH

Total entries: 50

Qualifying: Minimum 100 MPH for 10 laps. 33 fastest.

FIN	ENTRANT	LAPS	SPEED, REASON OUT	RELIEF DRIVER	FIN
1	Lou Meyer	200	109.069	—	1
2	Harry Hartz	200	108.170	—	2
3	Kelly Petillo	200	107.460	Kelly Petillo	3
4	Four Wheel Drive Auto	200	107.272	—	4
5	Boyle Motor Products	200	106.919	—	5
6	Clarence Felker	200	105.253	—	6
7	W. Wilbur Shaw	200	104.233	—	7
8	Phil Shafer	200	102.630	—	8
9	Boyle Motor Products	200	101.331	—	9
10	Joe Marks	200	98.931	—	10
11	Midwest Racing Team	199	Flagged	—	11
12	Ralph Hepburn	196	Flagged	—	12
13	Alden Sampson II	196	Out of gas	—	13
14	William S. White	194	Out of gas	—	14
15	Paul Weirick	192	Out of gas	—	15
16	Race Car Corp.	192	Out of gas	—	16
17	Lou Moore	185	Out of gas	Cliff Bergere	17
18	J. Stewart Carew	184	Flagged	Jimmy Snyder	18
19	Joe Lencki	183	Out of gas	—	19
20	Elgin Piston Pin	180	Out of gas	—	20
21	Boyle Motor Products	119	Wrecked	—	21
22	Bowes Seal Fast Corp.	116	Loose engine support	Tony Gulotta, Herb Ardinger	22
23	A. B. Litz	108	Crankshaft	Louis Tomei	23
24	Gil Pirrung	89	Crankshaft	—	24
25	James M. Winn	78	Crankshaft	—	25
26	Charles Worley	51	Crankshaft	—	26
27	Babe Stapp	44	Engine support arm	—	27
28	Bowes Seal Fast Corp.	38	Transmission	—	28
29	Chester L. Gardner	38	Clutch	—	29
30	Murrell Belanger	21	Oil leak	—	30
31	William L. Cantlon	13	Clutch	—	31
32	Moore & Fengler	4	Piston	—	32
33	Boyle Motor Products	0	Clutch	—	33

BR = Brisko   O = Offenhauser
BU = Buick   SP = Sparks
CR = Crager   STU = Studebaker
M = Miller

1937

FIN	START	QUAL. SPEED	NUMBER,	TYPE,	CYLINDERS	DRIVER	CAR NAME	CHASSIS	FIN
1	2	122.791	6	O	4	Wilbur Shaw	Shaw-Gilmore Spl.	Shaw	1
2	6	118.809	8	O	4	Ralph Hepburn	Hamilton & Harris Spl.	Stevens	2
3	32	118.608	3	M	8	Ted Horn	Miller-Hartz Spl.	Wetteroth	3
4	5	119.619	2	M	8	Louis Meyer	Boyle Products Spl.	Miller	4
5	16	117.546	45	O	4	Cliff Bergere	Midwest Red Lion Spl.	Stevens	5
6	1	123.455	16	O	4	Bill Cummings	Boyle Products Spl.	Miller	6
7	14	120.192	28	M	4	Billy DeVore	Miller Spl.	Stevens	7
8	7	118.788	38	O	4	Tony Gulotta	Burd Piston Ring Spl.	Rigling	8
9	12	120.240	17	M	4	George Connor	Marks Spl.	Adams	9
10	18	116.437	53	STU	8	Louis Tomei	Sobonite Plastics Spl.	Rigling	10
11	9	117.342	31	O	4	Chet Gardner	Burd Piston Ring Spl.	Duesenberg	11
12	10	116.464	23	M	4	Ronney Householder	Topping Spl.		12
13	17	116.996	62	M	4	Floyd Roberts	Thorne Engineering Spl.	Miller	13
14	11	116.372	35	M	4	Deacon Litz	Motorola Auto Radio Spl.	Miller	14
15	24	118.942	32	M	4	Floyd Davis	Thorne Engineering Spl.	Snowberger	15
16	25	118.555	34	M	4	Shorty Cantlon	Bowes Seal Fast Spl.	Weil	16
17	26	118.518	42	M	4	Al Miller	Thorne Engineering Spl.	Snowberger	17
18	8	118.540	1	O	4	Mauri Rose	Burd Piston Ring Spl.	Miller	18
19	29	117.421	41	McD	4	Ken Fowler	Lucky Teeter Spl.	Wetteroth	19
20	20	124.129	25	O	4	Kelly Petillo	Petillo Spl.	Wetteroth	20
21	28	117.497	43	M	4	George Bailey	Duray-Sims Spl.	Stevens	21
22	3	121.983	54	O	4	Herb Ardinger	Chicago Rawhide Oil Seal Spl.	Welch	22
23	15	118.213	24	BR	6	Frank Brisko	Elgin Piston Pin Spl.	Stevens	23
24	33	118.220	44	M	4	Frank Wearne	Duray Spl.	Stevens	24
25	27	118.242	26	M	4	Tony Willman	F.W.D. Spl.	Miller	25
26	4	119.922	10	M	4	Billy Winn	Harry A. Miller Spl.	Miller	26
27	30	117.354	12	PA	8	Russ Snowberger	R.S. Spl.	Snowberger	27
28	21	121.920	33	SP	4	Bob Swanson	Fink Auto Spl.	Adams	28
29	22	121.822	47	M	4	Harry McQuinn	Sullivan & O'Brien Spl.	Stevens	29
30	13	119.213	7	M	8	Chet Miller	Boyle Products Spl .	Summers	30
31	31	117.226	15	MAS	8	Babe Stapp	Topping Spl.	Maserati	31
32	19	125.287	5	SP	6	Jimmy Snyder	Sparks Spl.	Adams	32
33	23	119.968	14	AR	8	Rex Mays	Bowes Seal Fast Spl.	Alfa Romeo	33

Qualified, did not start: Emil Andres, Kennedy Tank Spl., #46, BU, 116.243
Joel Thorne, Thorne Engineering Spl., #22, O, 115.60, Bumped

Total entries: 54

Qualifying: Minimum of 105 MPH for 10 laps. Fastest 33.

FIN	ENTRANT	LAPS	SPEED, REASON OUT	RELIEF DRIVER	FIN
1	W. Wilbur Shaw	200	113.580	—	1
2	Louis Meyer	200	113.565	Bob Swanson	2
3	Harry Hartz	200	113.434	—	3
4	H. C. Henning	200	110.730	—	4
5	George H. Lyons	200	108.935	George Barringer	5
6	H. C. Henning	200	107.124	Chet Miller	6
7	H. E. Winn	200	106.995	Fred Frame	7
8	Joe Lencki	200	105.015	Rex Mays, Jimmy Snyder	8
9	Joe Marks	200	103.830	—	9
10	S. S. Engineering	200	101.825	—	10
11	Chester Gardner	199	Flagged	Billy Winn	11
12	Henry J. Topping, Jr.	194	Flagged	Al Putnam, Henry Banks, Ken Fowler	12
13	Joel Thorne, Inc.	194	Flagged	—	13
14	A. B. Litz	191	Out of oil	Harry McQuinn	14
15	Joel Thorne, Inc.	190	Wrecked	—	15
16	Bill White Race Cars	182	Flagged	Rex Mays	16
17	Joel Thorne, Inc.	170	Carburetor	Emil Andres, Mauri Rose	17
18	Lou Moore	127	Oil line	—	18
19	E. M. "Lucky" Teeter	116	Disqualified	—	19
20	Kelly Petillo	109	Out of oil	—	20
21	Sims & Duray	107	Clutch	—	21
22	Lewis W. Welch	106	Con. rod	Jimmy Snyder	22
23	Frank Brisko	105	No oil pressure	—	23
24	Leon Duray	99	Carburetor	—	24
25	Pete DePaolo	95	Con. rod	—	25
26	James M. Winn	85	Oil line	—	26
27	Russ Snowberger	66	Clutch	Johnny Seymour	27
28	Paul Weirick	52	Carburetor	—	28
29	Thomas O'Brien	47	Piston	—	29
30	H. C. Henning	36	Ignition	—	30
31	Henry J. Topping, Jr.	36	Clutch	Fred Frame	31
32	Joel Thorne, Inc.	27	Transmission	—	32
33	Bill White Race Cars	24	Overheating	—	33

AR = Alfa Romeo
BR = Brisko
BU = Buick
M = Miller

MAS = Maserati
McD = McDowell
O = Offenhauser

PA = Packard
SP = Sparks
STU = Studebaker

1938

FIN	START	QUAL. SPEED	NUMBER, TYPE, CYLINDERS			DRIVER	CAR NAME	CHASSIS	FIN
1	1	125.681	23	M	4	Floyd Roberts	Burd Piston Ring Spl.	Wetteroth	1
2	7	120.987	1	O	4	Wilbur Shaw	Shaw Spl.	Shaw	2
3	5	121.898	3	O	4	Chet Miller	I.B.E.W. Spl.	Summers	3
4	6	121.327	2	M	8	Ted Horn	Miller-Hartz Spl.	Wetteroth	4
5	18	120.435	38	O	4	Chet Gardner	Burd Piston Ring Spl.	Rigling	5
6	14	119.022	54	O	4	Herb Ardinger	Offenhauser Spl.	Miller-Ford	6
7	25	119.492	45	M	8	Harry McQuinn	Marchese Spl.	Marchese	7
8	30	116.339	58	O	4	Billy DeVore	P.R. & W. Spl.	Stevens	8
9	13	119.155	22	O	4	Joel Thorne	Thorne Engineering Spl.	Shaw	9
10	17	121.405	29	O	4	Frank Wearne	Indiana Fur Co. Spl.	Adams	10
11	33	113.828	43	M	8	Duke Nalon	Kohlert Spl.	Fengler	11
12	29	116.393	12	DUR	4	George Bailey	Leon Duray Barbasol Spl.	Weil	12
13	9	119.796	27	MAS	6	Mauri Rose	I.B.E.W. Spl.	Maserati	13
14	10	125.769	16	SP	6	Ronney Householder	Sparks-Thorne Engin. Spl.	Adams	14
15	15	123.506	6	SP	6	Jimmy Snyder	Sparks-Thorne Engin. Spl.	Adams	15
16	12	120.525	5	WIN	8	Louis Meyer	Bowes Seal Fast Spl.	Stevens	16
17	4	122.499	17	O	4	Tony Gulotta	Hamilton & Harris Spl.	Stevens	17
18	22	119.420	55	M	4	Al Miller	Domont's Pepsi Cola Spl.	Miller	18
19	19	120.326	15	M	4	George Connor	Marks Spl.	Adams	19
20	32	114.464	9	M	8	Cliff Bergere	Kraft's Real Rye Spl.	Stevens	20
21	31	116.279	33	VO	12	Henry Banks	Kimmel Spl.	Miller	21
22	21	119.827	35	O	4	Kelly Petillo	Petillo Spl.	Wetteroth	22
23	24	121.599	21	M	4	Louis Tomei	P.O.B. Perfect Seal Spl.	Miller	23
24	16	122.393	7	M	8	Bill Cummings	I.B.E.W. Spl.	Miller	24
25	2	124.027	14	M	4	Russ Snowberger	D-X Spl.	Snowberger	25
26	8	120.595	34	M	4	Babe Stapp	McCoy Auto Service Spl.	Weil	26
27	26	118.458	10	M	8	Tony Willman	Belanger Motors Spl.	Stevens	27
28	3	122.845	8	AR	8	Rex Mays	Alfa Romeo Spl.	A. R. Weil	28
29	28	117.126	42	BR	6	Emil Andres	Elgin Piston Pin Spl.	Adams	29
30	27	118.255	37	STU	8	Ira Hall	Greenfield Super Service Spl.	Nowiak	30
31	11	121.921	26	BR	6	Frank Brisko	Shurr-Stop Mechanical Brake Equalizer Spl.	Stevens	31
32	23	116.791	36	M	4	Al Putnam	Troy Tydol Spl.	Stevens	32
33	20	120.906	47	M	4	Shorty Cantlon	Kamm's Spl.	Stevens	33

Qualified, did not start: Charlie Crawford, Shafer Buick '8' Spl., #31, BU, 112.762 MPH, Too slow

Total entries: 49

Qualifying: Minimum of 110 MPH for 10 laps. Fastest 33.

FIN	ENTRANT	LAPS	SPEED, REASON OUT	RELIEF DRIVER	FIN
1	Lou Moore	200	117.200	—	1
2	W. Wilbur Shaw	200	115.580	—	2
3	Boyle Racing Hdqtrs.	200	114.946	—	3
4	Harry Hartz	200	112.203	—	4
5	Joe Lencki	200	110.311	—	5
6	Lewis W. Welch	199	109.843	Russ Snowberger, Cliff Bergere	6
7	Carl Marchese	197	108.694	Tony Willman	7
8	Joel Thorne, Inc.	185	102.080	—	8
9	Joel Thorne, Inc.	185	102.009	—	9
10	Paul Weirick	181	99.543	—	10
11	Henry Kohlert	178	Flagged	—	11
12	Leon Duray	166	Clutch	—	12
13	Boyle Racing Hdqtrs.	165	Supercharger	—	13
14	Joel Thorne, Inc.	154	Supercharger hose	Billy Winn	14
15	Joel Thorne, Inc.	150	Supercharger	—	15
16	Bowes Racing, Inc.	149	Oil pump	—	16
17	Tony Gulotta	130	Con rod	Kelly Petillo	17
18	Jack Holly	125	Clutch	—	18
19	Joseph Marks	119	Engine trouble	—	19
20	George H. Lyons	111	Piston	—	20
21	Louis Kimmel	109	Rod bearing	—	21
22	Kelly Petillo	100	Camshaft	—	22
23	H. E. Winn	88	Con. rod	—	23
24	Boyle Racing Hdqtrs.	72	Radiator tank leak		24
25	Russell Snowberger	56	Con. rod	—	25
26	Bill White Race Cars	54	Valve	—	26
27	Murrell Belanger	47	Valve	—	27
28	Bill White Race Cars	45	Supercharger	—	28
29	Elgin Piston Pin	45	Wrecked	—	29
30	Nowiak & Magnee	44	Hit wall	—	30
31	Frank Brisko	39	Oil line	—	31
32	Arthur M. Sims	15	Crankshaft	—	32
33	Thomas O'Brien	13	Supercharger	—	33

AR = Alfa Romeo   M. = Miller   STU = Studebaker
BR = Brisko   MAS = Maserati   VO = Voelker
BU = Buick   O = Offenhauser   WIN = Winfield
DUR = Duray   SP = Sparks

1939

FIN	START	QUAL. SPEED	NUMBER, TYPE, CYLINDERS			DRIVER	CAR NAME	CHASSIS	FIN
1	3	128.977	2	MAS	8	Wilbur Shaw	Boyle Valve Spl.	Maserati	1
2	1	130.138	10	SP	6	Jimmy Snyder	Thorne Engineering Spl.	Adams	2
3	10	123.835	54	O	4	Cliff Bergere	Offenhauser Spl.	Miller-Ford	3
4	4	127.723	4	M	8	Ted Horn	Boyle Valve Spl.	Miller	4
5	16	125.000	31	AR	8	Babe Stapp	Alfa Romeo Spl.	AR-Weil	5
6	15	120.935	41	O	4	George Barringer	Bill White Spl.	Weil	6
7	20	122.177	8	SP	6	Joel Thorne	Thorne Engineering Spl.	Adams	7
8	8	124.896	16	O	4	Mauri Rose	Wheeler's Spl.	Shaw	8
9	17	125.074	14	O	4	Frank Wearne	Burd Piston Ring Spl.	Wetteroth	9
10	33	116.527	26	DUR	4	Billy DeVore	Leon Duray Barbasol Spl.	Weil	10
11	27	121.749	62	O	4	Tony Gulotta	Burd Piston Ring Spl.	Stevens	11
12	2	130.067	45	WIN	8	Louis Meyer	Bowes Seal Fast Spl.	Stevens	12
13	12	123.208	18	O	4	George Connor	Marks Spl.	Adams	13
14	26	122.771	51	LN	6	Tony Willman	Burd Piston Ring Spl.	Lencki	14
15	30	118.426	58	AR	8	Louis Tomei	Alfa Romeo Spl.	Alfa Romeo	15
16	19	126.413	15	SP	6	Rex Mays	Thorne Engineering Spl.	Adams	16
17	9	124.125	9	M	8	Herb Ardinger	Miller-Hartz Spl.	Wetteroth	17
18	24	123.660	35	O	4	Kelly Petillo	Kay Jewelers Spl.	Wetteroth	18
19	14	121.683	49	O	4	Mel Hansen	Joel Thorne, Inc. Spl.	Shaw	19
20	32	117.287	38	BR	6	Harry McQuinn	Elgin Piston Pin Spl.	Blume	20
21	5	126.318	3	M	4	Chet Miller	Boyle Valve Spl.	Summers	21
22	13	122.204	25	O	4	Ralph Hepburn	Hamilton & Harris Spl.	Stevens	22
23	23	128.968	1	O	4	Floyd Roberts	Burd Piston Ring Spl.	Wetteroth	23
24	18	121.188	37	STU	8	Ira Hall	Greenfield Super Service Spl.	Nowiak	24
25	25	123.199	21	M	4	Russ Snowberger	D-X Spl.	Snowberger	25
26	6	125.821	17	M-RE	6	George Bailey	Miller Spl.	Miller	26
27	29	119.375	56	O	4	Floyd Davis	W.B.W. Spl.	Miller	27
28	28	123.233	42	O	4	Al Miller	Kennedy Tank Spl.	Adams	28
29	11	123.351	29	BR	6	Frank Brisko	National Seal Spl.	Stevens	29
30	21	121.212	44	O	4	Emil Andres	Chicago Flash Spl.	Stevens	30
31	22	129.431	32	SA	16	Bob Swanson	Sampson Motors, Inc. Spl.	Stevens	31
32	7	125.567	47	O	4	Shorty Cantlon	Automotive Service Spl.	Stevens	32
33	31	117.979	53	MAS	8	Deacon Litz	Maserati Spl.	Maserati	33

Qualified, did not start: George Robson, Deacon Litz Spl., #28, M, 116.305 MPH, Bumped

Total entries: 49

Qualifying: Minimum 110 MPH for 4 laps. Fastest 33.

FIN	ENTRANT	LAPS	SPEED, REASON OUT	RELIEF DRIVER	FIN
1	Boyle Racing Hdqtrs.	200	115.035	—	1
2	Joel Thorne, Inc.	200	114.245	—	2
3	Lewis W. Welch	200	113.698	—	3
4	Boyle Racing Hdqtrs.	200	111.879	—	4
5	Bill White Race Cars	200	111.230	—	5
6	Bill White Race Cars	200	111.025	—	6
7	Joel Thorne, Inc.	200	110.416	—	7
8	W. Wilbur Shaw	200	109.544	—	8
9	Moore & Roberts	200	107.806	—	9
10	Leon Duray	200	104.267	Henry Banks	10
11	George Lyons	200	103.938	Harry McQuinn	11
12	Bowes Racing, Inc.	197	Wrecked	—	12
13	Joseph Marks	195	Stalled	—	13
14	Joe Lencki	188	Fuel pump	—	14
15	Frank T. Griswold	186	Flagged	Mel Hansen	15
16	Thorne Engineering	145	Rings	—	16
17	Harry Hartz	141	Clutch	Frank Brisko, Mel Hansen	17
18	Kelly Petillo	141	Pistons	—	18
19	Joel Thorne, Inc.	113	Hit wall	—	19
20	F. Burren	110	Ignition	Al Putnam, Frank Brisko, George Robson	20
21	Boyle Racing Hdqtrs.	107	Wrecked	—	21
22	Anthony Gulotta	107	Wrecked	Bob Swanson	22
23	Lou Moore, Inc.	106	Wrecked	—	23
24	Magnee & Nowiak	89	Head gasket	—	24
25	Russell Snowberger	50	Leaking radiator	—	25
26	Harry A. Miller	47	Valve	—	26
27	Ed Walsh	43	Shock absorber	—	27
28	Paul Weirick	41	Accel. pedal bracket	—	28
29	Frank Brisko	38	Air pump	—	29
30	Jimmy Snyder	22	Stripped plug threads	—	30
31	Sampson Motors	19	Rear axle	—	31
32	Associated Enterprises	15	Main bearing	—	32
33	Richard T. Wharton	7	Valve	—	33

AR = Alfa Romeo
BR = Brisko
DUR = Duray
LN = Lencki

M = Miller
MAS = Maserati
O = Offenhauser
RE = Rear engine

SA = Sampson
SP = Sparks
STU = Studebaker
WIN = Winfield

1940

FIN	START	QUAL. SPEED	NUMBER, TYPE, CYLINDERS			DRIVER	CAR NAME	CHASSIS	FIN
1	2	127.065	1	MAS	8	Wilbur Shaw	Boyle Spl.	Maserati	1
2	1	127.850	33	WIN	8	Rex Mays	Bowes Seal Fast Spl.	Stevens	2
3	3	125.624	7	O	4	Mauri Rose	Elgin Piston Pin Spl.	Wetteroth	3
4	4	125.545	3	M	8	Ted Horn	Boyle Spl.	Miller	4
5	10	122.434	8	SP	6	Joel Thorne	Thorne & Donnelly Spl.	Adams	5
6	20	124.882	32	SA	16	Bob Swanson	Sampson '16' Spl.	Stevens	6
7	7	123.216	9	O	4	Frank Wearne	Boyle Spl.	Stevens	7
8	5	124.753	31	M	8	Mel Hansen	Hartz Spl.	Wetteroth	8
9	8	122.716	16	BR	6	Frank Brisko	Elgin Piston Pin Spl.	Stevens	9
10	31	118.981	49	MAS	8	Rene LeBegue, France	Lucy O'Reilly Schell Spl.	Maserati	10
11	15	122.486	41	AR	8	Harry McQuinn	Hollywood Pay Day Spl.	AR-Weil	11
12	22	122.963	25	O	4	Emil Andres	Belanger-Folz Spl.	Stevens	12
13	14	123.064	28	DUR	4	Sam Hanks	Leon Duray Spl.	Weil	13
14	16	121.889	6	O	4	George Barringer	Hollywood Pay Day Spl.	Weil	14
15	26	121.757	42	O	4	Joie Chitwood	Kennedy Tank Spl.	Adams	15
16	18	119.980	26	O	4	Louis Tomei	Falstaff Spl.	Miller	16
17	27	121.392	34	AR	8	Chet Miller	Alfa Romeo Spl.	Alfa Romeo	17
18	32	122.197	14	O	4	Billy DeVore	Bill Holabird Spl.	Shaw	18
19	28	120.818	44	O	4	Al Putnam	Refinoil Motor Oil Spl.	Adams	19
20	33	120.797	61	LN	4	Floyd Davis	Lencki Two Weeks Spl.	Lencki	20
21	13	125.331	35	O	4	Kelly Petillo	Indiana Fur Co. Spl.	Wetteroth	21
22	25	121.790	21	O	4	Duke Nalon	Marks Spl.	Silnes	22
23	23	122.562	17	O	4	George Robson	Keller Spl.	Miller-Ford	23
24	12	123.367*	24	O	4	Babe Stapp*	Surber Spl.	Stevens	24
25	19	122.963	36	M	4	Doc Williams	Quillen Bros. Refrig. Spl.	Cooper	25
26	17	124.585	10	LN	6	George Connor	Lencki Spl.	Lencki	26
27	6	123.673	5	O	4	Cliff Bergere	Noc-Out Hose Clamp Spl.	Wetteroth	27
28	29	120.809	38	BR	6	Paul Russo	Elgin Piston Pin Spl.	Blume	28
29	21	123.860	54	O	4	Ralph Hepburn	Bowes Seal Fast Spl.	Miller-Ford	29
30	30	120.288	58	AR	8	Al Miller	Alfa Romeo Spl.	Alfa Romeo	30
31	11	121.564	19	M	4	Russ Snowberger	Snowberger Spl.	Snowberger	31
32	9	122.614	27	O	4	Tommy Hinnershitz	Marks Spl.	Adams	32
33	24	121.827	29	MAS	8	Raoul Riganti, Argentina	Maserati Spl.	Maserati	33

Qualified, did not start: Tony Willman, Leader Card Spl., #45, M, 118.914 MPH
Rene Dreyfus, Lucy O'Reilly Schell Spl., #22, MAS, 118.831 MPH, Bumped
Louis Durant, Schoof Spl., #12, O, 117.218 MPH, Bumped

Total entries: 49

Qualifying: Minimum of 115 MPH for 4 laps. Fastest 33.

*Qualified by Shorty Cantlon

FIN	ENTRANT	LAPS	SPEED, REASON OUT	RELIEF DRIVER	FIN
1	Boyle Racing Hdqtrs.	200	114.277	—	1
2	Bowes Racing	200	113.742	—	2
3	Lou Moore	200	113.572	—	3
4	Boyle Racing Hdqtrs.	199	Flagged	—	4
5	Joel Thorne, Inc.	197	Flagged	—	5
6	Sampson Motors	196	Flagged	—	6
7	Boyle Racing Hdqtrs.	195	Flagged	—	7
8	Harry Hartz	194	Flagged	—	8
9	Frank Brisko	193	Flagged	—	9
10	Lucy O'Reilly Schell	192	Flagged	Rene Dreyfus	10
11	Bill White Race Cars	192	Flagged	—	11
12	Murrell Belanger	192	Flagged	—	12
13	Leon Duray	192	Flagged	—	13
14	Bill White Race Cars	191	Flagged	—	14
15	Paul Weirick	190	Flagged	—	15
16	Ed Walsh	190	Exhaust pipe	—	16
17	Wharton-Dewart Motor Racing	189	Flagged	Henry Banks	17
18	W. Wilbur Shaw	181	Flagged	George Connor	18
19	Anthony Gulotta	179	Flagged	—	19
20	Joseph Lencki	157	Flagged	Lou Webb, George Connor	20
21	Kelly Petillo	128	Rear main bearing	—	21
22	Joseph Marks	120	Con. rod	—	22
23	Marty Keller	67	Shock absorber	—	23
24	Fred Surber	64	Oil line	Tony Willman	24
25	Doc Williams	61	Oil line	—	25
26	Joseph Lencki	52	Con. rod	—	26
27	Lou Moore, Inc.	51	Oil line	—	27
28	Elgin Piston Pin	48	Oil leak	—	28
29	W. C. Winfield	47	Spun	—	29
30	Frank T. Griswold, Jr.	41	Clutch	—	30
31	Russell Snowberger	38	Water pump	—	31
32	Joseph Marks	32	Hit wall	—	32
33	Raoul Riganti	24	Wrecked	—	33

AR = Alfa Romeo   M = Miller   SA = Sampson
BR = Brisko   MAS = Maserati   SP = Sparks
DUR = Duray   O = Offenhauser   WIN = Winfield
LN = Lencki

1941

FIN	START	QUAL. SPEED	NUMBER, TYPE, CYLINDERS			DRIVER	CAR NAME	CHASSIS	FIN
1	17	121.106	16	O	4	Floyd Davis/M. Rose	Noc-Out Hose Clamp Spl.	Wetteroth	1
2	2	128.301	1	WIN	8	Rex Mays	Bowes Seal Fast Spl.	Stevens	2
3	28	124.297	4	SP	6	Ted Horn	T.E.C. Spl.	Adams	3
4	10	120.653	54	NO	8	Ralph Hepburn	Bowes Seal Fast Spl.	Miller-Ford	4
5	7	123.890	34	O	4	Cliff Bergere	Noc-Out Hose Clamp Spl.	Wetteroth	5
6	9	121.540	41	M	8	Chet Miller	Boyle Valve Spl.	Miller	6
7	4	125.449	15	AR	8	Harry McQuinn	Ziffrin Spl.	AR-Weil	7
8	6	123.890	7	O	4	Frank Wearne	Bill Holabird Spl.	Shaw	8
9	18	125.217	45	M	8	Paul Russo	Leader Card Spl.	Marchese	9
10	20	121.021	27	O	4	Tommy Hinnershitz	Marks Spl.	Adams	10
11	24	121.074	53	O	4	Louis Tomei	H-3 Spl.	Miller-Ford	11
12	31	121.951	55	O	4	Al Putnam	Schoof Spl.	Wetteroth	12
13	26	116.298	26	M	8	Overton Phillips	Phillips Spl.	Bugatti	13
14	27	120.329	25	LN	6	Joie Chitwood	Blue Crown Spark Plug Spl.	Lencki	14
15	30	122.951	17	MAS	8	Duke Nalon	Elgin Piston Pin Spl.	Maserati	15
16	13	123.984	14	O	4	George Connor	Boyle Valve Spl.	Stevens	16
17	12	119.860	47	O	4	Everett Saylor	Mark Bowles Spl.	Weil	17
18	3	127.836	2	MAS	8	Wilbur Shaw	Boyle Valve Spl.	Maserati	18
19	8	121.770	23	O	4	Billy DeVore	Hollywood Payday Candy Bar Spl.	Stevens	19
20	25	123.920	62	O	4	Tony Willman	Lyons Spl.	Stevens	20
21	11	120.104	42	O	4	Russ Snowberger	Jim Hussy's Sportsman Club Spl.	Snowberger	21
22	29	123.440	32	SA	16	Deacon Litz	Sampson '16' Spl.	Stevens	22
23	22	123.381	8	BR	6	Frank Brisko	Zollner Piston Spl.	Stevens	23
24	5	124.014	36	O	4	Doc Williams	Indiana Fur Co. Spl.	Cooper	24
25	16	121.576	10	DUR	4	George Robson	Gilmore Red Lion Spl.	Weil	25
26	1	128.691	3	MAS	8	Mauri Rose	Elgin Piston Pin Spl.	Maserati	26
27	19	124.417	22	O	4	Kelly Petillo	American Air Liner Sandwich Shop Spl.	Wetteroth	27
28	14	123.478	12	M-RE	6	Al Miller	Miller Spl.	Miller	28
29	21	124.599	9	O	4	Mel Hansen	Fageol Spl.	Miller-Ford	29
30	15	122.266	19	LN	6	Emil Andres	Kennedy Tank Spl.	Lencki	30
31	23	121.163	5	SP	6	Joel Thorne	Thorne Engineering Spl.	Adams	31
32	—	122.299	35	M-RE	6	George Barringer	Miller Spl.	Miller	32
33	—	118.211	28	O	4	Sam Hanks	Tom Joyce 7-Up Spl.	Kurtis	33

Qualified, did not start: Louis Durant, J & S Spl., #44, MER, 116.152 MPH, Bumped
Rene LeBegue, Talbot, #21, T, 115.603 MPH, Too slow

Total entries: 42

Qualifying: Minimum 115 MPH for 4 laps. Fastest 33.

FIN	ENTRANT	LAPS	SPEED, REASON OUT	RELIEF DRIVER	FIN
1	Lou Moore, Inc.	200	115.117	Mauri Rose	1
2	Bowes Racing	200	114.459	—	2
3	Art Sparks	200	113.864	—	3
4	Bowes Racing	200	113.631	—	4
5	Cliff Bergere	200	113.528	—	5
6	Boyle Racing Hdqtrs.	200	111.921	—	6
7	Bill White	200	111.795	Kelly Petillo	7
8	Arthur Sims	200	110.818	—	8
9	Carl Marchese	200	105.628	Louis Durant	9
10	Joe Marks	200	105.152	George Robson	10
11	Hughes Bros.	200	104.926	—	11
12	Val Johnson	200	101.381	Louis Durant	12
13	Overton Phillips	187	Flagged	Mel Hansen	13
14	Joe Lencki	177	Flagged	—	14
15	Elgin Piston Pin	173	Flagged	—	15
16	Boyle Racing Hdqtrs.	167	Transmission	—	16
17	Mark E. Bowles, M.D.	155	Wreck	—	17
18	Boyle Racing Hdqtrs.	151	Wreck	—	18
19	Fred Surber	121	Con. rod	—	19
20	George Lyons	117	Con. rod	—	20
21	Russell Snowberger	107	Water pump	—	21
22	Sampson Motors	89	Oil trouble	—	22
23	Frank Brisko	70	Valve Spring	—	23
24	Aero Marine Finishes	68	Radiator leak	—	24
25	Leon Duray	66	Oil leak	—	25
26	Lou Moore, Inc.	60	Spark plug	—	26
27	Kelly Petillo	48	Con. rod	—	27
28	Eddie Offutt	22	Transmission	—	28
29	Lou Fageol	11	Con. rod	—	29
30	Joe Lencki	5	Wreck	—	30
31	Joel Thorne, Inc.	5	Wreck	—	31
32	Eddie Offutt		Destroyed, garage fire—DNS	—	32
33	Ed Walsh Corp.		Wrecked before race—DNS	—	33

AR = Alfa Romeo   M = Miller   NO = Novi   SA = Sampson
BR = Brisko   MAS = Maserati   O = Offenhauser   SP = Sparks
DUR = Duray   MER = Mercury   RE = Rear engine   WIN = Winfield
LN = Lencki

1946

FIN	START	QUAL. SPEED	NUMBER, TYPE, CYLINDERS			DRIVER	CAR NAME	CHASSIS	FIN
1	15	125.541	16	SP	6	George Robson	Thorne Engineering Spl.	Adams	1
2	5	120.257	61	O	4	Jimmy Jackson	Jackson Spl.	Miller	2
3	7	123.980	29	MAS	8	Ted Horn	Boyle Maserati	Maserati	3
4	11	121.139	18	MAS	8	Emil Andres	Elgin Piston Pin Spl.	Maserati	4
5	12	119.816	24	O	4	Joie Chitwood	Noc-Out Hose Clamp Spl.	Wetteroth	5
6	6	118.973	33	AR	8	Louis Durant	Alfa Romeo	Alfa Romeo	6
7	28	121.249	52	MAS	8	Luigi Villoresi, Italy	Maserati	Maserati	7
8	29	121.233	7	O	4	Frank Wearne	Wolfe Motor Co. Spl.	Shaw	8
9	25	120.611	39	O	4	Bill Sheffler	Jack Maurer Spl.	Bromme	9
10	31	119.876	17	O	4	Billy DeVore	Schoof Spl.	Wetteroth	10
11	27	121.431	41	DUR	4	Mel Hansen	Ross Page Spl.	Kurtis	11
12	10	121.593	25	MAS	8	Russ Snowberger	Jim Hussy's Spl.	Maserati	12
13	18	124.499	14	SP	6	Harry McQuinn	Mobilgas Spl.	Adams	13
14	19	133.944	2	NO	8	Ralph Hepburn	Novi Governor Spl.	Kurtis	14
15	13	116.283	12	O	4	Al Putnam	L.G.S. Spring Clutch Spl.	Stevens	15
16	1	126.471	3	O	4	Cliff Bergere	Noc-Out Hose Clamp Spl.	Wetteroth	16
17	8	123.279	45	O	4	Duke Dinsmore	Johnston Spl.	Adams	17
18	17	124.649	5	O	4	Chet Miller	Miller Spl.	Cooper	18
19	16	125.113	63	AR	8	Jimmy Wilburn	Mobiloil Spl.	AR-Weil	19
20	26	123.094	42	M	8	Tony Bettenhausen	Bristow-McManus	Wetteroth	20
21	33	118.890	59	FV8	8	Danny Kladis	Grancor V8 Spl.	Miller-Ford	21
22	32	119.682	54	MAS	4	Duke Nalon	Maserati	Maserati	22
23	9	124.065	8	LN	6	Mauri Rose	Blue Crown Spark Plug Spl.	Lencki	23
24	30	120.006	38	O	4	George Connor	Ed Walsh Spl.	Kurtis	24
25	23	121.466	48	M	8	Hal Robson	Phillips Spl.	Bugatti	25
26	22	119.193	15	BR	6	Louis Tomei	Boxar Tool Spl.	Stevens	26
27	21	120.220	31	O	4	Henry Banks	Automobile Shippers Spl.	Snowberger	27
28	20	122.432	64	O	4	Shorty Cantlon	H-3 Spl.	Miller-Ford	28
29	24	120.628	26	M-RE	6	George Barringer	Tucker Torpedo Spl.	Miller	29
30	14	128.861	1	WIN	8	Rex Mays	Bowes Seal Fast Spl.	Stevens	30
31	3	124.762	32	SA	16	Sam Hanks	Spike Jones Spl.	Stevens	31
32	4	120.728	47	AR	8	Hal Cole	Don Lee Spl.	Alfa Romeo	32
33	2	126.183	10	O	8	Paul Russo	Fageol Twin Coach Spl.	Fageol	33

Qualified, did not start: Buddy Rush, Army Recruiting Spl., #37, STU, 116.268, Bumped
Charlie Van Acker, Singer Spl., #62, VO, 115.666, Too slow
Tony Bettenhausen, Marchese Spl., #27, M, 121.860, Qualified—withdrew, broken crankshaft

Total Entries: 58

Qualifying: Minimum 115 MPH for 4 laps. Fastest 33.

FIN	ENTRANT	LAPS	SPEED, REASON OUT	RELIEF DRIVER	FIN
1	Thorne Engineering	200	114.820	—	1
2	Jimmy Jackson	200	114.498	—	2
3	Boyle Racing Hdqtrs.	200	109.819	—	3
4	Frank Brisko	200	108.902	—	4
5	Fred Peters	200	108.399	Sam Hanks	5
6	Milt Marion	200	105.073	—	6
7	Corvorado Filippini	200	100.783	—	7
8	Ervin Wolfe	197	Flagged	—	8
9	Bill Sheffler	139	Flagged	—	9
10	William Schoof	167	Spun	—	10
11	Ross Page	143	Crankshaft	—	11
12	R. A. Cott	134	Differential	Duke Nalon	12
13	Robert Flavell	124	Out of oil	Jimmy Wilburn	13
14	W. C. Winfield	121	Stalled	—	14
15	George Kuehn	120	Magneto, frame	George Connor	15
16	Shirley Bergere	82	Out of oil	Rex Mays	16
17	Fred Johnston	82	Con. rod	—	17
18	Chet Miller	64	Oil line	Louis Tomei	18
19	Bill White	52	Engine trouble	—	19
20	Robert McManus	47	Con. rod	—	20
21	Grancor	46	Towed, disqualified	—	21
22	Corvorado Filippini	45	Universal	—	22
23	Joe Lencki	40	Wreck	—	23
24	Ed Walsh	38	Piston	—	24
25	Overton Phillips	37	Con. rod	—	25
26	Joseph Hosso	34	Oil line	—	26
27	Louis Rassey	32	Stalled	—	27
28	Charles J. Hughes	28	Clutch	—	28
29	George Barringer	27	Gear trouble	—	29
30	Bowes Racing	26	Manifold	—	30
31	Gordon Schroeder	18	Oil line	—	31
32	Don Lee, Inc.	16	Fuel leak	—	32
33	Lou Fageol	16	Wreck	—	33

AR = Alfa Romeo
BR = Brisko
DUR = Duray
FV8 = Ford V8

LN = Lencki
M = Miller
MAS = Maserati
NO = Novi

O = Offenhauser
RE = Rear engine
SA = Sampson

SP = Sparks
VO = Voelker
WIN = Winfield

1947

FIN	START	QUAL. SPEED	NUMBER, TYPE, CYLINDERS			DRIVER	CAR NAME	CHASSIS	FIN
1	3	124.040	27	O	4	Mauri Rose	Blue Crown Spark Plug Spl.	Deidt	1
2	8	128.756	16	O	4	Bill Holland	Blue Crown Spark Plug Spl.	Deidt	2
3	1	126.564	1	MAS	8	Ted Horn	Bennett Bros. Spl.	Maserati	3
4	4	120.733*	54	NO	8	Herb Ardinger*	Novi Governor Mobil Spl.	Kurtis	4
5	10	122.266	7	O	4	Jimmy Jackson	Jim Hussey Spl.	Miller	5
6	20	124.412	9	WIN	8	Rex Mays	Bowes Seal Fast Spl.	Kurtis	6
7	14	118.355	33	AR	8	Walt Brown	Permafuse Spl.	Alfa Romeo	7
8	28	115.644	34	AR	8	Cy Marshall	Tattersfield Spl.	AR-Weil	8
9	23	121.478	41	DUR	8	Fred Agabashian	Ross Page Spl.	Kurtis	9
10	27	119.840	10	O	4	Duke Dinsmore	Schoof Spl.	Wetteroth	10
11	7	118.425	58	O	4	Les Anderson	Kennedy Tank Spl.	Maserati	11
12	17	117.218	59	FV8	8	Pete Romcevich	Camco Motors Ford Spl.	Miller-Ford	12
13	30	116.781	3	LN	6	Emil Andres	Preston Tucker Partner Spl.	Lencki	13
14	15	117.716	31	O	4	Frank Wearne	Superior Industries Spl.	Miller	14
15	9	123.423	47	AR	8	Ken Fowler	Don Lee Alfa Romeo Spl.	Alfa Romeo	15
16	18	128.082	46	MS	12	Duke Nalon	Don Lee Mercedes Spl.	Mercedes	16
17	12	119.526	28	M	8	Roland Free	Bristow-McManus Spl.	Wetteroth	17
18	25	120.980	29	O	4	Tony Bettenhausen	Belanger Motors Spl.	Stevens	18
19	6	121.331	25	MAS	8	Russ Snowberger	Federal Engineering, Detroit Spl.	Maserati	19
20	16	122.096	52	O	4	Hal Robson	Palmer Spl.	Adams	20
21	2	124.957	18	NO	8	Cliff Bergere	Novi Governor Mobil Spl.	Kurtis	21
22	22	123.157	8	O	4	Joie Chitwood	Peters Spl.	Wetteroth	22
23	5	121.462	24	M	16	Shorty Cantlon	Automobile Shippers Spl.	Snowberger	23
24	26	120.923	43	O	4	Henry Banks	Federal Engineering, Detroit Spl.	Miller-Ford	24
25	19	124.848	66	M-RE	6	Al Miller	Preston Tucker Spl.	Miller	25
26	13	124.874	14	O	4	George Connor	Ed Walsh Spl.	Curtis	26
27	29	117.298	38	SP	6	Mel Hansen	Flavell-Duffy Spl.	Adams	27
28	21	123.967	15	O	4	Paul Russo	Wolfe Motor Co. Spl.	Shaw	28
29	24	121.049	44	LN	4	Charles Van Acker	Preston Tucker Partner Spl.	Stevens	29
30	11	119.932	53	O	4	Milt Fankhouser	Jack Maurer's Club Southern Spl.	Stevens	30

Qualified, did not start: Danny Kladis, Camco Motors Spl., #57, MER, 112.591 MPH, Below 115 MPH minimum
Frank Brisko, Boxar Tool Spl., 110.732 MPH, Below 115 MPH minimum

Total entries: 51

Qualifying: Minimum of 115 MPH for 4 laps. Fastest 33.

*Qualified by Doc Williams

FIN	ENTRANT	LAPS	SPEED, REASON OUT	RELIEF DRIVER	FIN
1	Lou Moore	200	116.338	—	1
2	Lou Moore	200	116.097	—	2
3	H. C. Henning	200	114.997	—	3
4	W. C. Winfield	200	113.404	Cliff Bergere	4
5	H. C. Henning	200	112.834	—	5
6	Bowes Racing	200	111.056	—	6
7	Milt Marion	200	101.744	—	7
8	Bill White	197	Flagged	—	8
9	Ross Page	191	Flagged	—	9
10	Bill Schoof	167	Flagged	Billy DeVore	10
11	Les Anderson	131	Flagged	—	11
12	Andy Granatelli	168	Mechanical failure	—	12
13	Joe Lencki	150	Magneto	George Connor	13
14	Louis Rassey	128	Spun	Louis Tomei	14
15	Don Lee, Inc.	121	Axle	—	15
16	Don Lee, Inc.	119	Piston	—	16
17	Robert J. McManus	87	Spun	—	17
18	Murrell Belanger	79	Timing gear	—	18
19	R. A. Cott	74	Oil pump	—	19
20	Richard L. Palmer	67	Transmission	—	20
21	W. C. Winfield	62	Piston	—	21
22	Fred Peters	51	Gears	—	22
23	Louis Rassey	40	Wreck	—	23
24	H. C. Henning	36	Oil line	—	24
25	Clay Ballinger	33	Magneto	—	25
26	Ed Walsh	32	Fuel leak	—	26
27	Robert J. Flavell	32	Pushed, disqualified	—	27
28	Ervin Wolfe	24	Wreck	—	28
29	Joe Lencki	24	Wreck	—	29
30	Milt Fankhouser	16	Stalled	—	30

AR = Alfa Romeo M = Miller MS = Mercedes RE = Rear engine
DUR = Duray MAS = Maserati O = Offenhauser SP = Sparks
FV8 = Ford V8 MER = Mercury NO = Novi WIN = Winfield
LN = Lencki

1948

FIN	START	QUAL. SPEED	NUMBER, TYPE, CYLINDERS			DRIVER	CAR NAME	CHASSIS	FIN
1	3	129.129	3	O	4	Mauri Rose	Blue Crown Spark Plug Spl.	Deidt	1
2	2	129.515	2	O	4	Bill Holland	Blue Crown Spark Plug Spl.	Deidt	2
3	11	131.603	54	NO	8	Duke Nalon	Novi Grooved Piston Spl.	Kurtis	3
4	5	126.565	1	MAS	8	Ted Horn	Bennett Bros. Spl.	Maserati	4
5	21	127.968	35	O	4	Mack Hellings	Don Lee Spl.	KK 2000	5
6	14	124.391	63	O	4	Hal Cole	City of Tacoma Spl.	KK 2000	6
7	28	128.420	91	O	4	Lee Wallard	Iddings Spl.	Meyer	7
8	27	121.790	33	AR	8	Johnny Mauro	Phil Kraft Spl.	Alfa Romeo	8
9	23	125.122	7	O	4	Tommy Hinnershitz	Kurtis-Kraft Spl.	Kurtis	9
10	4	127.510	61	O	4	Jimmy Jackson	Howard Keck Spl.	Deidt	10
11	12	125.440	4	O	4	Charles Van Acker	City of South Bend Spl.	Stevens	11
12	20	123.967	19	O*	4	Billy DeVore	Pat Clancy Spl.	Kurtis	12
13	8	122.791	98	O	4	Johnny Mantz	Kurtis-Kraft Spl.	KK 2000	13
14	22	126.396	6	O	4	Tony Bettenhausen	Belanger Motors Spl.	Stevens	14
15	18	122.796	64	O	4	Hal Robson	Palmer Construction Spl.	Adams	15
16	7	123.733	36	FA	6	Bill Cantrell	Fageol Twin Coach Spl.	Stevens	16
17	10	124.619	55	O	4	Joie Chitwood	Nyquist Spl.	Shaw	17
18	24	124.529	53	O	4	Bill Sheffler	Jack Maurer Spl.	Bromme	18
19	1	130.577	5	WIN	8	Rex Mays	Bowes Seal Fast Spl.	Kurtis	19
20	19	127.249	31	MS	12	Chet Miller	Don Lee Mercedes Spl.	Mercedes	20
21	13	124.580	52	O	4	Jack McGrath	Sheffler Spl.	Bromme	21
22	29	126.015	16	O	4	Duane Carter	Belanger Motors Spl.	Wetteroth	22
23	32	122.737	26	DUR	4	Fred Agabashian	Ross Page Spl.	Kurtis	23
24	9	122.337	34	O	4	Les Anderson	Kennedy Tank Spl.	Kurtis	24
25	33	122.117	17	SP	4	Mel Hansen	Schafer Gear Works Spl.	Adams	25
26	15	124.266	76	SP	6	Sam Hanks	Flavell Spl.	Adams	26
27	30	125.545	51	O	4	Spider Webb	Fowle Bros. Spl.	Bromme	27
28	17	123.018	9	M	8	George Connor	Bennett Bros. Spl.	Stevens	28
29	6	124.151	74	O	4	Doc Williams	Clarke Auto Co. Spl.	Cooper	29
30	31	123.393	86	O	4	Mike Salay	Terman Marine Supply	Wetteroth	30
31	16	123.550	8	O	4	Emil Andres	Tuffy's Spl.	KK 2000	31
32	25	122.595	25	MAS	8	Paul Russo	Federal Engineering, Detroit Spl.	Maserati	32
33	26	122.154	65	MAS	8	Harry McQuinn	Frank Lynch Motors, Inc. Spl.	Maserati	33

Qualified, did not start: Johnny Shackleford, Johnston Spl., #48, O, 121.745, Bumped
Myron Fohr, Marchese Spl., #32, O, 121.531, Bumped
Spider Webb, Anderson Spl., #72, O, 121.421, Bumped
Ken Fowler, Don Lee Alfa Romeo Spl., #42, AR, 120.446, Bumped
Louis Durant, Automobile Shippers Spl., #29, M, 117.666, Too slow

Total entries: 80

Qualifying: Minimum 115 MPH for 4 laps. Fastest 33.

*Six-wheel car

FIN	ENTRANT	LAPS	SPEED, REASON OUT	RELIEF DRIVER	FIN
1	Lou Moore	200	119.814	—	1
2	Lou Moore	200	119.147	—	2
3	W. C. Winfield	200	118.034	—	3
4	H. C Henning	200	117.844	—	4
5	Don Lee Division	200	113.361	—	5
6	Hal Cole	200	111.587	—	6
7	John Iddings	200	109.177	—	7
8	Johnny Mauro	198	Flagged	Louis Durant	8
9	Kurtis-Kraft Inc.	198	Flagged	—	9
10	Howard Keck Co.	193	Spun	—	10
11	Walter Redmer	192	Flagged	—	11
12	Pat Clancy	190	Flagged	—	12
13	Smith & Jones Co.	185	Flagged	—	13
14	Murrell Belanger	167	Clutch	—	14
15	Palmer Racing	164	Valve	—	15
16	Lou Fageol	161	Steering	—	16
17	Ted Nyquist	138	Fuel leak	Paul Russo, Johnny Shackleford	17
18	Bayard T. Sheffler	132	Plugs	—	18
19	Bowes Racing	129	Fuel leak	—	19
20	Don Lee Division	108	Oil trouble	Ken Fowler, Louis Tomei	20
21	Bayard T. Sheffler	70	Stalled	—	21
22	Murrell Belanger	59	Lost wheel	—	22
23	Ross Page	58	Oil line	—	23
24	Les Anderson	58	Gears	—	24
25	Paul Weirick	42	Disqualified, slow	—	25
26	Robert J. Flavell	34	Clutch	—	26
27	Louis Bromme	27	Oil line	—	27
28	H. C. Henning	24	Drive shaft	—	28
29	Ford Moyer	19	Clutch	—	29
30	John Lorenz	13	Stalled	—	30
31	C. George Tuffanelli	11	Steering	—	31
32	R. A. Cott	7	Oil leak	—	32
33	Gerald Brisko	1	Supercharger	—	33

AR = Alfa Romeo   MAS = Maserati   O = Offenhauser
DUR = Duray   MS = Mercedes   SP = Sparks
FA = Fageol   NO = Novi   WIN = Winfield
M = Miller

1949

FIN	START	QUAL. SPEED	NUMBER, TYPE, CYLINDERS			DRIVER	CAR NAME	CHASSIS	FIN
1	4	128.673	7	O	4	Bill Holland	Blue Crown Spark Plug Spl.	Deidt	1
2	12	132.900	12	O	4	Johnnie Parsons	Kurtis-Kraft Spl.	Kurtis	2
3	6	128.228	22	O	4	George Connor	Blue Crown Spark Plug Spl.	Lesovsky	3
4	13	129.776	2	O	4	Myron Fohr	Marchese Spl.	Marchese	4
5	16	126.863	77	O	4	Joie Chitwood	Wolfe Motor Co. Spl.	KK 2000	5
6	7	128.023	61	O	4	Jimmy Jackson	Howard Keck Spl.	Deidt	6
7	9	127.786	98	O	4	Johnny Mantz	Agajanian Spl.	KK 2000	7
8	19	129.487	19	O	4	Paul Russo	Tuffy's Spl.	KK 2000	8
9	32	126.042	9	O	4	Emil Andres	Tuffy's Spl.	KK 2000	9
10	24	127.756	71	O	4	Norm Houser	Troy Oil Co. Spl.	Langley	10
11	21	126.516	68	O	4	Jim Rathman	Pioneer Auto Repair Spl.	Wetteroth	11
12	18	125.945	64	O	4	Troy Ruttman	Carter Spl.	Wetteroth	12
13	10	127.759	3	O	4	Mauri Rose	Blue Crown Spark Plug Spl.	Deidt	13
14	5	128.233	17	O	4	Duane Carter	Belanger Motors Spl.	Stevens	14
15	15	127.750	29	O	4	Duke Dinsmore	Norm Olson Spl.	Olson	15
16	14	128.260	8	O	4	Mack Hellings	Don Lee Spl.	KK 2000	16
17	22	128.521	4	O	4	Bill Sheffler	Sheffler Spl.	Bromme	17
18	28	126.139	32	O	4	Johnny McDowell	Iddings Spl.	Meyer	18
19	11	127.168	14	O	4	Hal Cole	Grancor Spl.	KK 2000	19
20	25	127.289	38	SP	6	George Fonder	Ray Brady Spl.	Adams	20
21	30	127.191	74	O	4	Bill Cantrell	Kennedy Tank Spl.	Kurtis	21
22	17	128.087	57	O*	4	Jackie Holmes	Pat Clancy Spl.	Kurtis	22
23	20	128.912	6	MAS	8	Lee Wallard	IRC Inc. Spl.	Maserati	23
24	29	129.236	69	O	4	Bayliss Levrett	Wynn's Friction Proofing Oil Spl.	KK 2000	24
25	2	129.552	5	NO	8	Rex Mays	Novi Mobil Spl.	Kurtis	25
26	3	128.884	33	O	4	Jack McGrath	City of Tacoma Spl.	KK 2000	26
27	31	127.007	15	MAS	8	Fred Agabashian	IRC Inc. Spl.	Maserati	27
28	33	125.799	52	O	4	Manuel Ayulo	Sheffler Spl.	Bromme	28
29	1	132.939	54	NO	8	Duke Nalon	Novi Mobil Spl.	Kurtis	29
30	23	127.809	18	O	4	Sam Hanks	Love Machine & Tool Spl.	KK 2000	30
31	27	126.524	10	O	4	Charles Van Acker	Redmer Spl.	Stevens	31
32	8	127.823	26	O	4	George Lynch	Automobile Shippers Spl.	Snowberger	32
33	26	127.002	37	O	4	Spider Webb	Grancor Spl.	Bromme	33

Qualified, did not start: Ralph Pratt, Belanger Motors Spl., #34, O, 125.764, Bumped
Tony Bettenhausen, Flavell Spl., #46, SP, 125.764, Bumped
Doc Williams, Tom Sarafoff Spl., #65, O, 125.161, Bumped
Tony Bettenhausen, Mauro Alfa Romeo Spl., #16, AR, 125.156, Too slow
Bill Cantrell, Fageol's Twin Coach Spl., #36, FA, 125.022, Bumped
Henry Banks, Federal Engineering Detroit Spl., #21, O, 124.939, Bumped
Pat Flaherty, Grancor Spl., #43, MER, 120.846, Bumped
Manny Ayulo, Karl Hall Spl., #73, O, 120.490, Too slow
Henry Banks, Federal Engineering, Detroit Spl., #35, MAS, 94.867, Too slow

Total entries: 65

Qualifying: Minimum of 115 MPH for 4 laps. Fastest 33.

*Six-wheel car

FIN	ENTRANT	LAPS	SPEED, REASON OUT	RELIEF DRIVER	FIN
1	Lou Moore	200	121.327	—	1
2	Kurtis-Kraft, Inc.	200	119.785	—	2
3	Lou Moore	200	119.595	—	3
4	Carl Marchese	200	118.791	—	4
5	Ervin Wolfe	200	118.757	—	5
6	Howard Keck Co.	200	117.870	—	6
7	J. C. Agajanian	200	117.142	—	7
8	Charles Pritchard	200	111.862	—	8
9	Charles Pritchard	197	Flagged	Walt Brown	9
10	Joe Langley	181	Flagged	—	10
11	John Lorenz	175	Flagged	—	11
12	Ray W. Carter	151	Flagged	—	12
13	Lou Moore	192	Magneto	—	13
14	Murrell Belanger	182	Steering	—	14
15	Norm Olson	174	Radius rod	—	15
16	Don Lee Motors	172	Valve	—	16
17	Bill Sheffler	160	Con. rod	—	17
18	Henry Meyer	142	Magneto	—	18
19	Grancor Auto Specialists	117	Rod bearing insert	—	19
20	Ray T. Brady	116	Valve	Mel Hansen	20
21	Leslie M. Anderson	95	Drive shaft	—	21
22	Pat Clancy	65	Drive shaft	—	22
23	Indpls. Race Cars Inc.	55	Gears	—	23
24	Bayliss Levrett	52	Drain plug	—	24
25	W. C. Winfield	48	Engine trouble	—	25
26	Leo Dobry	39	Oil pump	—	26
27	Indpls. Race Cars, Inc.	38	Overheating	—	27
28	Bill Sheffler	24	Con. rod	—	28
29	W. C. Winfield	23	Rear axle	—	29
30	Milt Marion	20	Oil leak	—	30
31	Geneva Van Acker	10	Wreck	—	31
32	Louis Rassey	1	Wreck	—	32
33	Lou & Bruce Bromme	0	Transmission—DNS	—	33

AR = Alfa Romeo   NO = Novi
FA = Fageol   O = Offenhauser
MAS = Maserati   SP = Sparks
MER = Mercury

1950

FIN	START	QUAL. SPEED	NUMBER, TYPE, CYLINDERS			DRIVER	CAR NAME	CHASSIS	FIN
1	5	132.044	1	O	4	Johnnie Parsons	Wynn's Friction Proofing Spl.	Kurtis	1
2	10	130.482	3	O	4	Bill Holland	Blue Crown Spark Plug Spl.	Deidt	2
3	3	132.319	31	O	4	Mauri Rose	Howard Keck Spl.	Deidt	3
4	12	132.910	54	O	4	Cecil Green	John Zink Spl.	KK 3000	4
5	9	130.757	17	O	4	Joie Chitwood	Wolfe Motor Co. Spl.	KK 2000	5
6	23	132.436	8	O	4	Lee Wallard	Blue Crown Spark Plug Spl.	Moore	6
7	1	134.343	98	O	4	Walt Faulkner	Agajanian's Grant Piston Ring Spl.	KK 2000	7
8	4	132.163	5	O	4	George Connor	Blue Crown Spark Plug Spl. Jnr.	Lesovsky	8
9	19	130.790	7	O	4	Paul Russo	Russo-Nichels Spl.	Nichels	9
10	11	129.608	59	O	4	Pat Flaherty	Granatelli-Sabourin Spl.	KK 3000	10
11	16	131.714	2	O	4	Myron Fohr	Bardahl Spl.	Marchese	11
12	13	131.666	18	OS	4	Duane Carter	Belanger Motors Spl.	Stevens	12
13	26	130.687	15	O	4	Mack Hellings	Tuffy's Spl.	KK 2000	13
14	6	131.868	49	O	4	Jack McGrath	Hinkle Spl.	KK 3000	14
15	24	131.912	55	O	4	Troy Ruttman	Bowes Seal Fast Spl.	Lesovsky	15
16	31	129.213	75	O	4	Gene Hartley	Troy Oil Spl.	Langley	16
17	27	130.402	22	O	4	Jimmy Davies	Pat Clancey Spl.	Ewing	17
18	33	129.692	62	O	4	Johnny McDowell	Wales Trucking Spl.	KK 2000	18
19	20	130.454	4	O	4	Walt Brown	Tuffy's Spl.	KK 2000	19
20	14	129.748	21	O	4	Spider Webb	Fadely-Anderson Spl.	Maserati	20
21	15	129.520	81	O	4	Jerry Hoyt	Doc Morris Spl.	KK 2000	21
22	29	129.940	27	OS	4	Walt Ader	Sampson Spl.	Rae	22
23	30	129.697	77	O	4	Jackie Holmes	Norm Olson Spl.	Olson	23
24	28	129.959	76	O	4	Jim Rathmann	Pioneer Auto Repair Spl.	Wetteroth	24
25	21	129.646	12	OS	4	Henry Banks	IRC, Inc. Spl.	Maserati	25
26	22	132.690	67	O	4	Bill Schindler	Auto Shippers Spl.	Snowberger	26
27	17	131.181	24	O	4	Bayliss Levrett	Palmer Spl.	Adams	27
28	2	132.792	28	OS	4	Freddie Agabashian	Wynn's Friction Proofing Spl.	KK 3000	28
29	32	129.208	61	CS	6	Jimmy Jackson	Cummins Diesel Spl.	Kurtis	29
30	25	131.593	23	O	4	Sam Hanks	Merz Engineering Spl.	KK 2000	30
31	8	130.947	14	O	4	Tony Bettenhausen	Blue Crown Spark Plug Spl.	Deidt	31
32	18	130.928	45	O	4	Dick Rathmann	City of Glendale Spl.	Watson	32
33	7	131.066	69	O	4	Duke Dinsmore	Brown Motor Co. Spl.	KK 2000	33

Qualified, did not start: Cliff Griffith, Tom Sarafoff Spl., #66, O, 129.014, Bumped
George Fonder, Ray Brady Spl., #26, SP-S, 127.918, Too slow
Joe James, Esmerelda Spl., #63, O, 127.438, Too slow
Joe James, Bob Estes Lincoln-Mercury Spl., #82, AM, 124.176, Bumped
Chuck Leighton, Cantarano Spl., #79, WC, 121.065, Too slow
Manny Ayulo, Coast Grain Spl., #85, O, 106.000, Too slow

Total entries: 68

Qualifying: Minimum of 115 MPH for 4 laps. Fastest 33.

FIN	ENTRANT	LAPS	SPEED, REASON OUT	RELIEF DRIVER	FIN
1	Kurtis Kraft, Inc.	138	124.002	—	1
2	Lou Moore	137	122.638	—	2
3	Howard Keck Co.	137	121.778	—	3
4	M. A. Walker	137	121.766	—	4
5	Ervin Wolfe	136	121.755	Tony Bettenhausen	5
6	Lou Moore	136	121.009	—	6
7	J. C. Agajanian	135	121.094	—	7
8	Lou Moore	135	121.086	—	8
9	Paul Russo & Ray Nichels	135	119.961	—	9
10	Grancor Automotive Specialists	135	119.952	—	10
11	Carl Marchese	133	Flagged	—	11
12	Murrell Belanger	133	Flagged	—	12
13	Charles Pritchard	132	Flagged	—	13
14	Jack B. Hinkle	131	Spun	—	14
15	Bowes Racing, Inc.	130	Flagged	—	15
16	Joe Langley	128	Flagged	—	16
17	Pat Clancy	128	Flagged	—	17
18	M. Pete Wales	128	Flagged	—	18
19	Charles Pritchard	127	Flagged	—	19
20	R. A. Cott	126	Flagged	—	20
21	Ludson D. Morris, M. D.	125	Flagged	—	21
22	Sampson Manufacturing Co.	123	Flagged	—	22
23	Norm Olsen	123	Spun	—	23
24	John Lorenz	122	Flagged	—	24
25	Indianapolis Race Cars, Inc.	112	Flagged	Freddie Agabashian	25
26	Louis Rassey	111	Universal joint	—	26
27	Richard L. Palmer	108	No oil pressure	Bill Cantrell	27
28	Kurtis-Kraft, Inc.	64	Oil line	—	28
29	Cummins Engine Co.	52	Supercharger	—	29
30	Milt Marion	42	No oil pressure	—	30
31	Lou Moore	30	Wheel bearing	—	31
32	A. J. Watson	25	Stalled	—	32
33	Verlin Brown	10	Oil leak	—	33

AM = Ardun Mercury   O = Offenhauser   SP-S = Sparks
CS = Cummins Diesel   OS = Offenhauser   Supercharged
     Supercharged   Supercharged   WC = Wayne Chevrolet

1951

FIN	START	QUAL. SPEED	NUMBER, TYPE, CYLINDERS			DRIVER	CAR NAME	CHASSIS	FIN
1	2	135.039	99	O	4	Lee Wallard	Belanger Motors Spl.	Kurtis	1
2	7	132.183	83	O	4	Mike Nazaruk	Jim Robbins Spl.	Kurtis	2
3	3	134.303	9	O	4	Jack McGrath	Hinkle Spl.	KK 3000	3
4	31	132.228	57	O	4	Andy Linden	Leitenberger Spl.	Sherman	4
5	29	134.098	52	O	4	Bobby Ball	Blakely Oil Spl.	Schroeder	5
6	17	133.899	1	O	4	Henry Banks	Blue Crown Spark Plug Spl.	Moore	6
7	24	132.890	68	O	4	Carl Forberg	Auto Shippers Spl.	KK 3000	7
8	4	133.749	27	O	4	Duane Carter	Mobilgas Spl.	Deidt	8
9	9	131.950	5	O	4	Tony Bettenhausen	Mobiloil Spl.	Deidt	9
10	1	136.498	18	NS	8	Duke Nalon	Novi Purelube Spl.	Kurtis	10
11	22	133.102	69	O	4	Gene Force	Brown Motor Co. Spl.	KK 2000	11
12	12	132.998	25	O	4	Sam Hanks	Pete Schmidt Spl.	KK 3000	12
13	16	134.033	10	O	4	Bill Schindler	Chapman Spl.	KK 2000	13
14	5	133.422	16	O	4	Mauri Rose	Pennzoil Spl.	Deidt	14
15	14	136.872	2	O	4	Walt Faulkner	Agajanian's Grant Piston Ring Spl.	Kuzma	15
16	27	133.516	76	O	4	Jimmy Davies	Parks Spl.	Pawl	16
17	11	135.029	59	O	4	Freddie Agabashian	Granatelli-Bardahl Spl.	KK 3000	17
18	15	135.614	73	O	4	Carl Scarborough	McNamara Spl.	KK 2000	18
19	33	131.473	71	O	4	Bill Mackey	Karl Hall Spl.	—	19
20	19	133.764	8	O	4	Chuck Stevenson	Bardahl Spl.	Marchese	20
21	8	132.154	3	O	4	Johnnie Parsons	Wynn's Friction Proofing Spl.	KK 3000	21
22	10	131.892	4	O	4	Cecil Green	John Zink Spl.	KK 3000	22
23	6	132.314	98	O	4	Troy Ruttman	Agajanian's Featherweight Spl.	KK 2000	23
24	32	131.974	6	O	4	Duke Dinsmore	Brown Motor Co. Spl.	Schroeder	24
25	28	135.798	32	NS	8	Chet Miller	Novi Purelube Spl.	Kurtis	25
26	13	131.907	44	O	4	Walt Brown	Federal Engineering, Detroit Spl.	KK 3000	26
27	25	134.867	48	O	4	Rodger Ward	Deck Manufacturing Spl.	Bromme	27
28	18	133.839	23	O	4	Cliff Griffith	Doc Morris Spl.	KK 2000	28
29	20	133.725	81	O	4	Bill Vukovich	Central Excavating Spl.	Trevis	29
30	21	133.353	22	O	4	George Connor	Blue Crown Spark Plug Spl.	Lesovsky	30
31	23	132.925	19	O	4	Mack Hellings	Tuffanelli-Derrico Spl.	Deidt	31
32	26	132.475	12	OS	4	Johnny McDowell	W. & J. Spl.	Maserati	32
33	30	134.098	26	O	4	Joe James	Bob Estes Spl.	Watson	33

Qualified, did not start: Bob Sweikert, Marion Engineering Spl., #37, O, 131.224, Bumped
Manny Ayulo, Coast Grain Spl., #31, O, 131.128, Too slow
Frank Armi, Bardahl Spl., #64, DUR, 130.842, Bumped
Jackie Holmes, Palmer Spl., #24, O, 129.259, Too slow
Bayliss Levrett, Safety Seal Spl., #46, O, 128.329, Bumped
George Fonder, Lutes Truck Parts Spl., #53, O, 128.242, Too slow
Jerry Hoyt, Pat Clancy Spl., #14, O, 127.700, Too slow
Jimmy Bryan, Viking Trailer Spl., #72, O, 124.176, Bumped
Paul Russo, Kennedy Tank Spl., #7, O, 121.914, Too slow

Total entries: 72

Qualifying: Minimum 115 MPH for 4 laps. Fastest 33.

FIN	ENTRANT	LAPS	SPEED, REASON OUT	RELIEF DRIVER	FIN
1	Murrell Belanger	200	126.244	—	1
2	J. M. Robbins	200	125.302	—	2
3	Jack B. Hinkle	200	124.745	Manny Ayulo	3
4	George H. Leitenberger	200	123.812	—	4
5	John L. McDaniel	200	123.709	—	5
6	Lindsey Hopkins	200	123.304	—	6
7	Louis Rassey	193	Flagged	—	7
8	Rotary Engineering Corp.	180	Flagged	—	8
9	Rotary Engineering Corp.	178	Spun	—	9
10	Jean Marcenac	151	Stalled	—	10
11	Brown Motor Co.	142	No oil pressure	—	11
12	Peter Schmidt	135	Spun	—	12
13	H. A. Chapman	129	Con. rod	—	13
14	Howard Keck Co.	126	Broke wheel, wreck	—	14
15	J. C. Agajanian	123	Crankshaft	—	15
16	L. E. Parks	110	Rear end gears	—	16
17	Grancor Automotive Specialists	109	Clutch	—	17
18	Lee Elkins	100	Axle	—	18
19	Karl Hall	97	Clutch shaft	—	19
20	Carl Marchese	93	Caught fire	—	20
21	Ed Walsh	87	Magneto	—	21
22	M. A. Walker	80	Con. rod	—	22
23	J. C. Agajanian	78	Bearing	—	23
24	Brown Motor Co.	73	Overheating	—	24
25	Jean Marcenac	56	Ignition	—	25
26	Federal Automotive Associates	55	Magneto	—	26
27	Louis & Bruce Bromme	34	Oil line	—	27
28	Ludson D. Morris, M.D.	30	Axle	—	28
29	Pete Salemi	29	Oil tank	—	29
30	Lou Bromme	29	Universal joint	—	30
31	George Tuffanelli & Jimmy Derrico	18	Piston	—	31
32	Maserati Race Cars	15	Gas tank	—	32
33	Bob Estes	8	Drive shaft	—	33

DUR = Duray
NS = Novi Supercharged
O = Offenhauser
OS = Offenhauser
     Supercharged

1952

FIN	START	QUAL. SPEED	NUMBER, TYPE, CYLINDERS			DRIVER	CAR NAME	CHASSIS	FIN
1	7	135.364	98	O	4	Troy Ruttman	Agajanian Spl.	Kuzma	1
2	10	136.343	59	O	4	Jim Rathmann	Grancor-Wynn Oil Spl.	KK 3000	2
3	5	135.736	18	O	4	Sam Hanks	Bardahl Spl.	KK 3000	3
4	6	135.522	1	O	4	Duane Carter	Belanger Motors Spl.	Lesovsky	4
5	20	134.288	33	O	4	Art Cross	Bowes Seal Fast Spl.	KK 4000	5
6	21	134.142	77	O	4	Jimmy Bryan	Pete Schmidt Spl.	KK 3000	6
7	23	133.993	37	O	4	Jimmy Reece	John Zink Spl.	KK 4000	7
8	14	135.609	54	O	4	George Connor	Federal Engineering, Detroit Spl.	KK 3000	8
9	9	136.617	22	O	4	Cliff Griffith	Tom Sarafoff Spl.	KK 2000	9
10	31	135.328	5	O	4	Johnnie Parsons	Jim Robbins Spl.	Kurtis	10
11	3	136.664	4	O	4	Jack McGrath	Hinkle Spl.	KK 3000	11
12	26	133.904	29	O	4	Jim Rigsby	Bob Estes Spl.	Watson	12
13	16	134.953	14	O	4	Joe James	Bardahl Spl.	KK 4000	13
14	15	134.988	7	O	4	Bill Schindler	Chapman Spl.	Stephens	14
15	13	135.947	65	O	4	George Fonder	Leitenberger Spl.	Sherman	15
16	24	133.973	81	O	4	Eddie Johnson	Central Excavating Spl.	Trevis	16
17	8	138.212	26	O	4	Bill Vukovich	Fuel Injection Engineering Spl.	KK 500A	17
18	11	136.142	16	O	4	Chuck Stevenson	Springfield Welding's Clay Smith Spl.	KK 4000	18
19	12	135.962	2	O	4	Henry Banks	Blue Crown Spark Plug Spl.	Lesovsky	19
20	28	135.982	8	O	4	Manny Ayulo	Coast Grain Spl.	Lesovsky	20
21	33	133.939	31	O	4	Johnny McDowell	McDowell Spl.	Kurtis	21
22	29	135.962	48	O	4	Spider Webb	Granatelli Racing Enterprises Spl.	Bromme	22
23	22	134.139	34	O	4	Rodger Ward	Federal Engineering, Detroit Spl.	KK 4000	23
24	30	135.384	27	O	4	Tony Bettenhausen	Blue Crown Spark Plug Spl.	Deidt	24
25	4	136.188	36	NS	8	Duke Nalon	Novi Pure Oil Spl.	Kurtis	25
26	32	134.983	73	O	4	Bob Sweikert	McNamara Spl.	KK 2000	26
27	1	138.010	28	CS	6	Freddie Agabashian	Cummins Diesel Spl.	Kurtis	27
28	18	134.343	67	O	4	Gene Hartley	Mel-Rae Spl.	KK 4000	28
29	25	133.953	93	O	4	Bob Scott	Doc Morris Spl.	KK 2000	29
30	27	139.034	21	NS	8	Chet Miller	Novi Pure Oil Spl.	Kurtis	30
31	19	134.308	12	F	12	Alberto Ascari, Italy	Ferrari Spl.	Ferrari	31
32	17	134.725	55	O	4	Bobby Ball	Ansted-Rotary Spl.	Stevens	32
33	2	137.002	9	OS	4	Andy Linden	Miracle Power Spl.	KK 4000	33

Qualified, did not start: Mike Nazaruk, John Zink Spl., #66, O, 133.844, Bumped
Jimmy Jackson, Auto Shippers Spl., #61, O, 133.824, Bumped
Gene Force, Brown Motor Co. Spl., #96, O, 133.789, Too slow
George Tichenor, Peter Schmidt Spl., #88, O, 133.427, Bumped
Spider Webb, Blue Crown Spark Plug Spl., #51, O, 132.660, Bumped
Bob Sweikert, Pat Clancy Spl., #52, O, 132.553, Bumped

Total entries: 71

Qualifying: Fastest 33 over 4 laps.

FIN	ENTRANT	LAPS	SPEED, REASON OUT	RELIEF DRIVER	FIN
1	J. C. Agajanian	200	128.922	—	1
2	Grancor Automotive Specialists	200	126.723	—	2
3	Ed. Walsh	200	125.580	—	3
4	Murrell Belanger	200	125.259	—	4
5	Ray T. Brandy	200	124.292	—	5
6	Peter Schmidt	200	123.914	—	6
7	John Zink	200	123.312	—	7
8	Federal Automotive Associates	200	122.595	—	8
9	Tom Sarafoff	200	122.402	—	9
10	J. M. Robbins	200	121.789	—	10
11	Jack B. Hinkle	200	121.428	—	11
12	Bob Estes	200	120.587	—	12
13	Ed Walsh	200	120.108	—	13
14	H. A. Chapman	200	119.280	—	14
15	George H. Leitenberger	197	Flagged	—	15
16	Pete Salemi	193	Flagged	—	16
17	Howard Keck Co.	191	Steering pin broke, hit wall	—	17
18	Bessie Lee Paoli	187	Flagged	—	18
19	Lindsey Hopkins	184	Flagged	—	19
20	Coast Grain Co.	184	Flagged	—	20
21	Roger G. Wolcott	182	Flagged	—	21
22	Vincent Granatelli	162	Oil leak	—	22
23	Federal Automotive Associates	130	Oil pressure	—	23
24	Earl F. Slick	93	Starter	—	24
25	Lewis W. Welch	84	Supercharger shaft	—	25
26	Lee Elkins	77	Differential	—	26
27	Cummins Engine Co.	71	Supercharger	—	27
28	Mel B. Wiggers	65	Exhaust pipe	—	28
29	Ludson D. Morris, M.D.	49	Drive shaft	—	29
30	Lewis W. Welch	41	Supercharger shaft	—	30
31	Enzo Ferrari	40	Wheel broke, spun	—	31
32	Rotary Engineering Corp.	34	Gear case	—	32
33	Hart Fullerton	20	Oil leak	—	33

CS = Cummins Diesel   O = Offenhauser
    Supercharged   OS = Offenhauser
F = Ferrari   Supercharged
NS = Novi Supercharged

1953

FIN	START	QUAL. SPEED	NUMBER, TYPE, CYLINDERS			DRIVER	CAR NAME	CHASSIS	FIN
1	1	138.392	14	O	4	Bill Vukovich	Fuel Injection Engineering Spl.	KK 500A	1
2	12	137.310	16	O	4	Art Cross	Springfield Welding's Clay Smith Spl.	KK 4000	2
3	9	137.531	3	O	4	Sam Hanks	Bardahl Spl.	KK 4000	3
4	2	137.546	59	O	4	Freddie Agabashian	Grancor-Elgin Piston Pin Spl.	KK 500B	4
5	3	136.602	5	O	4	Jack McGrath	Hinkle Spl.	KK 4000	5
6	21	135.747	48	O	4	Jimmy Daywalt	Sumar Spl.	KK 3000	6
7	25	135.666	2	O	4	Jim Rathmann	Travelon Trailer Spl.	KK 500B	7
8	20	135.926	12	O	4	Ernie McCoy	Chapman Spl.	Stevens	8
9	6	136.024	98	O	4	Tony Bettenhausen	Agajanian Spl.	Kuzma	9
10	32	135.262	53	O	4	Jimmy Davies	Pat Clancy Spl.	KK 500B	10
11	26	135.461	9	NS	8	Duke Nalon	Novi Governor Spl.	Kurtis	11
12	19	135.936	73	O	4	Carl Scarborough	McNamara Spl.	KK 2000	12
13	4	136.384	88	O	4	Manny Ayulo	Pete Schmidt Spl.	Kuzma	13
14	31	135.506	8	O	4	Jimmy Bryan	Blakely Oil Spl.	Schroeder	14
15	28	137.868	49	O	4	Bill Holland	Crawford Spl.	KK 500B	15
16	10	137.468	92	O	4	Rodger Ward	M. A. Walker Electric Spl.	Kurtis	16
17	14	137.117	23	O	4	Walt Faulkner	Auto Shippers Spl.	KK 500A	17
18	22	135.721	22	O	4	Marshall Teague	Hart Fullerton Spl.	KK 4000	18
19	18	136.168	62	O	4	Spider Webb	Lubri-Loy Spl.	KK 3000	19
20	29	136.872	51	O	4	Bob Sweikert	Dean Van Lines Spl.	Kuzma	20
21	23	135.706	83	O	4	Mike Nazaruk	Kalamazoo Spl.	Turner	21
22	24	135.668	77	O	4	Pat Flaherty	Pete Schmidt Spl.	KK 3000	22
23	7	135.731	55	O	4	Jerry Hoyt	John Zink Spl.	KK 4000	23
24	27	135.267	4	O	4	Duane Carter	Belanger's Miracle Power Spl.	Lesovsky	24
25	17	136.219	7	O	4	Paul Russo	Federal Engineering, Detroit Spl.	KK 3000	25
26	8	137.667	21	O	4	Johnnie Parsons	Belond Equaflow Exhaust Spl.	KK 500B	26
27	15	136.867	38	O	4	Don Freeland	Bob Estes Spl.	Watson	27
28	13	137.263	41	O	4	Gene Hartley	Federal Engineering, Detroit Spl.	KK 4000	28
29	16	136.560	97	O	4	Chuck Stevenson	Agajanian Spl.	Kuzma	29
30	30	136.096	99	O	4	Cal Niday	Belanger's Miracle Power Spl.	Kurtis	30
31	11	137.431	29	O	4	Bob Scott	Belond Equaflow Exhaust Spl.	Bromme	31
32	33	135.262	56	O	4	Johnny Thomson	Doc Sabourin Spl.	Del Roy	32
33	5	136.060	32	O	4	Andy Linden	Cop-Sil-Loy Brake Spl.	Stevens	33

Qualified, did not start: Eddie Johnson, City of Detroit Spl., #26, O, 135.237, Bumped
Cal Niday, Storey-Ricketts Spl., #78, O, 134.927, Bumped
Johnnie Tolan, Blakely Oil Spl., #85, O, 134.852, Too slow
Potsy Goacher, Sid Street Motor Co. Spl., #36, O, 134.620, Bumped
Bill Holland, Slick Racers, Inc. Spl., #61, O, 134.439, Bumped
Pat O'Connor, Brown Motor Co. Spl., #74, O, 134.363, Bumped
Pat O'Connor, Engle & Stanko Spl., #64, O, 133.571, Too slow
Len Duncan, Caccia Motors Spl., #31, O, 133.487, Bumped

FIN	ENTRANT	LAPS	SPEED, REASON OUT	RELIEF DRIVER	FIN
1	Howard Keck Co.	200	128.740	—	1
2	Bessie Lee Paoli	200	126.827	—	2
3	Ed Walsh	200	126.465	Duane Carter	3
4	Grancor Automotive Specialists	200	126.219	Paul Russo	4
5	Jack B. Hinkle	200	124.556	—	5
6	Chapman S. Root	200	124.379	—	6
7	Ernest L. Ruiz	200	124.072	Eddie Johnson	7
8	H. A. Chapman	200	123.404	—	8
9	J. C. Agajanian	196	Wreck	Chuck Stevenson, Gene Hartley	9
10	Pat Clancy	193	Flagged	—	10
11	Jean Marcenac	191	Spun	—	11
12	Lee Elkins	190	Flagged	Bob Scott	12
13	Peter Schmidt	184	Con. rod	—	13
14	John L. McDaniel	183	Flagged	—	14
15	Ray Crawford	177	Cam gear	Jim Rathman	15
16	M. A. Walker	177	Stalled	Andy Linden, Duke Dinsmore	16
17	Eugene A. Casaroll	176	Flagged	Johnny Mantz	17
18	Hart Fullerton	169	Oil leak	—	18
19	3-L Racing Team	166	Oil leak	Johnny Thomson, Jackie Holmes	19
20	A. E. Dean	151	Radius rod	—	20
21	Lee Elkins	146	Stalled	—	21
22	Peter Schmidt	115	Wreck	—	22
23	John Zink	107	Overheating	Andy Linden, Chuck Stevenson	23
24	Murrell Belanger	94	Ignition	—	24
25	Federal Automotive Associates	89	Magneto	—	25
26	J. S. Belond	86	Crankshaft	—	26
27	Bob Estes	76	Wreck	—	27
28	Federal Automotive Associates	53	Wreck	—	28
29	J. C. Agajanian	42	Fuel leak	—	29
30	Murrell Belanger	30	Magneto	—	30
31	Louis & Bruce Bromme	14	Oil leak	—	31
32	Dr. Ray N. Sabourin	6	Ignition	—	32
33	Rotary Engineering Corp.	3	Wreck	—	33

George Fonder, Leitenberger Spl., #76, O, 133.457, Too slow
Joe Barzda, California Speed & Sport Shop Spl., #69, MAS, 121.918, Bumped

MAS = Maserati
NS = Novi Supercharged
O = Offenhauser

Total entries: 82

Qualifying: Fastest 33 over 4 laps.

1954

FIN	START	QUAL. SPEED	NUMBER, TYPE, CYLINDERS			DRIVER	CAR NAME	CHASSIS	FIN
1	19	138.478	14	O	4	Bill Vukovich	Fuel Injection Engineering Spl.	KK 500A	1
2	3	139.665	9	O	4	Jimmy Bryan	Dean Van Lines Spl.	Kuzma	2
3	1	141.033	2	O	4	Jack McGrath	Hinkle Spl.	KK 500C	3
4	11	137.736	34	O	4	Troy Ruttman	Auto Shippers Spl.	KK 500A	4
5	14	139.589	73	O	4	Mike Nazaruk	McNamara Spl.	KK 500C	5
6	24	137.746	77	O	4	Freddie Agabashian	Merz Engineering Spl.	KK 500C	6
7	6	138.339	7	O	4	Don Freeland	Bob Estes Spl.	Phillips	7
8	32	137.678	5	O	4	Paul Russo	Ansted Rotary Engineering Spl.	KK 500A	8
9	25	139.557	28	O	4	Larry Crockett	Federal Engineering, Detroit Spl.	KK 3000	9
10	13	139.828	24	O	4	Cal Niday	Jim Robbins Spl.	Stevens	10
11	27	138.675	45	O	4	Art Cross	Bardahl Spl.	KK 4000	11
12	5	138.776	98	O	4	Chuck Stevenson	Agajanian Spl.	Kuzma	12
13	22	138.164	88	O	4	Manny Ayulo	Pete Schmidt Spl.	Kuzma	13
14	9	138.206	17	O	4	Bob Sweikert	Lutes Truck Parts Spl.	KK 4000	14
15	8	138.238	16	O	4	Duane Carter	Auto Shippers Spl.	KK 4000	15
16	20	138.419	32	O	4	Ernie McCoy	Crawford Spl.	KK 500B	16
17	7	138.312	25	O	4	Jimmy Reece	Malloy Spl.	Pankratz	17
18	31	137.794	27	O	4	Ed Elisian	Chapman Spl.	Stevens	18
19	33	137.673	71	O	4	Frank Armi	Martin Bros. Spl.	Curtis	19
20	10	137.994	1	O	4	Sam Hanks	Bardahl Spl.	KK 4000	20
21	12	138.084	35	O	4	Pat O'Connor	Hopkins Spl.	KK 500C	21
22	16	139.297	12	O	4	Rodger Ward	Doc Sabourin Spl.	Pawl	22
23	17	139.061	31	O	4	Gene Hartley	John Zink Spl.	KK 4000	23
24	4	138.787	43	O	4	Johnny Thompson	Chapman Spl.	Nichels	24
25	23	137.820	74	O	4	Andy Linden	Brown Motor Co. Spl.	Schroeder	25
26	30	137.825	99	O	4	Jerry Hoyt	Belanger Motors Spl.	Kurtis	26
27	2	139.789	19	O	4	Jimmy Daywalt	Sumar Spl.	KK 500C	27
28	28	138.228	38	O	4	Jim Rathmann	Bardahl Spl.	KK 500C	28
29	21	138.275	10	O	4	Tony Bettenhausen	Mel Wiggers Spl.	KK 500C	29
30	29	137.979	65	O	4	Spider Webb	Advance Muffler Spl.	Bromme	30
31	26	139.217	33	O	4	Len Duncan	Ray Brady Spl.	Schroeder	31
32	15	139.578	15	O	4	Johnnie Parsons	Belond Equaflow Exhaust Spl.	KK 500C	32
33	18	138.948	51	O	4	Bill Homeier	Jones & Maley Spl.	KK 500C	33

Qualified, did not start: Eddie Johnson, McNamara Spl., #83, O, 137.599, Bumped
Jimmy Davies, Pat Clancy Spl., #53, O, 137.583, Bumped
Marshall Teague, Hart Fullerton Spl., #3, O, 137.552, Bumped
Bob Scott, Travelon Trailer Spl., #21, O, 137.504, Bumped
Art Cross, Springfield Welding Clay Smith Spl., #6, O, 137.362, Bumped
Danny Oakes, Micro-Nut Spl., #49, O, 137.237, Bumped
Jim Rathmann, Grancor-Elgin Piston Pin Spl., #59, O, 137.132, Bumped
Duke Dinsmore, Commercial Motor Freight Spl., #62, O, 137.096, Too slow
Walt Faulkner, Pete Schmidt Spl., #44, O, 137.065, Bumped
Ed Elisian, Wales Trucking Spl., #68, O, 136.581, Bumped
Duke Nalon, Novi Governor Spl., #8, NS, 136.395, Bumped

Total entries: 65

Qualifying: Fastest 33 over 4 laps.

FIN	ENTRANT	LAPS	SPEED, REASON OUT	RELIEF DRIVER	FIN
1	Howard Keck Co.	200	130.840	—	1
2	A. E. Dean	200	130.178	—	2
3	Jack B. Hinkle	200	130.086	—	3
4	Eugene A. Casaroll	200	129.218	Duane Carter	4
5	Lee Elkins	200	128.923	—	5
6	Miklos Sperling	200	128.711	—	6
7	Bob Estes	200	128.474	—	7
8	Hoosier Race Team, Inc.	200	128.037	Jerry Hoyt	8
9	Federal Automotive Associates	200	126.899	—	9
10	Jim Robbins Co.	200	126.895	—	10
11	Ed Walsh	200	126.232	Johnnie Parsons, Sam Hanks, Andy Linden, Jimmy Davies	11
12	J. C. Agajanian	199	Flagged	Walt Faulkner	12
13	Peter Schmidt	197	Flagged	—	13
14	Francis Bardazon	197	Flagged	—	14
15	Eugene A. Casaroll	196	Flagged	Jimmy Jackson, Marshall Teague, Tony Bettenhausen	15
16	Ray Crawford	194	Flagged	—	16
17	Emmett J. Malloy	194	Flagged	—	17
18	H. A. Chapman	193	Flagged	Bob Scott	18
19	T. W. & W. T. Martin	193	Flagged	George Fonder	19
20	Ed Walsh	191	Broke crankshaft, spun	Jimmy Davies, Jim Rathmann	20
21	Motor Racers, Inc.	181	Spun	—	21
22	Dr. Ray N. Sabourin	172	Stalled	Eddie Johnson	22
23	John S. Zink	168	Engine trouble	Marshall Teague	23
24	H. A. Chapman	165	Stalled	Andy Linden, Bill Homeier	24
25	Brown Motor Co.	165	Torsion bar	Bob Scott	25
26	Murrell Belanger	130	Engine trouble	—	26
27	Chapman S. Root	111	Wreck	—	27
28	Ed Walsh	110	Wreck	Pat Flaherty	28
29	Mel B. Wiggers	105	Con. rod bearing	—	29
30	Bruce Bromme	104	Oil leak	Danny Kladis	30
31	Ray T. Brady	101	Brakes	George Fonder	31
32	So. Calif. Muffler Corp.	79	Stalled	—	32
33	Cars, Inc.	74	Pit accident	—	33

NS = Novi Supercharged
O = Offenhauser

1955

FIN	START	QUAL. SPEED	NUMBER, TYPE, CYLINDERS			DRIVER	CAR NAME	CHASSIS	FIN
1	14	139.996	6	O	4	Bob Sweikert	John Zink Spl.	KK 500C	1
2	2	139.985	10	O	4	Tony Bettenhausen	Chapman Spl.	KK 500C	2
3	10	140.274	15	O	4	Jimmy Davies	Bardahl Spl.	KK 500B	3
4	33	134.113	44	O	4	Johnny Thomson	Pete Schmidt Spl.	Kuzma	4
5	7	139.762	77	O	4	Walt Faulkner	Merz Engineering Spl.	KK 500C	5
6	8	139.098	19	O	4	Andy Linden	Massaglia Spl.	KK 4000	6
7	16	139.811	71	O	4	Al Herman	Martin Bros Spl.	Kurtis	7
8	19	139.195	29	O	4	Pat O'Connor	Ansted–Rotary Spl.	KK 500D	8
9	17	139.416	48	O	4	Jimmy Daywalt	Sumar Spl.	Kurtis	9
10	12	140.149	89	O	4	Pat Flaherty	Dunn Engineering Spl.	KK 500B	10
11	18	139.330	98	O	4	Duane Carter	Agajanian Spl.	Kuzma	11
12	25	138.063	41	O	4	Chuck Weyant	Federal Engineering, Detroit Spl.	KK 3000	12
13	32	134.449	83	O	4	Eddie Johnson	McNamara Spl.	Trevis	13
14	20	138.707	33	O	4	Jim Rathmann	Belond Miracle Power Spl.	Epperly	14
15	21	139.866	12	O	4	Don Freeland	Bob Estes Spl.	Phillips	15
16	9	140.302	22	O	4	Cal Niday	D. A. Lubricant Spl.	KK 500B	16
17	24	138.750	99	O	4	Art Cross	Belanger Motors Spl.	KK 500C	17
18	31	135.014	81	O	4	Shorty Templeman	Central Excavating Spl.	Trevis	18
19	6	140.187	8	O	4	Sam Hanks	Jones & Maley Spl.	KK 500C	19
20	28	136.049	31	O	4	Keith Andrews	McDaniel Spl.	Schroeder	20
21	27	136.809	16	O	4	Johnnie Parsons	Trio Brass Foundry Spl.	KK 500C	21
22	13	140.116	37	O	4	Eddie Russo	Doc Sabourin Spl.	Pawl	22
23	23	139.206	49	O	4	Ray Crawford	Crawford Spl.	KK 500B	23
24	11	140.160	1	O	4	Jimmy Bryan	Dean Van Lines Spl.	Kuzma	24
25	5	141.071	4	O	4	Bill Vukovich	Hopkins Spl.	KK 500C	25
26	3	142.580	3	O	4	Jack McGrath	Hinkle Spl.	KK 500C	26
27	22	139.551	42	O	4	Al Keller	Sam Traylor Spl.	KK 2000	27
28	30	135.049	27	O	4	Rodger Ward	Aristo Blue Spl.	Kuzma	28
29	26	136.981	39	O	4	Johnny Boyd	Sumar Spl.	KK 500D	29
30	29	135.333	68	O	4	Ed Elisian	Westwood Tool & Gauge Spl.	KK 4000	30
31	1	140.045	23	O	4	Jerry Hoyt	Jim Robbins Spl.	Stevens	31
32	4	141.933	14	O	4	Freddie Agabashian	Federal Engineering, Detroit Spl.	KK 500C	32
33	15	139.991	5	O	4	Jimmy Reece	Malloy Spl.	Pankratz	33

Qualified, did not start: Len Duncan, Ray Brady Spl., #24, O, 133.245, Bumped
Ernie McCoy, La Villa Spl., #69, O, 133.038, Bumped
Johnny Kay, Leitenberger Spl., #76, O, 132.193, Bumped
Russ Klar, Ray Brady Spl., #61, O, 131.301, Bumped

Total entries: 58

Qualifying: Fastest 33 over 4 laps.

FIN	ENTRANT	LAPS	SPEED, REASON OUT	RELIEF DRIVER	FIN
1	John Zink Co.	200	128.209	—	1
2	H. A. Chapman	200	126.733	Paul Russo	2
3	Pat Clancy	200	126.299	—	3
4	Peter Schmidt	200	126.241	—	4
5	Merz Engineering, Inc.	200	125.377	Bill Homeier	5
6	Joseph Massaglia, Jr.	200	125.022	—	6
7	T. W. & W. T. Martin	200	124.794	—	7
8	Rotary Engine Corp.	200	124.644	—	8
9	Chapman S. Root	200	124.401	—	9
10	Harry Dunn	200	124.086	—	10
11	J. C. Agajanian	197	Flagged	—	11
12	Federal Automotive Associates	196	Flagged	—	12
13	Kalamazoo Sports, Inc.	196	Flagged	—	13
14	Southern Calif. Muffler Corp.	191	Flagged	—	14
15	Bob Estes	178	Transmission	—	15
16	Racing Associates	170	Wreck	—	16
17	Murrell Belanger	168	Con. rod cap.	—	17
18	Pete Salemi	142	Stalled	—	18
19	Cars, Inc.	134	Transmission	—	19
20	John L. McDaniel	120	Ignition	—	20
21	Carl L. Anderson	119	Magneto	—	21
22	Dr. Ray N. Sabourin	112	Ignition	—	22
23	Ray Crawford	111	Valve	—	23
24	A. E. Dean	90	Fuel pump	—	24
25	Lindsey Hopkins	56	Wreck	—	25
26	Jack B. Hinkle	54	Magneto	—	26
27	Samuel W. Traylor III	54	Wreck	—	27
28	E. R. Casale	53	Wreck	—	28
29	Chapman S. Root	53	Wreck	—	29
30	M. Pete Wales	53	Stopped at wreck	—	30
31	Jim Robbins	40	Oil leak	—	31
32	Federal Automotive Associates	39	Spun	—	32
33	Emmett J. Malloy	10	Con. rod	—	33

O = Offenhauser

1956

FIN	START	QUAL. SPEED	NUMBER, TYPE, CYLINDERS			DRIVER	CAR NAME	CHASSIS	FIN
1	1	145.596	8	O	4	Pat Flaherty	John Zink Spl.	Watson	1
2	13	142.051	4	O	4	Sam Hanks	Jones & Maley Spl.	KK 500C	2
3	26	141.699	16	O	4	Don Freeland	Bob Estes Spl.	Phillips	3
4	6	144.144	98	O	4	Johnnie Parsons	Agajanian Spl.	Kuzma	4
5	4	144.471	73	O	4	Dick Rathmann	McNamara Spl.	KK 500C	5
6	10	143.033	1	O	4	Bob Sweikert	D-A Lubricant Spl.	Kuzma	6
7	23	142.535	14	O	4	Bob Veith	Federal Engineering, Detroit Spl.	KK 500C	7
8	15	141.171	19	O	4	Rodger Ward	Filter Queen Spl.	KK 500C	8
9	21	142.885	26	O	4	Jimmy Reece	Massaglia Hotels Spl.	Lesovsky	9
10	30	141.471	27	O	4	Cliff Griffith	Jim Robbins Spl.	Stevens	10
11	22	142.846	82	O	4	Gene Hartley	Central Excavating Spl.	Kuzma	11
12	7	144.069	42	O	4	Freddie Agabashian	Federal Engineering, Detroit Spl.	KK 500C	12
13	25	142.236	57	O	4	Bob Christie	Helse Spl.	KK 500D	13
14	28	141.193	55	O	4	Al Keller	Sam Traylor Spl.	KK 4000	14
15	32	139.093	81	O	4	Eddie Johnson	Central Excavation Spl.	Kuzma	15
16	29	140.559	41	O	4	Billy Garrett	Greenman-Casale Spl.	Kuzma	16
17	33	138.530	64	O	4	Duke Dinsmore	Shannon's Spl.	KK 500A	17
18	3	144.980	7	O	4	Pat O'Connor	Ansted Rotary Spl.	KK 500D	18
19	19	143.741	2	O	4	Jimmy Bryan	Dean Van Lines Spl.	Kuzma	19
20	2	145.120	24	O	4	Jim Rathmann	Hopkins Spl.	KK 500C	20
21	31	140.061	34	O	4	Johnny Tolan	Trio Brass Foundry Spl.	KK 500C	21
22	5	144.602	99	O	4	Tony Bettenhausen	Belanger Motors Spl.	KK 500C	22
23	14	141.382	10	O	4	Ed Elisian	Hoyt Machine Spl.	KK 500C	23
24	16	140.977	48	O	4	Jimmy Daywalt	Sumar Spl.	KK 500D	24
25	24	142.394	54	O	4	Jack Turner	Travelon Trailer Spl.	KK 500B	25
26	20	142.976	89	O	4	Keith Andrews	Dunn Engineering Spl.	KK 500B	26
27	9	143.056	5	O	4	Andy Linden	Chapman Spl.	KK 500C	27
28	27	141.610	12	O	4	Al Herman	Bardahl Spl.	KK 500B	28
29	17	140.884	49	O	4	Ray Crawford	Crawford Spl.	KK 500B	29
30	12	142.337	15	O	4	Johnny Boyd	Bowes Seal Fast Spl.	KK 500E	30
31	11	142.484	53	O	4	Troy Ruttman	John Zink Spl.	KK 500C	31
32	18	145.549	88	O	4	Johnny Thomson	Pete Schmidt Spl.	Kuzma	32
33	8	143.546	29	NS	8	Paul Russo	Novi Vespa Spl.	Kurtis	33

Qualified, did not start: Eddie Sachs, Ray Brady Spl., #58, O, 137.373, Bumped

Total entries: 59

Qualifying: Fastest 33 over 4 laps.

FIN	ENTRANT	LAPS	SPEED, REASON OUT	RELIEF DRIVER	FIN
1	John Zink Co.	200	128.490	—	1
2	Cars, Inc.	200	128.303	—	2
3	Bob Estes	200	127.668	—	3
4	J. C. Agajanian	200	126.631	—	4
5	Kalamazoo Sports, Inc.	200	126.133	—	5
6	Racing Associates	200	125.489	—	6
7	Federal Automotive Associates	200	125.048	—	7
8	Ed Walsh	200	124.990	—	8
9	Joseph Massaglia, Jr.	200	124.938	—	9
10	Jim Robbins	199	Flagged	—	10
11	Pete Salemi	196	Flagged	—	11
12	Federal Automotive Associates	196	Flagged	—	12
13	H. H. Johnson	196	Flagged	—	13
14	Samuel W. Traylor III	195	Flagged	—	14
15	Pete Salemi	195	Flagged	—	15
16	E. R. Casale	194	Flagged	—	16
17	Shannon Bros.	191	Flagged	—	17
18	Ansted Rotary Corp.	187	Flagged	—	18
19	Dean Van Lines, Race Division	185	Flagged	—	19
20	Lindsey Hopkins	175	Oil trouble	—	20
21	Carl L. Anderson	173	Flagged	—	21
22	Murrell Belanger	160	Wrecked	—	22
23	Fred Sommer	160	Stalled	Eddie Russo	23
24	Chapman S. Root	134	Wrecked	—	24
25	Ernest L. Ruiz	131	Engine trouble	—	25
26	Harry Dunn	94	Spun	—	26
27	H. A. Chapman	90	Oil leak	—	27
28	Pat Clancy	74	Wreck	—	28
29	Ray Crawford	49	Wreck	—	29
30	George Bignotti	35	Engine trouble	—	30
31	John S. Zink	22	Spun	—	31
32	Peter Schmidt	22	Spun	—	32
33	Novi Racing Corp., Inc.	21	Wreck	—	33

NS = Novi Supercharged
O = Offenhauser

1957

FIN	START	QUAL. SPEED	NUMBER, TYPE, CYLINDERS			DRIVER	CAR NAME	CHASSIS	FIN
1	13	142.812	9	O	4	Sam Hanks	Belond Exhaust Spl.	Epperly	1
2	32	139.806	26	O	4	Jim Rathmann	Chiropractic Spl.	Epperly	2
3	15	141.188	1	O	4	Jimmy Bryan	Dean Van Lines Spl.	Kuzma	3
4	10	144.817	54	NS	8	Paul Russo	Novi Automotive Air Cond. Spl.	Kurtis	4
5	12	143.244	73	O	4	Andy Linden	McNamara–Veedol Spl.	KK 500G	5
6	5	142.102	6	O	4	Johnny Boyd	Bowes Seal Fast Spl.	KK 500G	6
7	28	140.329	48	O	4	Marshall Teague	Sumar Spl.	KK 500D	7
8	1	143.948	12	O	4	Pat O'Connor	Sumar Spl.	KK 500G	8
9	16	141.016	7	O	4	Bob Veith	Bob Estes Spl.	Phillips	9
10	14	141.271	22	O	4	Gene Hartley	Massaglia Hotels Spl.	Lesovsky	10
11	19	140.367	19	O	4	Jack Turner	Bardahl Spl.	KK 500G	11
12	11	143.529	10	O	4	Johnny Thomson	D-A Lubricant Spl.	Kuzma	12
13	33	139.779	95	O	4	Bob Christie	Jones & Maley Spl.	KK 500C	13
14	25	141.105	82	O	4	Chuck Weyant	Central Excavating Spl.	Kuzma	14
15	22	142.439	27	NS	8	Tony Bettenhausen	Novi Automotive Air Cond. Spl.	Kurtis	15
16	17	140.784*	18	O	4	Johnnie Parsons*	Sumar Spl.	KK 500G	16
17	21	139.649	3	O	4	Don Freeland	Ansted-Rotary Spl.	KK 500D	17
18	6	142.006	5	O	4	Jimmy Reece	Hoyt Machine Spl.	KK 500C	18
19	27	140.449	92	O	4	Don Edmunds	Makay Spl.	KK 500G	19
20	31	139.844	28	O	4	Johnny Tolan	Greenman-Casale Spl.	Kuzma	20
21	30	140.007	89	O	4	Al Herman	Dunn Engineering Spl.	Dunn	21
22	4	142.557	14	O	4	Freddie Agabashian	Bowes Seal Fast Spl.	KK 500G	22
23	2	143.872	88	O	4	Eddie Sachs	Pete Schmidt Spl.	Kuzma	23
24	18	140.411	77	O	4	Mike Magill	Dayton Steel Foundry Spl.	KK 500G	24
25	20	140.171	43	O	4	Eddie Johnson	Chapman Spl.	KK 500G	25
26	23	141.565	31	O	4	Bill Cheesbourg	Shildmeiers Seal Line Spl.	KK 500G	26
27	8	141.398	16	O	4	Al Keller	Bardahl Spl.	KK 500G	27
28	29	140.203	57	O	4	Jimmy Daywalt	Helse Spl.	KK 500C	28
29	7	141.777	83	O	4	Ed Elisian	McNamara Spl.	KK 500C	29
30	24	141.321	8	OS	4	Rodger Ward	Wolcott Fuel Injection Spl.	Lesovsky	30
31	3	142.772	52	O	4	Troy Ruttman	John Zink Spl.	Watson	31
32	26	140.862	55	O	4	Eddie Russo	Sclavi & Amos Spl.	KK 500C	32
33	9	140.729	23	O	4	Elmer George	Travelon Trailer Spl.	KK 500B	33

Qualified, did not start: Billy Garrett, Federal Engineering, Detroit Spl., #33, O, 139.546, Bumped
George Amick, Federal Engineering, Detroit Spl., #4, O, 139.443, Bumped
Dempsey Wilson, Martin Bros. Spl., #42, O, 139.109, Bumped
Chuck Weyant, Jim Robbins Spl., #35, O, 139.104, Bumped
Ray Crawford, Meguiar Mirror Glaze Spl., #49, O, 139.093, Too slow
Jud Larson, John Zink Spl., #25, O, 139.061, Bumped
Johnnie Parsons, Agajanian Spl., #98, O, 138.975, Bumped
Bill Cheesbourg, Las Vegas Club Spl., #45, O, 138.878, Bumped
Jimmy Davies, Trio Brass Foundry Spl., #32, O, 138.462, Bumped
Don Edmunds, Braund Birch, #67, O, 136.400, Too slow
Danny Kladis, Morgan Engineering Spl., #72, MAS-S, 124.412, Bumped

Total entries: 54

Qualifying: Fastest 33 over 4 laps.

*Qualified by Dick Rathmann

FIN	ENTRANT	LAPS	SPEED, REASON OUT	RELIEF DRIVER	FIN
1	George Salih	200	135.601	—	1
2	Lindsey Hopkins	200	135.382	—	2
3	A. E. Dean	200	134.246	—	3
4	Novi Racing Corp., Inc.	200	133.818	—	4
5	Kalamazoo Sports, Inc.	200	133.645	—	5
6	George Bignotti	200	132.846	—	6
7	Chapman S. Root	200	132.745	—	7
8	Chapman S. Root	200	132.281	—	8
9	Bob Estes	200	131.855	—	9
10	Joseph Massaglia, Jr.	200	131.345	—	10
11	Pat Clancy	200	130.906	—	11
12	Racing Associates	199	Flagged	—	12
13	Cars, Inc.	197	Flagged	—	13
14	Pete Salemi	196	Flagged	—	14
15	Novi Racing Corp., Inc.	195	Flagged	—	15
16	Chapman S. Root	195	Flagged	—	16
17	Ansted-Rotary Corp.	192	Flagged	—	17
18	Fred & Richard Sommer	182	Throttle	—	18
19	Roy McKay	170	Spun	—	19
20	Lysle Greenman	138	Clutch	—	20
21	Harry Dunn	111	Wreck	—	21
22	George Bignotti	107	Fuel tank	—	22
23	Peter Schmidt	105	Piston	—	23
24	George Walther, Jr.	101	Wreck	—	24
25	H. A. Chapman	93	Front wheel bearing	—	25
26	J. S. Donaldson	81	Fuel leak	—	26
27	Pat Clancy	75	Wreck	—	27
28	H. H. Johnson	53	Wreck	—	28
29	Kalamazoo Sports, Inc.	51	Timing gear	—	29
30	Roger Wolcott	27	Supercharger bearing	—	30
31	John Zink Co.	13	Overheating	—	31
32	Fred Sclavi	0	Wreck pace lap	—	32
33	Ernest L. Ruiz	0	Wreck pace lap	—	33

MAS-S = Maserati Supercharged
O = Offenhauser
OS = Offenhauser Supercharged
NS = Novi Supercharged

1958

FIN	START	QUAL. SPEED	NUMBER, TYPE, CYLINDERS			DRIVER	CAR NAME	CHASSIS	FIN
1	7	144.185	1	O	4	Jimmy Bryan	Belond AP Spl.	Epperly	1
2	25	142.710	99	O	4	George Amick	Demler Spl.	Epperly	2
3	8	144.023	9	O	4	Johnny Boyd	Bowes Seal Fast Spl.	KK 500G	3
4	9	143.919	33	O	4	Tony Bettenhausen	Jones & Maley Spl.	Epperly	4
5	20	143.147	2	O	4	Jim Rathmann	Leader Card 500 Roadster Spl.	Epperly	5
6	3	145.513	16	O	4	Jimmy Reece	John Zink Spl.	Watson	6
7	13	143.033	26	O	4	Don Freeland	Bob Estes Spl.	Phillips	7
8	19	143.512	44	O	4	Jud Larson	John Zink Spl.	Watson	8
9	26	142.670	61	O	4	Eddie Johnson	Bryant Heating & Cooling Spl.	KK 500G	9
10	33	142.546	54	NS	8	Bill Cheesbourg	Novi Automotive Air Cond. Spl.	Kurtis	10
11	21	142.931	52	O	4	Al Keller	Bardahl Spl.	KK 500G-2	11
12	6	144.683	45	O	4	Johnnie Parsons	Gerhardt Spl.	Kurtis	12
13	30	142.309	19	O	4	Johnny Tolan	Greenman-Casale Spl.	Kuzma	13
14	17	142.253	65	O	4	Bob Christie	Federal Engineering, Detroit Spl.	KK 500C	14
15	32	143.272	59	O	4	Dempsey Wilson	Sorenson Spl.	Kuzma	15
16	12	143.130	29	O	4	A. J. Foyt	Dean Van Lines Spl.	Kuzma	16
17	31	142.276	77	O	4	Mike Magill	Dayton Steel Foundry Spl.	KK 500G	17
18	14	142.959	15	NS	8	Paul Russo	Novi Automotive Air Cond. Spl.	Kurtis	18
19	23	142.817	83	O	4	Shorty Templeman	McNamara Spl.	KK 500D	19
20	11	143.266	8	O	4	Rodger Ward	Wolcott Fuel Injection Spl.	Lesovsky	20
21	15	142.778	43	O	4	Billy Garrett	Chapman Spl.	KK 500G	21
22	18	144.660	88	O	4	Eddie Sachs	Pete Schmidt Spl.	Kuzma	22
23	22	142.908	7	O	4	Johnny Thomson	D-A Lubricant Spl.	Kurtis	23
24	29	142.608	89	O	4	Chuck Weyant	Dunn Engineering Spl.	Dunn	24
25	10	143.438	25	O	4	Jack Turner	Massaglia Hotels Spl.	Lesovsky	25
26	4	144.881	14	O	4	Bob Veith	Bowes Seal Fast Spl.	KK 500G	26
27	1	145.974	97	O	4	Dick Rathmann	McNamara Spl.	Watson	27
28	2	145.926	5	O	4	Ed Elisian	John Zink Spl.	Watson	28
29	5	144.823	4	O	4	Pat O'Connor	Sumar Spl.	KK 500G	29
30	16	142.744	31	O	4	Paul Goldsmith	City of Daytona Beach Spl.	KK 500G	30
31	24	142.755	92	O	4	Jerry Unser	Makay Spl.	KK 500G	31
32	27	142.653	68	O	4	Len Sutton	Jim Robbins Spl.	KK 500G	32
33	28	142.631	57	O	4	Art Bisch	Helse Spl.	Kuzma	33

Qualified, did not start: Gene Hartley, Hoyt Machine Spl., #24, O, 142.231, Bumped
Freddie Agabashian, City of Memphis, Tennessee Spl., #56, O, 142.135, Bumped
Dempsey Wilson, Hall-Mar Spl., #71, O, 142.029, Bumped
Ray Crawford, Maguiars Mirror Glaze Spl., #49, O, 141.688, Bumped
Art Bisch, Ansted-Rotary Spl., #17, O, 141.376, Bumped
Freddie Agabashian, D-A Lubricant Spl., #75, O, 141.011, Too slow
Rex Easton, Hoover Motor Express Spl., #10, O, 140.972, Bumped

Total entries: 56

Qualifying: Fastest 33 over 4 laps.

FIN	ENTRANT	LAPS	SPEED, REASON OUT	RELIEF DRIVER	FIN
1	George Salih	200	133.791	—	1
2	Norman C. Demler	200	133.517	—	2
3	Robert M. Bowes II	200	133.099	—	3
4	Cars, Inc.	200	132.855	—	4
5	Lindsey Hopkins	200	132.852	—	5
6	John Zink	200	132.443	—	6
7	Bob Estes	200	132.403	—	7
8	John Zink Co.	200	130.550	—	8
9	J. S. "Duke" Donaldson	200	130.156	—	9
10	Novi Racing Corp., Inc.	200	129.149	—	10
11	Pat Clancy	200	128.498	—	11
12	Fred Gerhardt	200	128.254	—	12
13	Lysle Greenman	200	128.150	—	13
14	Federal Automotive Associates	189	Spun	—	14
15	Bob Sorenson	151	Clutch pedal	—	15
16	Dean Van Lines	148	Spun	—	16
17	George Walther, Jr.	136	Flagged	—	17
18	Novi Racing Corp., Inc.	122	Radiator	—	18
19	Kalamazoo Sports, Inc.	116	Brakes	—	19
20	Roger Wolcott	93	Fuel pump	—	20
21	H. A. Chapman	80	Cam gear	—	21
22	Peter Schmidt	68	Universal joint	—	22
23	Racing Associates	52	Steering	—	23
24	Harry Dunn	38	Wreck	—	24
25	Joseph Massaglia, Jr.	21	Fuel pump	—	25
26	Robert M. Bowes II	1	Wreck	—	26
27	Kalamazoo Sports, Inc.	0	Wreck	—	27
28	Ellen McKinney Zink	0	Wreck	—	28
29	Chapman S. Root	0	Wreck	—	29
30	Smokey Yunick	0	Wreck	—	30
31	Roy McKay	0	Wreck	—	31
32	Jim Robbins	0	Wreck	—	32
33	H. H. Johnson	0	Wreck	—	33

NS = Novi Supercharged
O = Offenhauser

1959

FIN	START	QUAL. SPEED	NUMBER, TYPE, CYLINDERS			DRIVER	CAR NAME	CHASSIS	FIN
1	6	144.035	5	O	4	Rodger Ward	Leader Card 500 Roadster Spl.	Watson	1
2	3	144.433	16	O	4	Jim Rathmann	Simoniz Spl.	Watson	2
3	1	145.908	3	O	4	Johnny Thomson	Racing Associates Spl.	Lesovsky	3
4	15	142.721	1	O	4	Tony Bettenhausen	Hoover Motor Express Spl.	Epperly	4
5	16	142.670	99	O	4	Paul Goldsmith	Demler Spl.	Epperly	5
6	11	142.812	33	O	4	Johnny Boyd	Bowes Seal Fast Spl.	Epperly	6
7	12	142.795	37	O	4	Duane Carter	Smokey's Reserve Torque Spl.	Kurtis	7
8	8	144.000	19	O	4	Eddie Johnson	Bryant Heating & Cooling Spl.	KK 500G	8
9	27	142.383	45	O	4	Paul Russo	Bardahl Spl.	KK 500G	9
10	17	142.648	10	O	4	A. J. Foyt	Dean Van Lines Spl.	Kuzma	10
11	9	143.575	88	O	4	Gene Hartley	Drewry's Spl.	Kuzma	11
12	7	144.023	74	O	4	Bob Veith	John Zink Heater Spl.	Moore	12
13	23	141.939	89	O	4	Al Herman	Dunn Engineering Spl.	Dunn	13
14	13	144.683	66	O	4	Jimmy Daywalt	Federal Engineering, Detroit Spl.	Kurtis	14
15	21	142.118	71	O	4	Chuck Arnold	Hall-Mar Spl.	Kurtis	15
16	33	141.215	58	O	4	Jim McWithey	Ray Brady Spl.	KK 500C	16
17	2	145.425	44	O	4	Eddie Sachs	Pete Schmidt Spl.	Kuzma	17
18	28	142.057	57	O	4	Al Keller	Helse Spl.	Kuzma	18
19	18	142.399	64	O	4	Pat Flaherty	John Zink Heater Spl.	Watson	19
20	4	144.248	73	O	4	Dick Rathmann	McNamara-Chiropractic Spl.	Watson	20
21	30	141.788	53	O	4	Bill Cheesbourg	Greenman-Casale Spl.	Kuzma	21
22	25	143.056	15	O	4	Don Freeland	Jim Robbins Spl.	KK 500G	22
23	32	141.348	49	O	4	Ray Crawford	Meguiar's Mirror Glaze Spl.	Elder	23
24	10	143.312	9	O	4	Don Branson	Bob Estes Spl.	Phillips	24
25	24	143.244	65	O	4	Bob Christie	Federal Engineering, Detroit Spl.	KK 500C	25
26	5	144.225	48	O	4	Bobby Grim	Sumar Spl.	KK 500G	26
27	14	143.478	24	O	4	Jack Turner	Travelon Trailer Spl.	Christensen	27
28	29	141.950	47	O	4	Chuck Weyant	Makay Spl.	KK 500G	28
29	19	142.298	7	O	4	Jud Larson	Bowes Seal Fast Spl.	Kurtis	29
30	31	141.482	77	O	4	Mike Magill	Dayton Steel Foundry Spl.	Sutton	30
31	26	142.925	87	O	4	Red Amick	Wheelers-Foutch Spl.	KK 500C	31
32	22	142.107	8	OS	4	Len Sutton	Wolcott Spl.	Lesovsky	32
33	20	142.118	6	O	4	Jimmy Bryan	Belond AP Muffler Spl.	Epperly	33

Qualified, did not start: Rex Easton, Massaglia Hotels Spl., #39, O, 139.438, Bumped
Shorty Templeman, Braund Plywood Spl., #76, O, 139.023, Too slow
Ralph Liguori, Eldorado Italia Spl., #12, MAS, 136.395, Bumped
Bill Homeier, Radsco Battery Spl., #62, O, 130.928, Too slow

Total entries: 61

Qualifying: Fastest 33 over 4 laps.

FIN	ENTRANT	LAPS	SPEED, REASON OUT	RELIEF DRIVER	FIN
1	Leader Cards, Inc.	200	135.857	—	1
2	Lindsey Hopkins	200	135.619	—	2
3	Racing Associates	200	135.340	—	3
4	John R. Wills	200	134.768	—	4
5	Norman C. Demler	200	134.573	—	5
6	Bignotti-Bowes Racing	200	133.867	—	6
7	Yunick, Glover & Lathrop	200	133.342	—	7
8	J. S. "Duke" Donaldson	200	133.336	—	8
9	Fred Gerhardt	200	133.331	—	9
10	A. E. Dean	200	133.297	—	10
11	R. T. Marley, Sr.	200	132.434	—	11
12	John Zink Co.	200	132.169	—	12
13	Harry Dunn	200	131.872	—	13
14	Federal Automotive Associates	200	131.861	—	14
15	Karl Hall	200	130.918	—	15
16	Ray T. Brady	200	129.024	—	16
17	Peter Schmidt	182	Gear tower bolt	—	17
18	H. H. Johnson	163	Piston	—	18
19	John Zink Co.	162	Wreck	—	19
20	Kalamazoo Sports, Inc.	150	Caught fire	—	20
21	Lysle Greenman	147	Magneto	—	21
22	Jim Robbins	136	Valve spring	—	22
23	Ray Crawford	115	Wreck	—	23
24	Bob Estes	112	Torsion bar	—	24
25	Federal Automotive Associates	109	Rod bolt	—	25
26	Chapman S. Root	85	Piston	—	26
27	Ernest L. Ruiz	47	Fuel tank	—	27
28	Roy Makay	45	Wreck	—	28
29	Bignotti-Bowes Racing	45	Wreck	—	29
30	George Walther, Jr.	45	Wreck	—	30
31	LeRoy E. Foutch, Jr.	45	Wreck	—	31
32	Wolcott Memorial Racing Team	34	Wreck	—	32
33	George Salih	1	Clutch	—	33

MAS = Maserati
O = Offenhauser
OS = Offenhauser
    Supercharged

1960

FIN	START	QUAL. SPEED	NUMBER, TYPE, CYLINDERS			DRIVER	CAR NAME	CHASSIS	FIN
1	2	146.371	4	O	4	Jim Rathmann	Ken-Paul Spl.	Watson	1
2	3	145.560	1	O	4	Rodger Ward	Leader Card 500 Roadster Spl.	Watson	2
3	26	142.783	99	O	4	Paul Goldsmith	Demler Spl.	Epperly	3
4	8	144.753	7	O	4	Don Branson	Bob Estes Spl.	Phillips	4
5	17	146.443	3	O	4	Johnny Thomson	Adams Quarter Horse Farm Spl.	Lesovsky	5
6	7	145.003	22	O	4	Eddie Johnson	Jim Robbins Spl.	Trevis	6
7	12	144.208	98	O	4	Lloyd Ruby	Agajanian Spl.	Watson	7
8	25	143.363	44	O	4	Bob Veith	Pete Schmidt Spl.	Meskowski	8
9	28	142.354	18	O	4	Bud Tingelstad	Jim Robbins Spl.	Trevis	9
10	14	143.638	38	O	4	Bob Christie	Federal Engineering, Detroit Spl.	KK 500C	10
11	22	143.084	27	O	4	Red Amick	King O'Lawn Spl.	Epperly	11
12	27	142.631	17	O	4	Duane Carter	Thompson Industries Spl.	Kuzma	12
13	31	141.248	39	O	4	Bill Homeier	Ridgewood Builders Spl.	Kuzma	13
14	24	143.896	48	O	4	Gene Hartley	Sumar Spl.	KK 500G	14
15	9	144.665	65	O	4	Chuck Stevenson	Leader Card 500 Roadster Spl.	Watson	15
16	21	143.158	14	O	4	Bobby Grim	Bill Forbes Racing Team Spl.	Meskowski	16
17	19	143.856	26	O	4	Shorty Templeman	Federal Engineering, Detroit Spl.	KK 500C	17
18	23	149.056	56	O	4	Jim Hurtubise	Travelon Trailer Spl.	Christensen	18
19	10	144.532	10	O	4	Jimmy Bryan	Metal Cal Spl.	Epperly	19
20	6	145.366	28	O	4	Troy Ruttman	John Zink Heater Spl.	Watson	20
21	1	146.592	6	O	4	Eddie Sachs	Dean Van Lines Spl.	Ewing	21
22	11	144.352	73	O	4	Don Freeland	Ross-Babcock Traveler Spl.	Kurtis	22
23	18	145.214	2	O	4	Tony Bettenhausen	Dowgard Spl.	Watson	23
24	15	143.512	32	O	4	Wayne Weiler	Ansted-Rotary Spl.	Epperly	24
25	16	143.466	5	O	4	A. J. Foyt	Bowes Seal Fast Spl.	Kurtis	25
26	29	142.203	46	O	4	Eddie Russo	Go Kart Spl.	KK 500G	26
27	13	143.770	8	O	4	Johnny Boyd	Bowes Seal Fast Spl.	Epperly	27
28	20	143.472	37	O	4	Gene Force	Makay Spl.	KK 500G	28
29	32	140.378	16	O	4	Jim McWithey	Hoover Motor Express Spl.	Epperly	29
30	5	145.443	9	O	4	Len Sutton	S-R Racing Enterprises Spl.	Watson	30
31	4	145.543	97	O	4	Dick Rathmann	Jim Robbins Spl.	Watson	31
32	30	141.838	76	O	4	Al Herman	Joe Hunt Magneto Spl.	Ewing	32
33	33	143.215*	23	O	4	Dempsey Wilson*	Bryant Heating & Cooling Spl.	KK 500G	33

Qualified, did not start: Chuck Rodee, Dunn Engineering Spl., #89, O, 140.100, Bumped
Al Keller, Makay Spl., #35, O, 138.268, Too slow
Ebb Rose, Ellen Zink Spl., #41, O, 138.153, Bumped
Chuck Hulse, Sorenson Spl., #69, O, 137.174, Bumped

Total entries: 66

Qualifying: Fastest 33 over 4 laps.

*Qualified by Jimmy Daywalt

FIN	ENTRANT	LAPS	SPEED, REASON OUT	RELIEF DRIVER	FIN
1	Ken-Paul Inc.	200	138.767	—	1
2	Leader Cards Inc.	200	138.631	—	2
3	Norman C. Demler	200	136.792	—	3
4	Bob Estes	200	136.785	—	4
5	Racing Associates	200	136.750	—	5
6	Jim Robbins Co.	200	136.137	—	6
7	J. C. Agajanian	200	135.983	—	7
8	Peter Schmidt	200	135.452	—	8
9	Jim Robbins Co.	200	133.717	—	9
10	Federal Automotive Associates	200	133.416	—	10
11	Leonard A. Faas, Sr.	200	131.946	—	11
12	Jack Ensley & Shirley Murphy	200	131.882	—	12
13	Norman Hall	200	131.367	—	13
14	Chapman S. Root	196	Flagged	—	14
15	Leader Cards Inc.	196	Flagged	—	15
16	William P. Forbes	194	Flagged	—	16
17	Federal Automotive Associates	191	Flagged	—	17
18	Ernest L. Ruiz	185	Con. rod	—	18
19	George Salih	152	Fuel pump	—	19
20	John Zink Co.	134	Rear end gear	—	20
21	Dean Van Lines Racing Div.	132	Magneto	—	21
22	Racing Associates	129	Magneto	—	22
23	Lindsey Hopkins	125	Con. rod	—	23
24	Anstead-Rotary Corp.	103	Wrecked	—	24
25	Bignotti-Bowes Racing	90	Clutch	—	25
26	C. O. Prather	84	Wreck	—	26
27	Bignotti-Bowes Racing	77	Piston	—	27
28	Roy Makay	74	Brakes	—	28
29	Hoover Motor Express, Inc.	60	Brakes	—	29
30	Pete Salemi & Nick Rini	47	Engine trouble	—	30
31	Jim Robbins Co.	42	Brake line	—	31
32	Joe Hunt	34	Clutch	—	32
33	J. S. "Duke" Donaldson	11	Magneto	—	33

O = Offenhauser

1961

FIN	START	QUAL. SPEED	NUMBER, TYPE, CYLINDERS			DRIVER	CAR NAME	CHASSIS	FIN
1	7	145.903	1	O	4	A. J. Foyt	Bowes Seal Fast Spl.	Watson	1
2	1	147.481	12	O	4	Eddie Sachs	Dean Van Lines Spl.	Ewing	2
3	4	146.187	2	O	4	Rodger Ward	Del Webb's Sun City Arizona Spl.	Watson	3
4	18	144.341	7	O	4	Shorty Templeman	Bill Forbes Racing Team Spl.	Watson	4
5	26	146.157	19	O	4	Al Keller	Konstant Hot Spl.	Phillips	5
6	28	145.191	18	O	4	Chuck Stevenson	Metal Cal Spl.	Epperly	6
7	33	144.293	31	O	4	Bobby Marshman	Hoover Motor Express Spl.	Epperly	7
8	25	146.909	5	O	4	Lloyd Ruby	Autolite Dealer's Association Spl.	Epperly	8
9	13	145.144	17	RECC	4	Jack Brabham, Australia	Kimberly Cooper Climax Spl.	Cooper	9
10	32	144.555	34	O	4	Norman Hall	Federal Engineering, Detroit Spl.	K K 500C	10
11	15	144.817	28	O	4	Gene Hartley	John Chalik Spl.	Trevis	11
12	5	146.080	98	O	4	Parnelli Jones	Agajanian's Willard Battery Spl.	Watson	12
13	6	146.033	97	O	4	Dick Rathmann	Jim Robbins Spl.	Trevis	13
14	17	144.741	10	O	4	Paul Goldsmith	Racing Associates Spl.	Lesovsky	14
15	12	145.349	15	O	4	Wayne Weiler	Hopkins Coral Harbour Spl.	Watson	15
16	31	144.202	35	O	4	Dempsey Wilson	Lysle Greenman Spl.	Kuzma	16
17	16	144.782	32	O	4	Bob Christie	North Electric Spl.	Kurtis	17
18	10	145.843	33	O	4	Eddie Johnson	Jim Robbins Spl.	Kuzma	18
19	8	145.897	8	O	4	Len Sutton	Bryant Heating & Cooling Spl.	Watson	19
20	22	144.799	52	O	4	Troy Ruttman	John Zink Trackburner Spl.	Moore	20
21	20	144.092	41	O	4	Johnny Boyd	Leader Card 500 Roadster Spl.	Watson	21
22	3	146.306	99	O	4	Jim Hurtubise	Demler Spl.	Epperly	22
23	19	144.338	86	O	4	Ebb Rose	Meyer Speedway Spl.	Porter	23
24	30	145.038	26	O	4	Cliff Griffith	McCullough Engineering Spl.	Elder	24
25	21	144.904	45	O	4	Jack Turner	Bardahl Spl.	Kurtis	25
26	14	144.954	73	O	4	A. J. Shepherd	Travelon Trailer Spl.	Watson	26
27	29	145.068	22	O	4	Roger McCluskey	Racing Associates Spl.	Watson	27
28	9	145.873	14	O	4	Bill Cheesbourg	Dean Van Lines Spl.	Kuzma	28
29	27	145.349	83	O	4	Don Davis	Dart Kart by Rupp Spl.	Trevis	29
30	11	145.413	4	O	4	Jim Rathmann	Simoniz Golden Anniversary Spl.	Watson	30
31	23	144.219	55	O	4	Jimmy Daywalt	Shultz Fueling Equipment Spl.	K K 500G	31
32	24	144.029	16	O	4	Bobby Grim	Thompson Industries Spl.	Watson	32
33	2	146.843	3	O	4	Don Branson	Hoover Motor Express Spl.	Epperly	33

Qualified, did not start: Paul Russo, Bryant Heating & Cooling Spl., #21, O, 143.983, Bumped
Bob Cleberg, Bell Lines Trucking Spl., #6, O, 143.672, Bumped
Bob Veith, Bardahl Spl., #23, O, 143.581, Too slow
Bert Brooks, Hall-Mar Spl., #79, O, 143.415, Too slow
Bob Veith, Shaler-Rislone Spl., #25, O, 143.062, Bumped
Norman Hall, Concannon Car Co. Flying Spl., #92, O, 141.861, Bumped
Don Freeland, Joe Hunt Magneto Spl., #47, O, 141.476, Too slow

Total entries: 69

Qualifying: Fastest 33 over 4 laps.

FIN	ENTRANT	LAPS	SPEED, REASON OUT	RELIEF DRIVER	FIN
1	Bignotti-Bowes Racing Association	200	139.130	—	1
2	Dean Van Lines Racing Div.	200	139.041	—	2
3	Leader Cards, Inc.	200	138.539	—	3
4	William P. Forbes	200	136.873	—	4
5	Bruce Homeyer	200	136.034	—	5
6	C & H Supply Co.	200	135.742	—	6
7	Hoover Motor Express	200	135.534	—	7
8	Lindsey Hopkins	200	134.860	—	8
9	Cooper Car Co. Ltd.	200	134.116	—	9
10	Federal Automotive Associates	200	134.104	—	10
11	John Chalik	198	Flagged	—	11
12	J. C. Agajanian	192	Flagged	—	12
13	Jim Robbins Co.	164	Fuel pump	—	13
14	Racing Associates	160	Con. rod	—	14
15	Lindsey Hopkins	147	Wheel bearing	—	15
16	Lysle Greenman	145	Fuel pump	—	16
17	William Tucker, Inc.	132	Burned piston	—	17
18	Jim Robbins Co.	127	Wreck	—	18
19	Pete Salemi & Nick Rini	110	Clutch	—	19
20	John S. Zink	105	Clutch	—	20
21	Leader Cards, Inc.	105	Clutch	—	21
22	Norm Demler, Inc.	102	Piston	—	22
23	Racing Associates	93	Con. rod	—	23
24	Edgar R. Elder	55	Piston	—	24
25	Fred Gerhardt	52	Wreck	—	25
26	Ernest L. Ruiz	51	Wreck	—	26
27	Racing Associates	51	Wreck	—	27
28	Dean Van Lines Racing Div.	50	Wreck	—	28
29	Floyd Trevis & Gil Morcroft	49	Wreck	—	29
30	Ken-Paul, Inc.	48	Magneto	—	30
31	C. O. Prather	27	Brake line	—	31
32	Ansted-Thompson Racing, Inc.	26	Piston	—	32
33	Hoover Motor Express	2	Bent valves	—	33

O = Offenhauser
RECC = Rear Engine—
     Cooper Climax

1962

FIN	START	QUAL. SPEED	NUMBER, TYPE, CYLINDERS			DRIVER	CAR NAME	CHASSIS	FIN
1	2	149.371	3	O	4	Rodger Ward	Leader Card 500 Roadster Spl.	Watson	1
2	4	149.328	7	O	4	Len Sutton	Leader Card 500 Roadster Spl.	Watson	2
3	27	146.431	2	O	4	Eddie Sachs	Dean-Autolite Spl.	Ewing	3
4	12	147.209	27	O	4	Don Davis	J. H. Rose Truck Lines Spl.	Lesovsky	4
5	3	149.347	54	O	4	Bobby Marshman	Bryant Heating & Cooling Spl.	Epperly	5
6	7	149.025	15	O	4	Jim McElreath	Shultz Fueling Equipment Spl.	Kurtis	6
7	1	150.370	98	O	4	Parnelli Jones	Agajanian's Willard Battery Spl.	Watson	7
8	24	146.520	12	O	4	Lloyd Ruby	Thompson Industries Spl.	Watson	8
9	23	146.610	44	O	4	Jim Rathmann	Simoniz Vista Spl.	Watson	9
10	28	147.047	38	O	4	Johnny Boyd	Metal-Cal Spl.	Epperly	10
11	6	149.050	4	O	4	Shorty Templeman	Bill Forbes Racing Team Spl.	Watson	11
12	11	147.312	14	O	4	Don Branson	Mid-Continent Securities Spl.	Epperly	12
13	29	146.963	91	O	4	Jim Hurtubise	Jim Robbins Spl.	Trevis	13
14	32	146.336	86	O	4	Ebb Rose	J. H. Rose Truck Lines Spl.	Porter	14
15	10	147.753	5	O	4	Bud Tingelstad	Konstant Hot Spl.	Phillips	15
16	9	147.759	17	O	4	Roger McCluskey	Bell Lines Trucking Spl.	Watson	16
17	17	146.092	21	O	4	Elmer George	Sarkes-Tarzian Spl.	Lesovsky	17
18	30	146.765	26	O	4	Troy Ruttman	Jim Robbins Spl.	Kuzma	18
19	15	146.604	18	O	4	Bobby Grim	Morcroft Spl.	Trevis	19
20	8	147.886	34	REB	8	Dan Gurney	Mickey Thompson Harvey Aluminum Spl.	Thompson	20
21	16	146.377	19	O	4	Chuck Hulse	Federal Engineering, Detroit Spl.	KK 500C	21
22	33	146.318	79	O	4	Jimmy Daywalt	Albany N.Y. Spl.	Kurtis	22
23	5	149.074	1	O	4	A. J. Foyt	Bowes Seal Fast Spl.	Trevis	23
24	13	147.161	9	O	4	Dick Rathmann	Chapman Spl.	Watson	24
25	18	146.592	32	O	4	Eddie Johnson	Polyaire Foam Spl.	Trevis	25
26	26	146.437	53	O	4	Paul Goldsmith	American Rubber & Plastics Spl.	Epperly	26
27	20	146.969	88	O	4	Gene Hartley	Drewry's Spl.	Watson	27
28	14	146.687	62	O	4	Paul Russo	Denver-Chicago Trucking Co. Spl.	Watson	28
29	25	146.496	45	O	4	Jack Turner	Bardahl Spl.	Kurtis	29
30	31	146.341	29	O	4	Bob Christie	North Electric Spl.	Kurtis	30
31	22	146.831	83	O	4	Allen Crowe	S-R Racing Enterprises Spl.	Watson	31
32	21	146.969	67	O	4	Chuck Rodee	Travelon Trailer Spl.	Watson	32
33	19	146.157	96	O	4	Bob Veith	Maguires Mirror Glaze Spl.	Elder	33

Qualified, did not start: Dempsey Wilson, Lysle Greenman Spl., #31, O, 146.086, Bumped
Ronnie Duman, Stearly Motor Freight Spl., #28, O, 145.908, Bumped
Duane Carter, John Zink Trackburner Spl., #72, O, 145.867, Bumped
Don Freeland, Hart Fullerton Spl., #36, O, 145.366, Too slow
Chuck Arnold, Turtle Drilling Spl., #23, O, 145.366, Too slow
Bruce Jacobi, Froehde Mobil Homes Spl., #22, O, 144.939, Bumped

Total entries: 65

Qualifying: Fastest 33 over 4 laps.

FIN	ENTRANT	LAPS	SPEED, REASON OUT	RELIEF DRIVER	FIN
1	Leader Cards, Inc.	200	140.293	—	1
2	Leader Cards, Inc.	200	140.167	—	2
3	Dean Van Lines Racing Div.	200	140.075	—	3
4	Bob Philipp	200	139.768	—	4
5	Your Bryant Dealer	200	138.790	—	5
6	C. O. Prather	200	138.653	—	6
7	J. C. Agajanian	200	138.534	—	7
8	Ansted-Thompson Racing, Inc.	200	138.182	—	8
9	Smokey Yunick	200	136.913	—	9
10	C & H Supply Co.	200	136.600	—	10
11	William P. Forbes	200	135.844	—	11
12	Lindsey Hopkins	200	135.836	—	12
13	John Marco Pusilo	200	135.655	—	13
14	Herb Porter	200	134.001	—	14
15	Bruce Homeyer	200	133.170	—	15
16	Sclavi, Inc.	168	Spun	—	16
17	Mari George	146	Engine seized	A. J. Foyt, Paul Russo	17
18	Jim Robbins Co.	140	Burned piston	—	18
19	Gilbert E. Morcroft	96	Oil leak	—	19
20	Mickey Thompson	92	Rear end gear	—	20
21	Federal Automotive Associates	91	Fuel pump	—	21
22	Tassi Vatis	74	Transmission	—	22
23	Bignotti-Bowes Racing Association	69	Lost wheel	—	23
24	H. A. Chapman	51	Magneto	—	24
25	Peter G. Torosian	38	Magneto	—	25
26	Bignotti-Bowes Racing Association	26	Magneto	—	26
27	M & W Racing Associates	23	Steering	Bill Cheesbourg	27
28	Myron E. Osborn	20	Engine trouble	—	28
29	Fred Gerhardt	17	Wreck	—	29
30	William Tucker, Inc.	17	Wreck	—	30
31	Pete Salemi & Nick Rini	17	Wreck	—	31
32	Ernest L. Ruiz	17	Wreck	—	32
33	Ray Crawford	12	Engine trouble	—	33

O = Offenhauser
REB = Rear Engine—
    Buick

1963

FIN	START	QUAL. SPEED	NUMBER, TYPE, CYLINDERS			DRIVER	CAR NAME	CHASSIS	FIN
1	1	151.153	98	O	4	Parnelli Jones	Agajanian's Willard Battery Spl.	Watson	1
2	5	149.750	92	REF	8	Jim Clark, Scotland	Lotus Powered by Ford	Lotus	2
3	8	150.615	2	O	4	A. J. Foyt	Sheraton-Thompson Spl.	Trevis	3
4	4	149.800	1	O	4	Rodger Ward	Kaiser Aluminium Spl.	Watson	4
5	3	150.188	4	O	4	Don Branson	Leader Card 500 Roadster Spl.	Watson	5
6	6	149.744	8	O	4	Jim McElreath	Bill Forbes Racing Team Spl.	Watson	6
7	12	149.019	93	REF	8	Dan Gurney	Lotus Powered by Ford	Lotus	7
8	11	149.340	10	O	4	Chuck Hulse	Dean Van Lines Spl.	Ewing	8
9	31	149.613	84	REC	8	Al Miller	Mickey Thompson Harvey Aluminum Spl.	Thompson	9
10	17	149.130	22	O	4	Dick Rathmann	Chapman Spl.	Watson	10
11	30	147.832	29	O	4	Dempsey Wilson	Vita Fresh Orange Juice Spl.	Kuzma	11
12	33	148.374	17	O	4	Troy Ruttman	Jim Robbins Autocrat Seat Belt Spl.	Kuzma	12
13	18	149.124	65	O	4	Bob Christie	Travelon Trailer Spl.	Watson	13
14	32	148.545	32	O	4	Ebb Rose	Sheraton-Thompson Spl.	Watson	14
15	14	148.680	14	O	4	Roger McCluskey	Konstant Hot Spl.	Watson	15
16	7	149.458	5	O	4	Bobby Marshman	Econo Car Rentals Spl.	Epperly	16
17	10	149.570	9	O	4	Eddie Sachs	Bryant Heating & Cooling Spl.	Watson	17
18	9	150.163	99	O	4	Paul Goldsmith	Demler Spl.	Watson	18
19	19	149.123	52	O	4	Lloyd Ruby	John Zink Trackburner Spl.	Moore	19
20	21	148.509	88	O	4	Eddie Johnson	Drewry's Spl.	Watson	20
21	22	148.386	45	O	4	Chuck Stevenson	Bardahl Spl.	Watson	21
22	2	150.257	56	NS	8	Jim Hurtubise	Hotel Tropicana Las Vegas Spl.	Kurtis	22
23	15	148.002	83	REC	8	Duane Carter	Mickey Thompson Harvey Aluminum Spl.	Thompson	23
24	29	147.838	16	O	4	Jim Rathmann	Hopkins Coral Harbour Spl.	Watson	24
25	20	148.717	26	O	4	Bobby Grim	Morcroft Spl.	Trevis	25
26	24	148.289	86	O	4	Bob Veith	Sheraton-Thompson Spl.	Porter	26
27	13	148.877	35	O	4	Allen Crowe	Gabriel Shocker Spl.	Trevis	27
28	25	148.227	54	O	4	Bud Tingelstad	Hoover, Inc. Spl.	Epperly	28
29	26	148.063	37	O	4	Johnny Rutherford	U.S. Equipment Co. Spl.	Watson	29
30	28	147.893	21	O	4	Elmer George	Sarkes Tarzian Spl.	Lesovsky	30
31	23	148.343	75	NS	8	Art Malone	STP Spl.	Kurtis	31
32	27	148.038	23	O	4	Johnny Boyd	Bowes Seal Fast Spl.	Epperly	32
33	16	149.421	6	NS	8	Bobby Unser	Hotel Tropicana Las Vegas Spl.	Kurtis	33

Qualified, did not start: Len Sutton, Crawford Spl., #47, O, 147.620, Bumped
Ralph Liguori, Shultz Fueling Equipment Spl., #3, O, 147.620, Bumped
Masten Gregory, Harvey Aluminum Spl., #81, REC, 147.517, Bumped
Len Sutton, Leader Card Autolite Spl., #7, O, 147.372, Bumped
Ebb Rose, Racing Associates Spl., #46, O, 147.293, Bumped
Chuck Rodee, Konstant Hot Spl., #38, O, 147.197, Bumped
Pedro Rodriguez (Mexico), BMC Cooper Aston Martin Spl., #48, REAM, 146.687, Bumped

Total entries: 66

Qualifying: Fastest 33 over 4 laps.

FIN	ENTRANT	LAPS	SPEED, REASON OUT	RELIEF DRIVER	FIN
1	J. C. Agajanian	200	143.137	—	1
2	Lotus Indianapolis Project	200	142.752	—	2
3	Ansted-Thompson Racing	200	142.210	—	3
4	Leader Cards, Inc.	200	141.090	—	4
5	Leader Cards, Inc.	200	140.866	—	5
6	William P. Forbes	200	140.862	—	6
7	Lotus Indianapolis Project	200	140.071	—	7
8	Dean Van Lines	200	140.064	—	8
9	Mickey Thompson	200	139.524	—	9
10	H. A. Chapman	200	138.845	—	10
11	Gordon Van Liew	200	138.574	—	11
12	Jim Robbins Co.	200	138.244	—	12
13	Ernest L. Ruiz	200	136.104	—	13
14	Ansted-Thompson Racing	200	132.347	—	14
15	Bruce Homeyer	198	Spun	—	15
16	Lindsey Hopkins	196	Rear end	—	16
17	D. V. S. Inc.	181	Lost wheel	—	17
18	Norm Demler, Inc	149	Crankshaft bearing	—	18
19	John S. Zink	126	Hit wall	—	19
20	M & W Racing Associates	112	Hit wall	—	20
21	Fred Gerhardt	110	Valve	—	21
22	Novi, Inc.	102	Oil leak	—	22
23	Mickey Thompson	100	Threw rod	—	23
24	Lindsey Hopkins	99	Magneto	—	24
25	Gilbert E. Morcroft	79	Oil leak	—	25
26	Racing Associates	74	Valve	—	26
27	Pete Salemi & Nick Rini	47	Lost wheel	—	27
28	Tidewater Associates, Inc.	46	Hit wall	—	28
29	Ed Kostenuk	43	Transmission	—	29
30	Mari George	21	Handling	—	30
31	Novi, Inc.	18	Clutch	—	31
32	Salih-Paddock Corp.	12	Oil leak	—	32
33	Novi, Inc.	2	Hit wall	—	33

AM = Aston Martin   NS = Novi Supercharged
C = Chevrolet   O = Offenhauser
F = Ford   RE = Rear engine

1964

FIN	START	QUAL. SPEED	NUMBER, TYPE, CYLINDERS			DRIVER	CAR NAME	CHASSIS	FIN
1	5	154.672	1	O	4	A. J. Foyt	Sheraton-Thompson Spl.	Watson	1
2	3	156.406	2	REF	8	Rodger Ward	Kaiser Aluminum Spl.	Watson	2
3	7	153.932	18	O	4	Lloyd Ruby	Bill Forbes Racing Team Spl.	Watson	3
4	21	150.893	99	O	4	Johnny White	Demler Spl.	Watson	4
5	13	151.835	88	O	4	Johnny Boyd	Vita Fresh Orange Juice Spl.	Kuzma	5
6	19	151.210	15	O	4	Bud Tingelstad	Federal Engineering, Detroit Spl.	Trevis	6
7	12	151.860	23	O	4	Dick Rathmann	Chapman Spl.	Watson	7
8	27	151.573	4	O	4	Bob Harkey	Wally Weir's Mobilgas Spl.	Watson	8
9	32	149.869	68	O	4	Bob Wente	Morcroft-Taylor Spl.	Trevis	9
10	20	151.038	16	O	4	Bobby Grim	Konstant Hot Spl.	Kurtis	10
11	30	151.222	3	NS	8	Art Malone	Studebaker STP Spl.	Kurtis	11
12	9	152.672	5	REO	4	Don Branson	Wynn's Friction Proofing Spl.	Watson	12
13	10	152.581	53	REO	4	Walt Hansgen	M.G. Liquid Suspension Spl.	Huffaker	13
14	11	152.542	56	O	4	Jim Hurtubise	Tombstone Life Spl.	Hurtubise	14
15	8	153.813	66	REO	4	Len Sutton	Bryant Heating & Cooling Spl.	Vollstedt	15
16	33	148.711	62	O	4	Bill Cheesbourg	Arizona Apache Airlines Spl.	Epperly	16
17	6	154.487	12	REF	8	Dan Gurney	Lotus Powered by Ford	Lotus	17
18	18	151.292	14	O	4	Troy Ruttman	Dayton Steel Wheel Spl.	Watson	18
19	23	153.381	54	REO	4	Bob Veith	MG Liquid Suspension Spl.	Huffaker	19
20	25	152.504	52	REO	4	Jack Brabham, Australia	John Zink-Urschel Trackburner Spl.	Brabham	20
21	26	152.381	28	NS	8	Jim McElreath	Studebaker STP Spl.	Kurtis	21
22	28	151.451	77	O	4	Bob Mathouser	Dayton Disc Brake Spl.	Walther	22
23	4	155.099	98	O	4	Parnelli Jones	Agajanian's Bowes Seal Fast Spl.	Watson	23
24	1	158.828	6	REF	8	Jim Clark, Scotland	Lotus Powered by Ford	Lotus	24
25	2	157.857	51	REF	8	Bobby Marshman	Pure Oil Firebird Spl.	Lotus	25
26	24	152.905	84	REF	8	Eddie Johnson	Mickey Thompson Sears Allstate Spl.	Thompson	26
27	15	151.400	86	O	4	Johnny Rutherford	Bardahl Spl.	Watson	27
28	29	150.830	95	O	4	Chuck Stevenson	Diet Rite Cola-Leader Card Spl.	Watson	28
29	14	151.464	83	REF	8	Dave MacDonald	Mickey Thompson Sears Allstate Spl.	Thompson	29
30	17	151.439	25	REF	8	Eddie Sachs	American Red Ball Spl.	Halibrand	30
31	16	149.744	64	O	4	Ronnie Duman	Clean Wear Service Spl.	Trevis	31
32	22	154.865	9	NS	8	Bobby Unser	Studebaker STP Spl.	Ferguson	32
33	31	150.094	26	O	4	Norman Hall	B.K. Nothing Hurst Floor Shift Spl.	Watson	33

Qualified, did not start: Paul Russo, Sarkes Tarzian Spl., #21, O, 148.644, Bumped

Masten Gregory, Mickey Thompson Sears Allstate Spl., #82, REF, 148.038, Too slow

Bob Christie, Jim Robbins Autocrat Seat Belt Spl., #33, O, 147.583, Too slow

Jud Larson, Kaiser Aluminum Spl., #85, O, 147.432, Too slow

FIN	ENTRANT	LAPS	SPEED, REASON OUT	RELIEF DRIVER	FIN
1	Ansted-Thompson Racing	200	147.350	—	1
2	Leader Cards, Inc.	200	146.339	—	2
3	William P. Forbes	200	144.320	—	3
4	Norm Demler, Inc.	200	143.206	—	4
5	Gordon Van Liew	200	142.345	—	5
6	Federal Automotive Associates	198	Flagged	—	6
7	H. A. Chapman	197	Flagged	—	7
8	Walter Weir, Jr.	197	Flagged	—	8
9	G. E. Morcroft-Ralph Taylor	197	Flagged	—	9
10	Vatis Enterprises, Inc.	196	Flagged	—	10
11	STP Division of Studebaker	194	Flagged	—	11
12	Leader Cards, Inc.	187	Clutch	—	12
13	Kjell H. Qvale	176	Flagged	—	13
14	D.V.S. Inc.	141	Oil pressure	—	14
15	Vollstedt Enterprises, Inc.	140	Fuel pump	—	15
16	Myron E. Osborn	131	Engine trouble	—	16
17	Team Lotus, Ltd.	110	Tire wear	—	17
18	George Walther, Jr.	99	Spun	—	18
19	Kjell H. Qvale	88	Burned piston	—	19
20	Zink-Urschel-Slick, Inc.	77	Split fuel tank	—	20
21	STP Division of Studebaker	77	Engine trouble	—	21
22	George Walther, Jr.	77	Brakes	—	22
23	J. C. Agajanian	55	Pit fire	—	23
24	Team Lotus, Ltd.	47	Rear suspension	—	24
25	Lindsey Hopkins	39	Oil plug	—	25
26	Mickey Thompson	6	Fuel pump	—	26
27	Racing Associates	2	Wreck	—	27
28	Leader Cards, Inc.	2	Wreck	—	28
29	Mickey Thompson	1	Wreck	—	29
30	D.V.S. Inc.	1	Wreck	—	30
31	Nicholas E. Fulbright	1	Wreck	—	31
32	STP Division of Studebaker	1	Wreck	—	32
33	Pope-Hall Enterprises	1	Wreck	—	33

Al Miller, Gerhardt & DeOrian Spl., #93, O, 147.227, Too slow
Chuck Rodee, Joe Hunt Magneto Spl., #81, O, 146.466, Too slow

F = Ford
NS = Novi Supercharged
O = Offenhauser
RE = Rear engine

Total entries: 61   **Qualifying:** Fastest 33 over 4 laps.

1965

FIN	START	QUAL. SPEED	NUMBER, TYPE, CYLINDERS			DRIVER	CAR NAME	CHASSIS	FIN
1	2	160.729	82	REF	8	Jim Clark, Scotland	Lotus Powered by Ford	Lotus	1
2	5	158.625	98	REF	8	Parnelli Jones	Agajanian's Hurst Floor Shift Spl.	Lotus	2
3	4	158.849	12	REF	8	Mario Andretti	Dean Van Lines Spl.	Brawner	3
4	7	157.805	74	REF	8	Al Miller	Jerry Alderman Ford Spl.	Lotus	4
5	14	155.012	76	O	4	Gordon Johncock	Weinberger Homes Spl.	Watson	5
6	15	154.839	81	REO	4	Mickey Rupp	G. C. Murphy Stores Spl.	Gerhardt	6
7	22	155.481	83	REF	8	Bobby Johns	Lotus Powered by Ford	Lotus	7
8	18	155.501	4	REF	8	Don Branson	Wynn's Spl.	Watson	8
9	32	154.440	45	REF	8	Al Unser	Sheraton-Thompson Spl.	Lola	9
10	28	153.998	23	O	4	Eddie Johnson	Chapman Spl.	Watson	10
11	9	157.246	7	REF	8	Lloyd Ruby	Du Pont Golden 7 Spl.	Halibrand	11
12	12	156.121	16	REF	8	Len Sutton	Bryant Heating & Cooling Spl.	Vollstedt	12
13	29	155.172	14	REF	8	Johnny Boyd	George Bryant & Staff Spl.	BRP	13
14	21	155.662	53	REO	4	Walt Hansgen	MG Liquid Suspension Spl.	Huffaker	14
15	1	161.233	1	REF	8	A. J. Foyt	Sheraton-Thompson Spl.	Lotus	15
16	24	154.672	5	REF	8	Bud Tingelstad	American Red Ball Spl.	Lola	16
17	6	158.416	66	REO	4	Billy Foster, Canada	Jim Robbins Autotron Electronics Spl.	Vollstedt	17
18	19	154.513	18	O	4	Arnie Knepper	Konstant Hot Spl.	Kurtis	18
19	8	157.467	9	NS	8	Bobby Unser	STP Gasoline Treatment Spl.	Ferguson	19
20	13	155.878	52	REO	4	Jim McElreath	John Zink-Urschel Trackburner Spl.	Brabham	20
21	16	154.825	94	REO	4	George Snider	Gerhardt Spl.	Gerhardt	21
22	25	154.533	65	REO	4	Ronnie Duman	Travelon Trailer—H & H Bookbinding Spl.	Gerhardt	22
23	31	154.540	41	REF	8	Masten Gregory	Geroge Bryant & Staff Spl.	BRP	23
24	10	156.427	54	REO	4	Bob Veith	MG Liquid Suspension Spl.	Huffaker	24
25	26	154.275	88	O	4	Chuck Stevenson	Vita Fresh Orange Juice Spl.	Kuzma	25
26	3	158.898	17	REF	8	Dan Gurney	Yamaha Spl.	Lotus	26
27	17	154.606	48	REO	4	Jerry Grant	Bardahl—MG Liquid Suspension Spl.	Huffaker	27
28	30	154.546	19	REO	4	Chuck Rodee	Wally Weir's Mobiloil Spl.	Halibrand	28
29	27	154.268	29	REF	8	Joe Leonard	All American Racers Spl.	Halibrand	29
30	23	155.186	25	REF	8	Roger McCluskey	All American Racers Spl.	Halibrand	30
31	11	156.291	24	REF	8	Johnny Rutherford	Racing Associates Spl.	Halibrand	31
32	33	153.774	47	REO	4	Bill Cheesbourg	WIFE Good Guy Spl.	Gerhardt	32
33	20	156.863	59	NS	8	Jim Hurtubise	STP-Tombstone Life Spl.	Kurtis	33

Qualified, did not start: Rodger Ward, Moog St. Louis Spl., #2, REF, 153.623, Too slow
Mel Kenyon, Federal Engineering, Detroit Spl., #27, O, 153.597, Bumped
Bob Christie, Kemerly Chevy & Olds Spl., #21, O, 153.472, Bumped
Norman Hall, Pope-Hall Enterprises Spl., #8, O, 153.407, Bumped
Bobby Grim, Racing Associates Spl., #86, O, 153.309, Bumped

Total entries: 68

Qualifying: Fastest 33 over 4 laps.

FIN	ENTRANT	LAPS	SPEED, REASON OUT	RELIEF DRIVER	FIN
1	Team Lotus (Overseas) Ltd.	200	151.388	—	1
2	J. C. Agajanian	200	149.200	—	2
3	Auto Technics, Inc.	200	149.121	—	3
4	Jerry Alderman Ford Sales	200	146.581	—	4
5	Weinberger & Wilseck Ent.	200	146.417	—	5
6	Pete Salemi	198	Flagged	—	6
7	Team Lotus (Overseas) Ltd.	197	Flagged	—	7
8	Leader Cards, Inc.	197	Flagged	—	8
9	Ansted-Thompson Racing	196	Flagged	—	9
10	H. A. Chapman	195	Flagged	—	10
11	David R. McManus	184	Blew engine	—	11
12	Jim Robbins & Vollstedt Ent.	177	Flagged	—	12
13	George Bryant Racing Projects	140	Gearbox	—	13
14	Kjell H. Qvale	117	Fuel line	—	14
15	Ansted-Thompson Racing	115	Rear end gears	—	15
16	Lindsey Hopkins	115	Hit wall	—	16
17	Jim Robbins & Vollstedt Ent.	85	Water manifold	—	17
18	Vatis Enterprises, Inc.	80	Cylinder wall	—	18
19	STP Division of Studebaker	69	Oil connection	—	19
20	Zink-Urschel-Slick, Inc.	66	Rear end gears	—	20
21	Fred Gerhardt	64	Rear end gears	—	21
22	Ernest L. Ruiz	62	Rear end gears	—	22
23	George Bryant Racing Projects	59	Lost oil pressure	—	23
24	Kjell H. Qvale	58	Burned piston	—	24
25	Gordon Van Liew	50	Burned piston	—	25
26	All American Racers, Inc.	42	Timing gears	—	26
27	Kjell H. Qvale	30	Magneto	—	27
28	Walter Weir, Jr.	28	Rear end gears	—	28
29	All American Racers, Inc.	27	Oil leak	—	29
30	All American Racers, Inc.	18	Clutch	—	30
31	Racing Associates	15	Transmission	—	31
32	Lane-Fulbright Racing Team	14	Magneto	—	32
33	Chemical Compounds Division	1	Transmission	—	33

F = Ford
NS = Novi Supercharged
O = Offenhauser
RE = Rear engine

1966

FIN	START	QUAL. SPEED	NUMBER, TYPE, CYLINDERS			DRIVER	CAR NAME	CHASSIS	FIN
1	15	159.243	24	REF	8	Graham Hill, England	American Red Ball Spl.	Lola	1
2	2	164.114	19	REF	8	Jim Clark, Scotland	STP Gasoline Treatment Spl.	Lotus	2
3	7	160.908	3	REF	8	Jim McElreath	Zink-Urschel-Slick Trackburner Spl.	Brabham	3
4	6	161.059	72	REF	8	Gordon Johncock	Weinberger Homes Spl.	Gerhardt	4
5	17	158.555	94	REO	4	Mel Kenyon	Gerhardt Spl.	Gerhardt	5
6	11	159.972	43	REF	8	Jackie Stewart, Scotland	Bowes Seal Fast Spl.	Lola	6
7	29	158.898	54	REO	4	Eddie Johnson	Valvoline Spl.	Huffaker	7
8	28	159.109	11	REOT	4	Bobby Unser	Vita Fresh Orange Juice Spl.	Huffaker	8
9	20	159.560	6	REF	8	Joe Leonard	Yamaha Eagle Spl.	Eagle	9
10	10	160.335	88	REF	8	Jerry Grant	Bardahl-Pacesetter Homes Spl.	Eagle	10
11	5	162.433	14	REF	8	Lloyd Ruby	Bardahl Eagle Spl.	Eagle	11
12	23	162.372	18	REF	8	Al Unser	STP Oil Treatment Spl.	Lotus	12
13	21	159.271	8	REF	8	Roger McCluskey	G. C. Murphy Spl.	Eagle	13
14	4	162.484	98	REOS	4	Parnelli Jones	Agajanian's Rev 500 Spl.	Shrike	14
15	13	159.468	26	REOS	4	Rodger Ward	Bryant Heating & Cooling Spl.	Lola	15
16	25	159.645	77	REF	8	Carl Williams	Dayton Steel Wheel Spl.	Gerhardt	16
17	22	159.208	56	REOT	4	Jim Hurtubise	Gerhardt Spl.	Gerhardt	17
18	1	165.849	1	REF	8	Mario Andretti	Dean Van Lines Spl.	Brabham	18
19	3	162.521	82	REF	8	George Snider	Sheraton-Thompson Spl.	Coyote	19
20	8	160.844	12	REF	8	Chuck Hulse	Wynn's Spl.	Watson	20
21	27	159.144	22	REOS	4	Bud Tingelstad	Federal Engineering, Detroit Spl.	Gerhardt	21
22	14	159.384	28	REF	8	Johnny Boyd	Prestone Spl.	BRP	22
23	9	160.385	4	REF	8	Don Branson	Leader Card Racers Spl.	Gerhardt	23
24	12	159.490	27	REF	8	Billy Foster, Canada	Jim Robbins Company Spl.	Vollstedt	24
25	16	158.688	53	REO	4	Gary Congdon	Valvoline Spl.	Huffaker	25
26	18	161.355	2	REF	8	A. J. Foyt	Sheraton-Thompson Spl.	Lotus	26
27	19	160.499	31	REF	8	Dan Gurney	All American Racers Eagle Spl.	Eagle	27
28	24	159.794	66	REF	8	Cale Yarborough	Jim Robbins Company Spl.	Vollstedt	28
29	26	159.440	37	REF	8	Arnie Knepper	Sam Liosi Spl.	Cecil	29
30	30	158.681	75	REF	8	Al Miller	Jerry Alderman Ford Spl.	Lotus	30
31	31	158.367	39	OT-R	4	Bobby Grim	Racing Associates Spl.	Watson	31
32	32	159.144	34	REF	8	Larry Dickson	Michner Petroleum Spl.	Lola	32
33	33	158.646	96	REF	8	Ronnie Duman	Harrison Spl.	Eisert	33

Qualified, did not start: Dick Atkins, Agajanian's Rev 500 Spl., #97, REOS, 158.158, Bumped
Art Pollard, Heger 4 & Compton Spl., #44, REO, 157.985, Bumped

Total entries: 78

Qualifying: 4 laps, fastest 33.

FIN	ENTRANT	LAPS	SPEED, REASON OUT	RELIEF DRIVER	FIN
1	John Mecom, Jr.	200	144.317	—	1
2	STP Division of Studebaker	200	143.843	—	2
3	Zink-Urschel-Slick Corp.	200	143.742	—	3
4	W & W Enterprises, Inc.	200	143.084	—	4
5	Fred Gerhardt	198	Flagged	—	5
6	John Mecom, Jr.	190	Oil pressure	—	6
7	Vatis Enterprises, Inc.	175	Stalled	—	7
8	Gordon Van Liew	171	Flagged	—	8
9	All American Racers	170	Stalled	—	9
10	John Klug	167	Flagged	—	10
11	All American Racers	166	Broken cam stud	—	11
12	STP Division of Studebaker	161	Crash	—	12
13	Lindsey Hopkins	129	Oil leak	—	13
14	J. C. Agajanian	87	Wheel bearing	—	14
15	John Mecom, Jr.	74	Handling	—	15
16	George Walther, Jr.	38	Valve, oil	—	16
17	Fred Gerhardt	29	Oil line	—	17
18	Dean Racing Enterprises	27	Valve	—	18
19	Ansted-Thompson Racing	22	Wreck	—	19
20	Leader Cards, Inc.	22	Wreck	—	20
21	Federal Automotive Associates	16	Radiator overheating	—	21
22	George R. Bryant	5	Wreck	—	22
23	Leader Cards, Inc.	0	Wreck	—	23
24	J. M. Robbins	0	Wreck	—	24
25	Vatis Enterprises, Inc.	0	Wreck	—	25
26	Ansted-Thompson Racing	0	Wreck	—	26
27	All American Racers	0	Wreck	—	27
28	J. M. Robbins	0	Wreck	—	28
29	D.V.S. Inc.	0	Wreck	—	29
30	Jerry Alderman Ford Sales	0	Wreck	—	30
31	Herb Porter	0	Wreck	—	31
32	Michner Petroleum, Inc.	0	Wreck	—	32
33	J. Frank Harrison	0	Wreck	—	33

F = Ford
O = Offenhauser
R = Roadster
RE = Rear engine

OS = Offenhauser Supercharged
OT = Offenhauser Turbocharged

1967

FIN	START	QUAL. SPEED	NUMBER, TYPE, CYLINDERS			DRIVER	CAR NAME	CHASSIS	FIN
1	4	166.289	14	REF	8	A. J. Foyt	Sheraton-Thompson Spl.	Coyote	1
2	9	164.594	5	REF	8	Al Unser	Retzloff Chemical Spl.	Lola	2
3	5	166.098	4	REF	8	Joe Leonard	Sheraton-Thompson Spl.	Coyote	3
4	24	163.376	69	REF	8	Denis Hulme, New Zealand	City of Daytona Beach Spl.	Eagle	4
5	11	164.241	2	REF	8	Jim McElreath	John Zink Trackburner Spl.	Moore	5
6	6	166.075	40	T-PW—		Parnelli Jones	STP Oil Treatment Spl.	Paxton	6
7	27	162.925	8	REOT	4	Chuck Hulse	Hopkins Spl.	Lola	7
8	13	163.897	16	REOT	4	Art Pollard	Thermo King Auto Air Cond. Spl.	Gerhardt	8
9	8	164.752	6	REF	8	Bobby Unser	Rislone Spl.	Eagle	9
10	23	163.696	41	REF	8	Carl Williams	George R. Bryant Spl.	BRP	10
11	28	162.580	46	REOT	4	Bob Veith	Thermo-King Auto Air Cond. Spl.	Gerhardt	11
12	3	166.559	3	REF	8	Gordon Johncock	Gilmore Broadcasting Spl.	Gerhardt	12
13	12	164.084	39	REOT	4	Bobby Grim	Racing Associates Spl.	Gerhardt	13
14	25	163.228	10	REF	8	Bud Tingelstad	Federal Engineering, Detroit Spl.	Gerhardt	14
15	21	162.543	22	REF	8	Larry Dickson	Vita Fresh Orange Juice Spl.	Lotus	15
16	14	163.778	15	REOT	4	Mel Kenyon	Thermo King Auto Air Cond. Spl.	Gerhardt	16
17	20	162.830	21	REF	8	Cale Yarborough	Bryant Heating & Cooling Spl.	Vollstedt	17
18	29	164.099	24	REF	8	Jackie Stewart, Scotland	Bowes Seal Fast Spl.	Lola	18
19	22	165.563	12	REF	8	Roger McCluskey	G. C. Murphy Spl.	Eagle	19
20	30	163.808	42	REF	8	Jerry Grant	All American Racers Spl.	Eagle	20
21	2	167.224	74	REF	8	Dan Gurney	Wagner-Lockheed Brake Fluid Spl.	Eagle	21
22	18	162.900	19	REF	8	Arnie Knepper	M.V.S. Racers Spl.	Cecil	22
23	17	162.903	98	REOS	4	Ronnie Duman	Agajanian's Rev 500 Spl.	Shrike	23
24	32	163.051	48	REGWF	8	Jochen Rindt, Austria	Wagner-Lockheed Brake Fluid Spl.	Eagle	24
25	19	162.859	45	REF	8	Johnny Rutherford	Weinberger Homes Spl.	Eagle	25
26	10	164.256	26	REF	8	George Snider	Wagner-Lockheed Brake Fluid Spl.	Laycock	26
27	26	163.066	67	REF	8	LeeRoy Yarbrough	Jim Robbins Seat Belt Co. Spl.	Vollstedt	27
28	33	162.602	32	REF	8	Al Miller	Cleaver-Brooks Spl.	Gerhardt	28
29	15	163.540	53	REOT	4	Wally Dallenbach	Valvoline Spl.	Huffaker	29
30	1	168.982	1	REF	8	Mario Andretti	Dean Van Lines Spl.	Brawner	30
31	16	163.213	31	REF	8	Jim Clark, Scotland	STP Oil Treatment Spl.	Lotus	31
32	31	163.317	81	REF	8	Graham Hill, England	STP Oil Treatment Spl.	Lotus	32
33	7	165.229	25	REOT	4	Lloyd Ruby	American Red Ball Spl.	Laycock	33

Qualified, did not start: Lucien Bianchi, Belgium, Jim Robbins Co. Spl., #27, REF, 162.484, Bumped
Jim Hurtubise, Mallard Spl., #56, FEOT, 162.411, Bumped
Gary Congdon, Sheraton-Thompson Spl., #84, REF, 162.396, Bumped
Jochen Rindt, Austria, Friedkin Enterprises Spl., #87, REF, 162.389, Bumped
Jerry Grant, Friedkin Enterprises Spl., #78, REF, 162.352, Bumped
Pedro Rodriguez, Mexico, Leader Card Racers Spl., #90, REF, 162.352, Bumped
Ronnie Bucknam, Vita Fresh Orange Juice Spl., #23, REF, 162.243, Bumped

FIN	ENTRANT	LAPS	SPEED, REASON OUT	RELIEF DRIVER	FIN
1	Ansted-Thompson Racing, Inc.	200	151.207	—	1
2	Mecom Racing Enterprises, Inc.	198	Flagged	—	2
3	A. J. Foyt, Jr.	197	Flagged	—	3
4	Smokey Yunick, Inc.	197	Flagged	—	4
5	John S. Zink	197	Flagged	—	5
6	STP Division of Studebaker	196	Gear box	—	6
7	Interstate Racer Team	195	Wrecked	—	7
8	Don Gerhardt-Phil Casey	195	Flagged	—	8
9	Leader Cards, Inc.	193	Flagged	—	9
10	George R. Bryant Racing	189	Wrecked	—	10
11	Fred Gerhardt	189	Flagged	—	11
12	Johncock Race Team	188	Spun out	—	12
13	Racing Associates	187	Wreck	—	13
14	Federal Automotive Associates	182	Flagged	—	14
15	Gordon Van Liew	180	Wreck	—	15
16	Fred Gerhardt	177	Wreck	—	16
17	Vollstedt Enterprises, Inc.	176	Wreck	—	17
18	Mecom Racing Ent. Inc.	168	Blown engine	—	18
19	Lindsey Hopkins	165	Blown engine	—	19
20	All American Racers	162	Piston ring	—	20
21	All American Racers	160	Burned Piston	—	21
22	D.V.S. Inc.	158	Blown engine	—	22
23	J. C. Agajanian	153	Fuel flooding engine	—	23
24	All American Racers	108	Broken valve	—	24
25	W & W Enterprises, Inc.	103	Wreck	—	25
26	Vel's Ford Sales Co.	99	Spun out	Lloyd Ruby	26
27	Jim Robbins Co.	87	Spun out	—	27
28	Walter Weir, Inc.	74	Oil leak	—	28
29	Vatis Enterprises, Inc.	73	Wreck	—	29
30	Dean Racing Enterprises, Inc.	58	Lost wheel	—	30
31	STP Division of Studebaker	35	Burned piston	—	31
32	STP Division of Studebaker	23	Burned piston	—	32
33	Gene White Co. of Indy	3	Dropped valve	—	33

Jackie Stewart, Scotland, Bowes Seal Fast Spl., #43, REF, 162.221, Bumped
Bob Harkey, Kenny Brenn Spl., #57, REF, 162.140, Bumped
Jim Hurtubise, Autoteria Car Wash Mfrs. Spl., #11, REF, 161.936, Too slow
Bob Hurt, Rev 500 Spl., #29, REOT, 161.261, Bumped

F = Ford
FE = Front Engine
GWF = Gurney Weslake Ford

OS = Offenhauser Supercharged
OT = Offenhauser Turbocharged

RE = Rear Engine
T-PW = Pratt-Whitney Turbine

Total entries: 90

Qualifying: Fastest 33 over 4 laps.

1968

FIN	START	QUAL. SPEED	NUMBER, TYPE, CYLINDERS			DRIVER	CAR NAME	CHASSIS	FIN
1	3	169.507	3	REOT	4	Bobby Unser	Rislone Spl.	Eagle	1
2	10	166.512	48	REGWF	8	Dan Gurney	Olsonite Eagle	Eagle	2
3	17	165.191	15	REOT	4	Mel Kenyon	City of Lebanon, Ind. Spl.	Gerhardt	3
4	20	164.189	42	REF	8	Denis Hulme, New Zealand	Olsonite Eagle	Eagle	4
5	5	167.613	25	REOT	4	Lloyd Ruby	Gene White Company Spl.	Laycock	5
6	26	162.338	59	REOT	4	Ronnie Duman	Cleaver-Brooks Spl.	Hayhoe	6
7	23	163.510	98	REOT	4	Billy Vukovich	Wagner-Lockheed Brake Fluid Spl.	Shrike	7
8	27	162.499	90	REOT	4	Mike Mosley	Zecol-Lubaid Spl.	Watson	8
9	31	162.118	94	REOT	4	Sam Sessions	Valvoline Spl.	Finley	9
10	25	162.866	6	REOT	4	Bobby Grim	Gene White Company Spl.	Laycock	10
11	24	163.495	16	REOT	4	Bob Veith	Thermo King Auto Air Cond. Spl.	Gerhardt	11
12	1	171.559	60	T-PW—		Joe Leonard	STP Oil Treatment Spl.	Lotus	12
13	11	166.297	20	T-PW—		Art Pollard	STP Oil Treatment Spl.	Lotus	13
14	13	165.327	82	REF	8	Jim McElreath	Jim Greer Spl.	Coyote	14
15	28	162.323	84	REF	8	Carl Williams	Sheraton-Thompson Spl.	Coyote	15
16	18	164.444	10	REOT	4	Bud Tingelstad	Federal Engineering, Detroit Spl.	Gerhardt	16
17	12	165.548	54	REOT	4	Wally Dallenbach	Valvoline Spl.	Finley	17
18	21	163.830	18	REF	8	Johnny Rutherford	City of Seattle Spl.	Eagle	18
19	2	171.208	70	T-PW—		Graham Hill, England	STP Oil Treatment Spl.	Lotus	19
20	8	166.821	1	REF	8	A. J. Foyt	Sheraton-Thompson Spl.	Coyote	20
21	19	164.211	45	REF	8	Ronnie Bucknum	Weinberger Homes Spl.	Eagle	21
22	14	165.032	27	REFT	8	Jim Malloy	Jim Robbins Seat Belt Co. Spl.	Vollstedt	22
23	15	164.782	78	REFT	8	Jerry Grant	Bardahl Eagle	Eagle	23
24	22	163.562	11	REOT	4	Gary Bettenhausen	Thermo King Auto Air Cond. Spl.	Gerhardt	24
25	32	161.900	21	REFT	8	Arnie Knepper	Bryant Heating & Cooling Spl.	Vollstedt	25
26	6	167.069	24	REFT	8	Al Unser	Retzloff Chemical Spl.	Lola	26
27	9	166.775	4	REOT	4	Gordon Johncock	Gilmore Broadcasting Spl.	Gerhardt	27
28	33	161.124	64	REF	8	Larry Dickson	Overseas National Airways Spl.	Brawner	28
29	7	166.976	8	REOT	4	Roger McCluskey	G. C. Murphy Spl.	Eagle	29
30	30	162.191	56	R-OT	4	Jim Hurtubise	Pepsi-Cola-Frito-Lay Spl.	Mallard	30
31	29	162.264	29	REF	8	George Snider	Vel's Parnelli Jones Ford Spl.	Morris	31
32	16	164.144	35	RB	8	Jochen Rindt, Austria	Repco Brabham Spl.	Brabham	32
33	4	167.691	2	REFT	8	Mario Andretti	Overseas National Airways Spl.	Brawner	33

Qualified, did not start: Bruce Walkup, Cleaver-Brooks Spl., #62, 160.514, Bumped
Bob Harkey, Kenny Brenn Spl., #88, 159.915, Bumped
Larry Dickson, Jack Adams Aircraft Spl., #36, 159.652, Bumped
George Follmer, George R. Bryant Spl., #41, 158.877, Bumped
Sonny Ates, Federal Engineering, Detroit Spl., #31, 158.221, Bumped
Bill Puterbaugh, Dayton Steel Wheel Spl., #77, 157.301, Bumped
Bill Cheesbourg, Michner Petroleum Spl., #22, 157.274, Bumped
Al Miller, Wally Weir Spl., #32, 157.109, Too slow

FIN	ENTRANT	LAPS	SPEED, REASON OUT	RELIEF DRIVER	FIN
1	Leader Cards, Inc.	200	152.882	—	1
2	All American Racers, Inc.	200	152.187	—	2
3	Fred Gerhardt	200	149.224	—	3
4	All American Racers, Inc.	200	149.146	—	4
5	Gene White Co.	200	148.529	—	5
6	Hayhoe Racing Ent.	199	Flagged	—	6
7	J. C. Agajanian	198	Flagged	—	7
8	Leader Cards, Inc.	197	Flagged	—	8
9	Vatis Enter. Inc.	197	Flagged	—	9
10	Gene White Co.	196	Flagged	—	10
11	Don Gerhardt	196	Flagged	—	11
12	STP Corporation	191	Governor shaft	—	12
13	STP Corporation	188	Drive mechanism	—	13
14	James H. Greer	179	Stalled	—	14
15	Ansted-Thompson Racing	163	Wrecked, caught fire	—	15
16	Federal Automotive Assoc.	158	Overheating	—	16
17	Vatis Enter. Inc.	146	Excessive vibration	—	17
18	Alan Green	125	Ruptured fuel surge tank	—	18
19	STP Corporation	110	Hit wall	—	19
20	Ansted-Thompson Racing	86	Blown engine	—	20
21	W & W Enterprises	76	Broken transmission gear	—	21
22	Jim Robbins Co.	64	Broken gear	—	22
23	Friedkin Enterprises	50	Starter shaft	—	23
24	Don Gerhardt	43	Oil cooler	—	24
25	Vollstedt Enterprises	42	Oil cooler	—	25
26	Retzloff Racing Team	40	Hit wall	—	26
27	Johncock Racing Team	37	Gearbox	—	27
28	Andretti Racing Enterprises	24	Burned piston	Mario Andretti	28
29	Lindsey Hopkins	16	Oil cooler	—	29
30	Jim Hurtubise	9	Burned piston	—	30
31	Vel's Racing Team	9	Oil leak	—	31
32	Motor Racing Developments Ltd.	5	Burned piston	—	32
33	Andretti Racing Enterprises	2	Burned piston	—	33

Bob Harkey, Stewart-Warner Spl., #71, 156.257, Too slow
Jerry Titus, Bardahl Eagle, #76, 154.540, Too slow

Total entries: 77

Qualifying: Fastest 33 over 4 laps.

F = Ford
FT = Ford Turbocharged
GWF = Gurney Weslake Ford
OT = Offenhauser Turbocharged
R = Roadster
RB = Repco Brabham
RE = Rear engine
T-PW = Pratt-Whitney Turbine

1969

FIN	START	QUAL. SPEED	NUMBER, TYPE, CYLINDERS			DRIVER	CAR NAME	CHASSIS	FIN
1	2	169.851	2	REFT	8	Mario Andretti	STP Oil Treatment Spl.	Brawner	1
2	10	167.341	48	REG	8	Dan Gurney	Olsonite Eagle	Eagle	2
3	3	169.683	1	REOT	4	Bobby Unser	Bardahl Spl.	Lola	3
4	24	165.426	9	REOT	4	Mel Kenyon	Krohne Grain Transport Spl.	Gerhardt	4
5	33	160.851	92	RERB	8	Peter Revson	Repco-Brabham Spl.	Brabham	5
6	11	167.240	44	REFT	8	Joe Leonard	City of Daytona Beach Spl.	Eagle	6
7	4	168.903	66	REOT	4	Mark Donohue	Sunoco-Simoniz Spl.	Lola	7
8	1	170.568	6	REFT	8	A. J. Foyt	Sheraton-Thompson Spl.	Coyote	8
9	31	163.014	21	REFT	8	Larry Dickson	Bryant Heating & Cooling Spl.	Vollstedt	9
10	32	160.901	97	REOT	4	Bobby Johns	Wagner-Lockheed Brake Fluid Spl.	Shrike	10
11	13	167.092	10	REOT	4	Jim Malloy	Jim Robbins Company Spl.	Vollstedt	11
12	23	165.434	11	REOT	4	Sam Sessions	Valvoline Motor Oil Spl.	Finley	12
13	22	166.113	90	REOT	4	Mike Mosley	Zecol-Lubaid Spl.	Watson	13
14	6	168.350	82	REFT	8	Roger McCluskey	G. C. Murphy Spl.	Coyote	14
15	18	166.597	15	REFT	8	Bud Tingelstad	Vel's Parnelli Jones Ford Spl.	Lola	15
16	15	166.914	84	REFT	8	George Snider	Sheraton-Thompson Spl.	Coyote	16
17	14	166.968	59	REOT	4	Sonny Ates	Krohne Grain Transport Spl.	Brabham	17
18	25	165.092	42	REFT	8	Denis Hulme, New Zealand	Olsonite Eagle	Eagle	18
19	5	168.626	12	REOT	4	Gordon Johncock	Gilmore Broadcasting Spl.	Gerhardt	19
20	20	166.428	4	REOT	4	Lloyd Ruby	Wynn's Spitfire Spl.	Laycock	20
21	19	166.497	22	REOT	4	Wally Dallenbach	Sprite Spl.	Eagle	21
22	21	166.220	29	REFT	8	Arnie Knepper	M.V.S. Spl.	Morris	22
23	8	168.075	67	REFT	8	LeeRoy Yarbrough	Jim Robbins Company Spl.	Vollstedt	23
24	29	163.875	95	RERB	8	Jack Brabham, Australia	Repco-Brabham Spl.	Brabham	24
25	30	163.265	57	REOT	4	Carl Williams	STP Gasoline Treatment Spl.	Gerhardt	25
26	9	167.777	8	REOT	4	Gary Bettenhausen	Thermo King Auto Air Cond. Spl.	Gerhardt	26
27	27	164.286	62	REFT	8	George Follmer	Retzloff Chemical Spl.	Gilbert	27
28	7	168.224	38	REOT	4	Jim McElreath	Jack Adams Airplane Spl.	Brabham	28
29	17	166.628	36	REOT	4	Johnny Rutherford	Patrick Petroleum Spl.	Eagle	29
30	16	166.636	45	REOT	4	Ronnie Bucknum	Weinberger Homes Spl.	Eagle	30
31	12	167.123	40	REOT	4	Art Pollard	STP Oil Treatment Spl.	Lotus	31
32	26	164.843	98	REOT	4	Billy Vukovich	Wagner Lockheed Brake Fluid Spl.	Brabham	32
33	28	163.942	16	REOT	4	Bruce Walkup	Thermo King Auto Air Cond. Spl.	Gerhardt	33

Qualified, did not start: Rick Muther, Bulldog Stables Spl., #26, REOT, 158.744, Bumped
Al Miller, Jack Adams Airplanes Spl., #72, T-A, 156.440, Bumped-disqualified

Total entries: 87

Qualifying: Fastest 33 over 4 laps.

FIN	ENTRANT	LAPS	SPEED, REASON OUT	RELIEF DRIVER	FIN
1	STP Corporation	200	156.867	—	1
2	All American Racers	200	155.337	—	2
3	Leader Cards, Inc.	200	154.090	—	3
4	3-K Racing Enterprises	200	152.177	—	4
5	Motor Racing Developments	197	Flagged	—	5
6	Smokey Yunick, Inc.	193	Flagged	—	6
7	U.S. Racing, Inc.	190	Flagged	—	7
8	Ansted-Thompson Racing	181	Flagged	—	8
9	Vollstedt Enterprises	180	Flagged	—	9
10	J. C. Agajanian	171	Flagged	—	10
11	Jim Robbins Company	165	Flagged	—	11
12	Vatis Enterprises	163	Flagged	—	12
13	Leader Cards, Inc.	162	Broken piston	—	13
14	A. J. Foyt and James Greer	157	Broken manifold	—	14
15	Vel's Parnelli Jones Ford, Inc.	155	Blown engine	—	15
16	Ansted Thompson Racing	152	Flagged	—	16
17	3-K Racing Enterprises	146	Stalled	—	17
18	All American Racers	145	Clutch	—	18
19	Johncock Racing Team	137	Broken piston	—	19
20	Gene White Co. of Indy	105	Fuel coupling	—	20
21	Lindsey Hopkins	82	Clutch	—	21
22	M.V.S., Inc.	82	Wreck	—	22
23	Jim Robbins Company	65	Exhaust header	—	23
24	Motor Racing Developments	58	Ignition	—	24
25	STP Corporation	50	Clutch	—	25
26	Don Gerhardt	35	Broken piston	—	26
27	George Follmer Enterprises	26	Waste-gate	—	27
28	Two Jacks, Inc.	24	Engine caught fire	—	28
29	Michner Petroleum, Inc.	24	Split oil tank	—	29
30	W & W Enterprises	16	Burned piston	—	30
31	STP Corporation	7	Drive chain	—	31
32	J. C. Agajanian	1	Con. rod	—	32
33	Don Gerhardt	0	Gearbox	—	33

FT = Ford Turbocharged RB = Repco Brabham
G = Gurney RE = Rear engine
OT = Offenhauser T-A = Turbine-Adams
    Turbocharged

1970

FIN	START	QUAL. SPEED	NUMBER,	TYPE, CYLINDERS	DRIVER	CAR NAME	CHASSIS	FIN
1	1	170.221	2	REFT 8	Al Unser	Johnny Lightning "500" Spl.	P. J. Colt	1
2	5	168.911	66	REFT 8	Mark Donohue	Sunoco Spl.	Lola	2
3	11	166.860	48	REOT 4	Dan Gurney	Olsonite Eagle	Eagle	3
4	23	165.662	83	REFT 8	Donnie Allison	Greer-Foyt Spl.	Eagle	4
5	33	166.821	14	REFT 8	Jim McElreath	Greer-Foyt Spl.	Coyote	5
6	8	168.209	1	REFT 8	Mario Andretti	STP Oil Treatment Spl.	McNamara	6
7	29	165.983	89	REOT 4	Jerry Grant	Nelson Iron Works Spl.	Eagle	7
8	15	165.654	38	REOT 4	Rick Muther	The Tony Express	Brabham	8
9	19	166.590	75	REOT 4	Carl Williams	McLaren Spl.	McLaren	9
10	3	170.004	7	REFT 8	A. J. Foyt	Sheraton-Thompson ITT Spl.	Coyote	10
11	7	168.508	3	REFT 8	Bobby Unser	Wagner-Lockheed Brake Fluid Spl.	Eagle	11
12	32	165.373	67	REFT 8	Sam Sessions	Jim Robbins Co. Spl.	Eagle	12
13	26	166.397	32	REOT 4	Jack Brabham, Austr.	Gilmore Broadcasting Spl.	Brabham	13
14	31	165.548	44	REFT 8	Dick Simon	Bryant Heating & Cooling Spl.	Vollstedt	14
15	27	166.136	19	REFT 8	Ronnie Bucknum	M.V.S. Spl.	Morris	15
16	22	165.906	23	REOT 4	Mel Kenyon	Sprite Spl.	Coyote	16
17	24	165.601	22	REOT 4	Wally Dallenbach	Sprite Spl.	Eagle	17
18	2	170.213	18	REOT 4	Johnny Rutherford	Patrick Petroleum Spl.	Eagle	18
19	13	166.559	27	REFT 8	LeeRoy Yarbrough	Jim Robbins Co. Spl.	Eagle	19
20	10	167.660	84	REFT 8	George Snider	Sheraton Thompson Spl.	Coyote	20
21	12	166.651	9	REOT 4	Mike Mosley	G. C. Murphy Spl.	Eagle	21
22	16	167.942	73	REOT 4	Peter Revson	McLaren Spl.	McLaren	22
23	30	165.753	58	REOT 4	Billy Vukovich	Sugaripe Prune Spl.	Brabham	23
24	18	166.898	15	REFT 8	Joe Leonard	Johnny Lightning "500" Spl.	P. J. Colt	24
25	4	169.213	11	REFT 8	Roger McCluskey	QuicKick Spl.	Scorpion	25
26	20	166.451	16	REOT 4	Gary Bettenhausen	Thermo King Auto Air Cond. Spl.	Gerhardt	26
27	25	168.895	25	REOT 4	Lloyd Ruby	Daniels Cablevision Spl.	Laycock	27
28	17	167.015	5	REOT 4	Gordon Johncock	Gilmore Broadcasting Spl.	Gerhardt	28
29	14	166.459	97	REOT 4	Bruce Walkup	Wynn's Kwik Kool Spl.	Laycock	29
30	6	168.595	10	REOT 4	Art Pollard	Art Pollard Car Wash Systems Spl.	King	30
31	21	166.052	20	REFT 8	George Follmer	STP Gasoline Treatment Spl.	Brawner	31
32	28	166.121	93	REOT 4	Greg Weld	Art Pollard Car Wash Systems Spl.	Gerhardt	32
33	9	167.895	31	REOT 4	Jim Malloy	Stearn's Manufacturing Transi-Tread Spl.	Gerhardt	33

Qualified, did not start: Arnie Knepper, Caves Buick Spl., #53, REOT, 165.320, Too slow
Kevin Bartlett, George Walther's Tyrone Spl., #77 REFT, 165.259, Bumped
Tony Adamowicz, Patrick Petroleum Spl., #36 REOT, 164.820, Bumped
Bentley Warren, Vatis Enterprises Spl., #94 REOT, 164.805, Bumped
Jim McElreath, Caves Buick Spl., #74 REOT, 163.592, Bumped
Steve Krisiloff, VTM Finishing Corp. Spl., #92 REF, 162.448, Bumped

FIN	ENTRANT	LAPS	SPEED OR REASON OUT	RELIEF DRIVER	FIN
1	Vel's Parnelli Jones Ford	200	155.749	—	1
2	U. S. Racing, Inc.	200	155.317	—	2
3	Olsonite Div.	200	153.201	—	3
4	A. J. Foyt & J. H. Greer	200	152.777	—	4
5	A. J. Foyt & J. H. Greer	200	152.182	—	5
6	STP Corp.	199	Flagged	—	6
7	Jerry Grant Racing Ent.	198	Flagged	—	7
8	Two Jacks, Inc.	197	Flagged	—	8
9	Bruce McLaren Motor Racing	197	Flagged	—	9
10	Ansted-Thompson Racing	195	Gears	—	10
11	Leader Cards, Inc.	192	Flagged	—	11
12	Jim Robbins Co.	190	Flagged	—	12
13	Motor Racing Devel. (O'Seas)	175	Engine failure	—	13
14	Racing International	168	Flagged	—	14
15	M.V.S. Inc.	162	Wreck	—	15
16	Lindsey Hopkins	160	Wreck	Roger McCluskey	16
17	Lindsey Hopkins	143	Mag failure	—	17
18	Michner Petroleum, Inc.	135	Broken header	—	18
19	Jim Robbins Co.	107	Turbocharger	—	19
20	Ansted-Thompson Racing	105	Right rear suspension	—	20
21	Leader Cards, Inc.	96	Radiator leak	—	21
22	Bruce McLaren Motor Racing	87	Blown engine	—	22
23	Jerry O'Connell	78	Clutch	—	23
24	Vel's Parnelli Jones Ford	73	Engine failure	—	24
25	Hayhoe Racing Ent.	62	Suspension	—	25
26	Don Gerhardt	55	Engine failure	—	26
27	Gene White Co. of Indy	54	Rear end	—	27
28	Johncock Racing Team	45	Blown engine	—	28
29	Agajanian-Faas Racers	44	Timing gears	—	29
30	Race-Go Corp.	28	Broken piston	—	30
31	STP Corp.	18	Engine failure	—	31
32	Race-Go Corp.	12	Broken piston	—	32
33	Federal Automotive Assoc.	DNS	Suspension failure-wreck	—	33

Denny Zimmerman, Joe Hunt Magneto, #99 REOT, 158.982, Too slow
Larry Dickson, Canal 9, Buenos Aires Spl., #8 REOT, 158.489, Too slow
Jigger Sirois, City of Memphis Spl., #54 REGE, 157.487, Too slow

RE = Rear Engine
FT = Ford Turbocharged
OT = Offenhauser Turbocharged
F = Ford
GE = General Electric Turbine

Total entries: 84

Qualifying: Fastest 33 over 4 laps.

1971

FIN	START	QUAL. SPEED	NUMBER, TYPE, CYLINDERS		DRIVER	CAR NAME	CHASSIS	FIN
1	5	174.622	1	REFT 8	Al Unser	Johnny Lightning "500" Spl.	P. J. Colt	1
2	1	178.696	86	REOT 4	Peter Revson	McLaren Spl.	McLaren	2
3	6	174.317	9	REFT 8	A. J. Foyt	ITT Thompson Spl.	Coyote	3
4	10	171.838	42	REOT 4	Jim Malloy	Olsonite Eagle	Eagle	4
5	11	171.674	32	REOT 4	Billy Vukovich	Sugaripe Prune Spl.	Brabham	5
6	20	171.903	84	REFT 8	Donnie Allison	Purolator Spl.	Coyote	6
7	17	170.156	58	REOT 4	Bud Tingelstad	Sugaripe Prune Spl.	Brabham	7
8	28	169.755	43	REOT 4	Denny Zimmerman	Fiore Racing Enterprises Spl.	Vollstedt	8
9	22	171.241	6	REFT 8	Roger McCluskey	Sprite Spl.	Kuzma-Kenyon	9
10	13	171.233	16	REOT 4	Gary Bettenhausen	Thermo King Auto Air Cond. Spl.	Gerhardt	10
11	7	173.821	12	REFT 8	Lloyd Ruby	Utah Stars Spl.	Laycock	11
12	3	175.816	2	REOT 4	Bobby Unser	Olsonite Eagle	Eagle	12
13	19	169.579	4	REFT 8	Mike Mosley	G. C. Murphy Spl.	Eagle	13
14	33*	170.164	44	REFT 8	Dick Simon*	Travelodge Sleeper Spl.	Vollstedt	14
15	29	169.205	41	REOT 4	George Follmer	Spirit of Indianapolis Spl.	King	15
16	14	170.770	21	REFT 8	Cale Yarborough	Gene White Firestone Spl.	Laycock	16
17	4	174.910	85	REOT 4	Denis Hulme, N. Z.	McLaren Spl.	McLaren	17
18	24	171.151	18	REOT 4	Johnny Rutherford	Patrick Petroleum Spl.	Eagle	18
19	8	172.761	15	REFT 8	Joe Leonard	Samsonite Traveler Spl.	P. J. Colt	19
20	16	169.571	68	REFT 8	David Hobbs, England	Penske High Performance Products	Lola	20
21	18	169.972	38	REOT 4	Rick Muther	Arkansas Aviation Spl.	Brawner	21
22	32	169.197	99	REOT 4	Bob Harkey	Joe Hunt Magneto Spl.	Gerhardt	22
23	15	169.627	95	REOT 4	Bentley Warren	Classic Wax Spl.	Eagle	23
24	23	171.160	22	REOT 4	Wally Dallenbach	Sprite Spl.	Kuzma-Kenyon	24
25	2	177.087	66	REOT 4	Mark Donohue	Sunoco Spl.	McLaren	25
26	31	169.500	64	REFT 8	Art Pollard	Gilmore Racing Team Spl.	Brawner	26
27	25	170.358	98	REFT 8	Sam Sessions	Wynn's Kwik Kool Spl.	P. J. Colt	27
28	26	170.285	45	REOT 4	Larry Dickson	Spirit of Indianapolis Spl.	King	28
29	12	171.388	7	REOT 4	Gordon Johncock	Norris Industries Spl.	McLaren	29
30	9	172.612	5	REFT 8	Mario Andretti	STP Oil Treatment Spl.	McNamara	30
31	27	169.835	20	REFT 8	Steve Krisiloff	STP Gasoline Treatment Spl.	McNamara	31
32	30	170.205	23	REFT 8	Mel Kenyon	Sprite Spl.	Kuzma-Kenyon	32
33	21	171.600	80	REOT 4	George Snider	G. C. Murphy Spl.	Eagle	33

*Car qualified for 27th starting position by John Mahler. Simon replaced Mahler and was moved to last.

Qualified, did not start: Jim McElreath, Thermo King Auto Air Cond. Spl., #46 REOT 169.165, Bumped
Dick Simon, Travelodge Sleeper Spl., #10 REFT 168.903, Bumped
Carl Williams, Dayton Steel Foundry Spl., #77 REFT 168.784, Bumped
Sam Posey, Farrell's Ice Cream Parlor Restaurant, #78 REOT 168.775, Bumped
Jerry Grant, Norris Industries Spl., #92 REFT 168.492, Bumped
Art Pollard, Gilmore Racing Team Spl., #8 REFT 168.366, Bumped

FIN	ENTRANT	LAPS	SPEED OR REASON OUT	RELIEF DRIVER	FIN
1	Vel's Parnelli Jones Ford, Inc.	200	157.735	—	1
2	McLaren Cars Ltd.	200	157.419	—	2
3	Thompson Industries	200	156.069	—	3
4	Dan Gurney	200	154.577	—	4
5	Jerry O'Connell	200	154.563	—	5
6	A. J. Foyt-J. H. Greer	199	Flagged	—	6
7	Jerry O'Connell	198	Flagged	—	7
8	Frank J. Fiore	189	Flagged	—	8
9	Lindsey Hopkins	188	Flagged	—	9
10	Don Gerhardt	178	Flagged	—	10
11	Gene White Racing	174	Gearbox failure	—	11
12	Dan Gurney	164	Accident	—	12
13	Leader Cards, Inc.	159	Accident	—	13
14	Dick Simon Ltd.	151	Flagged	—	14
15	Grant King Racers	147	Broken piston	—	15
16	Gene White Racing	140	Broken stud, oil leak	—	16
17	McLaren Cars Ltd.	137	Dropped valve	—	17
18	Michner Petroleum, Inc.	128	Flagged	—	18
19	Vel's Parnelli Jones Ford, Inc.	123	Turbocharger	—	19
20	U. S. Racing, Inc.	107	Gearbox failure, accident	—	20
21	Two Jacks, Inc.	85	Accident, avoid Hobbs	—	21
22	Joe Hunt	77	Rear end failure	—	22
23	Vatis Enterprises	76	Broken gearbox	—	23
24	Lindsey Hopkins	69	Dropped valve	—	24
25	U. S. Racing, Inc.	66	Gearbox failure	—	25
26	Gilmore Championship Racing	45	Dropped valve	—	26
27	Agajanian-Faas Racers	43	Broken valve	—	27
28	Grant King Racers	33	Engine failure	—	28
29	Vollstedt Enterprises	11	Accident	—	29
30	STP Corp.	11	Accident	—	30
31	STP Corp.	10	Oil leak, spin	—	31
32	Lindsey Hopkins	10	Accident	—	32
33	Leader Cards, Inc.	6	Stalled	—	33

Bill Simpson, Wynn's Kwik Kool Spl., #28 REOT 168.271, Bumped
Donnie Allison, Purolator Spl., #83 REFT 168.130, Withdrawn
Jim McElreath, ITT Thompson Spl., #14 REFT 167.817, Bumped

OT = Offenhauser Turbocharged
FT = Ford Turbocharged
RE = Rear Engine

Total Entries: 77

Qualifying: Fastest 33 over 4 laps.